Fourteen Steps in Managing an Aging Work Force

Fourteen Steps in Managing an Aging Work Force

Helen Dennis
University of Southern California

Lexington Books
D.C. Heath and Company/Lexington, Massachusetts/Toronto

Library of Congress Cataloging-in-Publication Data

Fourteen steps in managing an aging work force.

Includes index.
1. Aged—Employment. 2. Personnel management. I. Dennis, Helen. [DNLM: 1. Aged. 2. Aging. 3. Employment. 4. Personnel Management—methods. WT 30 F781]
HF5549.5.044F68 1987 658.3′042 87-3322
ISBN 0-669-13206-3 (alk. paper)

Published simultaneously in Canada
Printed in the United States of America
Casebound International Standard Book Number: 0-669-13206-3
Library of Congress Catalog Card Number: 86-45185

The paper used in this publication meets the minimum requirements of American National Standard for Information Sciences—Permanence of Paper for Printed Library Materials, ANSI Z39.48-1984. ∞™

87 88 89 90 91 8 7 6 5 4 3 2 1

Dedicated to
my parents,
Hedy and Eric Gutman,
and in memory of
Barbara Heller

Contents

Preface

Aging is a unifying phenomenon. It cuts across racial, sexual, and ethnic lines; it affects senior management and line workers, those supervising and those being supervised. For those of us who work, we are or will become older workers, members of a large and growing group of individuals 40 years and older, protected by the Age Discrimination in Employment Act.

Yet, aging has assumed a rather amorphous role in the U.S. workplace. In most cases, it is addressed *only* when employees are ready to retire or in relationship to avoiding costly age-discrimination lawsuits.

This book is based on the premise that age issues must be addressed while individuals are still employed to ensure that employers continue to reap the best performance from older workers and that older workers attain the highest level of job satisfaction and appropriate remuneration.

The purpose of this book is to provide an up-to-date overview of subjects important to managing an aging work force. These subjects have been addressed in fourteen selected steps; each step is addressed by a chapter. To reflect the breadth of the issues, contributors represent diverse disciplines, including business, gerontology, law, sociology, psychology, medicine, biology, and public administration.

The following steps are recommended for effective management of an aging work force in the 1980s and beyond:

1. Understand the changing work force.
2. Implement the Age Discrimination in Employment Act and understand its implications for management policy and practice.
3. Know the facts about the normal aging process.
4. Prevent work-induced stress detrimental to older workers and encourage effective stress management.
5. Know the health-related cost/benefit issues of older workers and use cost-management strategies.

6. Use objective performance appraisals.
7. Offer well-designed retraining programs and encourage older workers to participate.
8. Implement alternative work schedules.
9. Use knowledge of life stages for job assignments and team building.
10. Conduct management training on the subject of aging to prevent age discrimination and to encourage effective use of older workers.
11. Use community resources for future employment and career-development opportunities for older employees.
12. Examine labor's history, policies, needs, and services regarding older union workers.
13. Capitalize on older workers' desires and abilities to extend their working career.
14. Offer comprehensive retirement-planning programs.

The reader is invited to add to this list.

Organization and Content

The fourteen chapters developing each of the fourteen steps are organized into seven areas. The first area provides a *broad background* to the changing work force and the law. Chapter 1 describes the work force in terms of demography, economic conditions, work expectations, and legislation as well as the meaning of these changes for management. Chapter 2 provides an overview of the Age Discrimination in Employment Act and describes several case studies.

The second area addresses *health issues*. Chapter 3 describes the normal physical aspects of aging. Stress as it applies to older workers and stress management techniques are presented in chapter 4. Chapter 5 concerns health care issues and cost-management strategies related to older workers.

The third area focuses on *effective management* of older workers. Chapter 6 describes the components of objective performance appraisals and their particular relevance to older workers. Chapter 7 presents the methods and significance of training older workers. Chapter 8 describes alternative work schedules that are useful for older workers. Chapter 9 presents a description of several theories of life stages and applies them to the management of work relationships with emphasis on intergenerational relationships.

The fourth area describes *resources for managers*. Chapter 10 describes a management training program that focuses on aging and the training impact on participating managers from across the United States. Chapter 11 presents resources available to managers that are useful to older workers for future employment, career development, training, and retirement.

The last three chapters represent very different areas. Chapter 12 represents a fifth area—*labor.* It describes a labor perspective on age issues in the workplace, focusing on age issues confronting labor and labor–management initiatives. Chapter 13 covers a rationale for a sixth area: *continued work and career development* in later life. Examples include artists, musicians, authors, and public policy leaders. Chapter 14 addresses the seventh and final area, *retirement planning.* It presents the role of the employer in retirement planning, the rationale for providing retirement-planning programs, and trends for the future.

Use of This Book

The information in this book can be used by various types of professional groups and students. It can be used by *employers.* Managers may find some of the information useful when making employment, retention, termination, retraining, and promotion decisions involving older workers. Human resource directors may find some of the information useful in matching human resources to corporate or organizational objectives. Trainers and educators specializing in management training may use the information to prevent age discrimination and to prepare managers to increase their effectiveness with older workers.

The information can be used by *business schools.* Typically, the subject of aging is addressed as a legal issue in business schools. This book can be used to present the subject of aging from a human resource perspective and can serve as an auxiliary text to human resource management courses.

The book can be used by *schools of gerontology and social work.* The subspecialties of industrial gerontology and industrial social work have focused on work-force issues that relate to aging, employment, and retirement.

The book also may be useful to *retirement specialists* who are broadening their role in the U.S. workplace. In addition to retirement planning, specialists are increasingly involved in issues of employment and retirement by working with employers on corporate policies and management practices, and with pre-retirees on planning for their future.

I hope that this book will enhance the readers' knowledge of what is involved in the effective management of an aging work force, and that some of that knowledge will be translated into action steps helpful to employers in meeting their objectives, while providing meaningful roles for society's vital older persons.

Helen Dennis

Acknowledgments

Appreciation is extended to Valerie Remnet, lecturer and project director at the Andrus Gerontology Center, University of Southern California, and David A. Peterson, director of the Leonard Davis School at the Andrus Center, for their commitment to the issues and their continued support of the development of this book. A special thank you goes to Rita Ivens, who prepared the manuscript and provided outstanding administrative support, and to Jon Pynoos for his constructive comments.

As always, my family has given me the support and confidence to pursue and create. Thank you, Lloyd, Laurie, and Susan.

Step 1: Understand the changing work force.

The Work Force of Tomorrow: Its Challenge to Management

Phoebe S. Liebig

The Challenge

The work force of tomorrow presents managers with multiple challenges that will be more pronounced than in the past decade. These challenges will affect employer policies and practices and involve changes primarily in demography, economic conditions, work expectations, and legislation. In particular, the issue of age has evolved as a major cutting edge in the workplace, especially in relationship to employment, retention, promotion, retirement, and termination. This issue will become even more significant in the next ten to fifteen years. While it is important for managers to understand age issues and apply that understanding to fair employment and management practices, managing an aging work force involves principles that are relevant to workers of all ages.

Demographic Changes and the Work Force

Population Trends

The aging of the United States is now a fact. This trend will continue through the rest of this century, then rise dramatically in the first three decades of the twenty-first century. Figure 1–1 describes the profile of America's aging society between the years 1982 and 2030. The figure shows that the U.S. population in 1982 departed from the classical population pyramid of proportionately more younger persons up to age 20 and fewer persons past the age of 65. These statistics also show that in the "squaring of the pyramid," the relative percentages of all age groups become roughly equivalent. This will be especially pronounced in the year 2030, when nearly all age groups up to age 75 will each be 6 percent of the total population.

The proportion of Americans today who are 65 and older is 11.2 percent. This percentage will increase to approximately 17 percent in the year 2030,

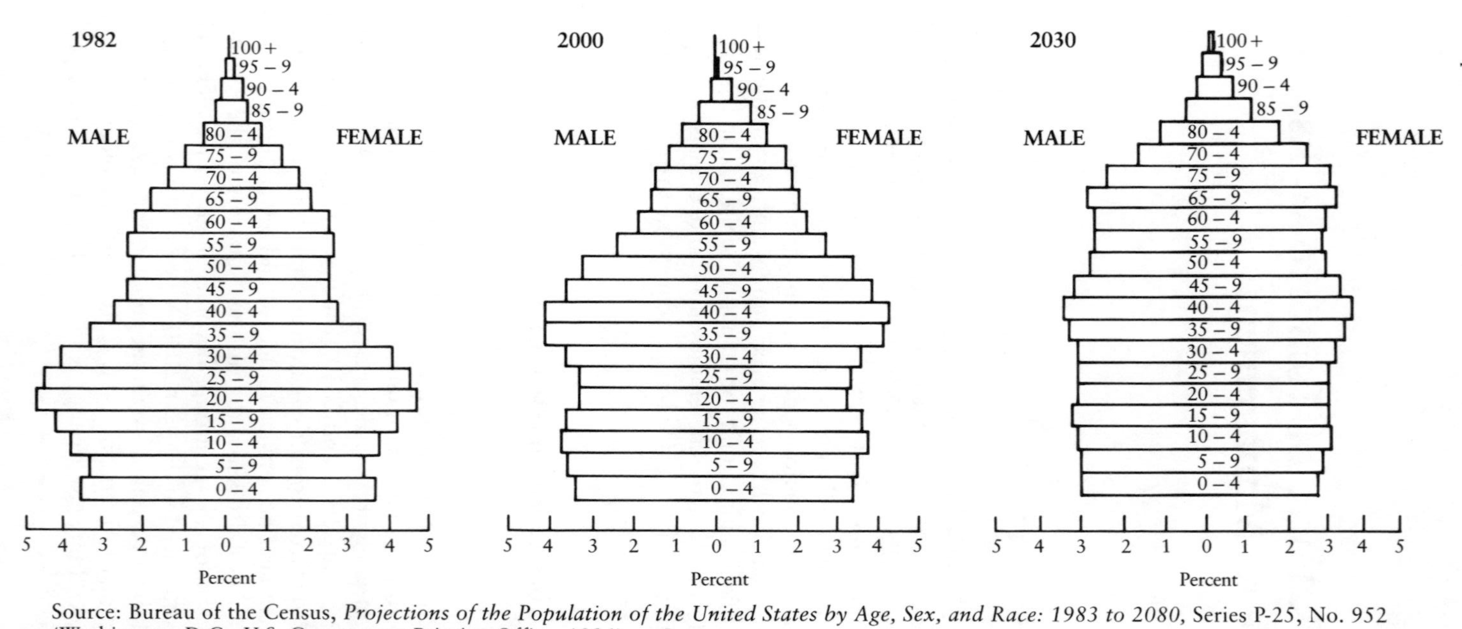

Source: Bureau of the Census, *Projections of the Population of the United States by Age, Sex, and Race: 1983 to 2080*, Series P-25, No. 952 (Washington, D.C.: U.S. Government Printing Office, 1984), p. 5.

Figure 1–1. Changes in Age Distribution by Sex, 1982, 2000, 2030

when those born during the baby boom will be between 66 and 84 years. The median age also has increased from 30 in 1980 to 31.5 years in 1985 (*USA Today* May 15, 1986). In fact, one-half of all Americans will be age 35 in the year 2000 and age 39 in 2020 (Bureau of the Census 1984). Based on these projections, all institutions will need to adapt to this "graying" of America.

This projected age distribution that began in the late 1970s will be accompanied by slower population and work force growth. From 1975 to 1984, the civilian noninstitutional population age 16 years and over grew from 153 million to 176 million. However, the average annual rate of change declined from 2.2 percent to 1.3 percent. From 1990 to 1995, it is projected that that same population will grow from more than 186 million to nearly 194 million, with average annual rates of change projected to decrease to .8 percent (Fullerton 1985).

An Aging Work Force

During most of the 1970s, the growth of the civilian work force was unprecedented. From 1960 to 1985, the total working population grew rapidly from 71.5 million to 117.2 million, increasing on average by 2.6 percent annually and peaking in 1980. From 1984 to 1995, the work force will grow more slowly, increasing from nearly 123 million to 129 million, with an average annual rate of change of 1.0 percent for the period 1990–95 (Fullerton 1985).

While the population grows and the slowdown in work force growth continues, the workers of the United States will be aging. The 25– to 54–year–old population group, the prime working-age component of the work force, will be the fastest growing group during the next decade. This group will increase by 21 percent. Based on Bureau of Labor Statistics (BLS) middle growth projections, the overall working population is anticipated to increase by only 15 million, as the number of those in the older and younger work forces drop (Fullerton 1985).

Labor force participation among persons 55 and older is expected to be about 25 percent in 1995. This is a decline from 30 percent in 1984 and 39 percent in 1970. The projected drop is due to continuing decreased labor force participation by older men. Between 1950 and 1980, the proportion of working men age 55 and older dropped from 69 to 46 percent (Rhine 1984). The youth work force, comprised of entry-level workers ages 16 to 24, grew rapidly during the 1970s and is projected to drop in absolute numbers during the late 1980s and early 1990s. The numbers of this baby bust generation will decline from 2.7 million to 1.1 million in 1995 (Axel and Brotman 1982; Fullerton 1985).

The net outcome of these work force shifts and the aging of the baby boom generation will result in nearly three-fourths of the 1995 working population being aged 25 to 54, compared with two-thirds of the 1984 work force. In the year 2000, the oldest of the baby boomers will be at the tail end of that prime working age group. Of even greater significance is the larger numbers of workers aged 45 and older. In 1960, the absolute number for this age group was 28 million; in the year 2000, it is predicted that this group will total 43 million or approximately one-third of the entire working population. Figure 1–2 depicts these emerging trends in labor force participation by age and sex between the years 1960 and 2000. The figure shows the continued decline in labor force participation of men aged 55 and over plus higher rates for older women and women in all age groups, until age 65.

Gender, Racial, and Household Shifts

In addition to age-distribution change, other population-related shifts of the past two decades will continue over the next ten to fifteen years. The proportion of the work force that is female increased from 32 percent in 1956 to 40 percent in 1975 and to 44 percent in 1984 (*USA Today* June 17, 1986). This increase is responsible for more than 62 percent of the growth of the entire civilian labor force (Segal Associates 1986). Female workers are projected to reach 46 percent of the total working population by 1995 (Fullerton 1985). Work force participation increased for women of all ages between 1960 and 1980, and doubled for women aged 45 to 54 (Axel and Brotman 1982). In 1984, the participation rate for women 45 to 54 years old, many of whom are displaced homemakers, was 63 percent; in 1995, it is projected to be 71 percent. The proportion of these women with at least one living parent is 65 percent, up from 37 percent in 1940 (Menken 1985). With increasing longevity, that proportion will increase.

As for younger women, who are also part of the prime working age group, participation rates for those aged 25 to 34 will increase from 55 percent in 1975 to 81 percent in 1995. Similarly, those aged 35 to 44 will increase from 56 percent in 1975 to 80.5 percent in 1995 (Fullerton 1985). As head of their own households or part of two-earner households, many are mothers as well. Within the past decade, the work force participation rate for married women with children under 1 year of age increased 70 percent (Bureau of National Affairs 1986). In 1984, nearly 20 million mothers, single and married, were working—most of them full-time, even if their youngest child was under 3 (Segal Associates 1986).

The racial composition of tomorrow's work force also will be different. In 1946, 1 birth in 7 was nonwhite compared with 1 birth in 5 in 1976 (Greenwald 1986). This growing trend is corroborated by 1980—85 shifts that show an 8.2 percent increase of black Americans, compared to a 4.1 percent increase of whites and a 5.4 increase of the total U.S. population

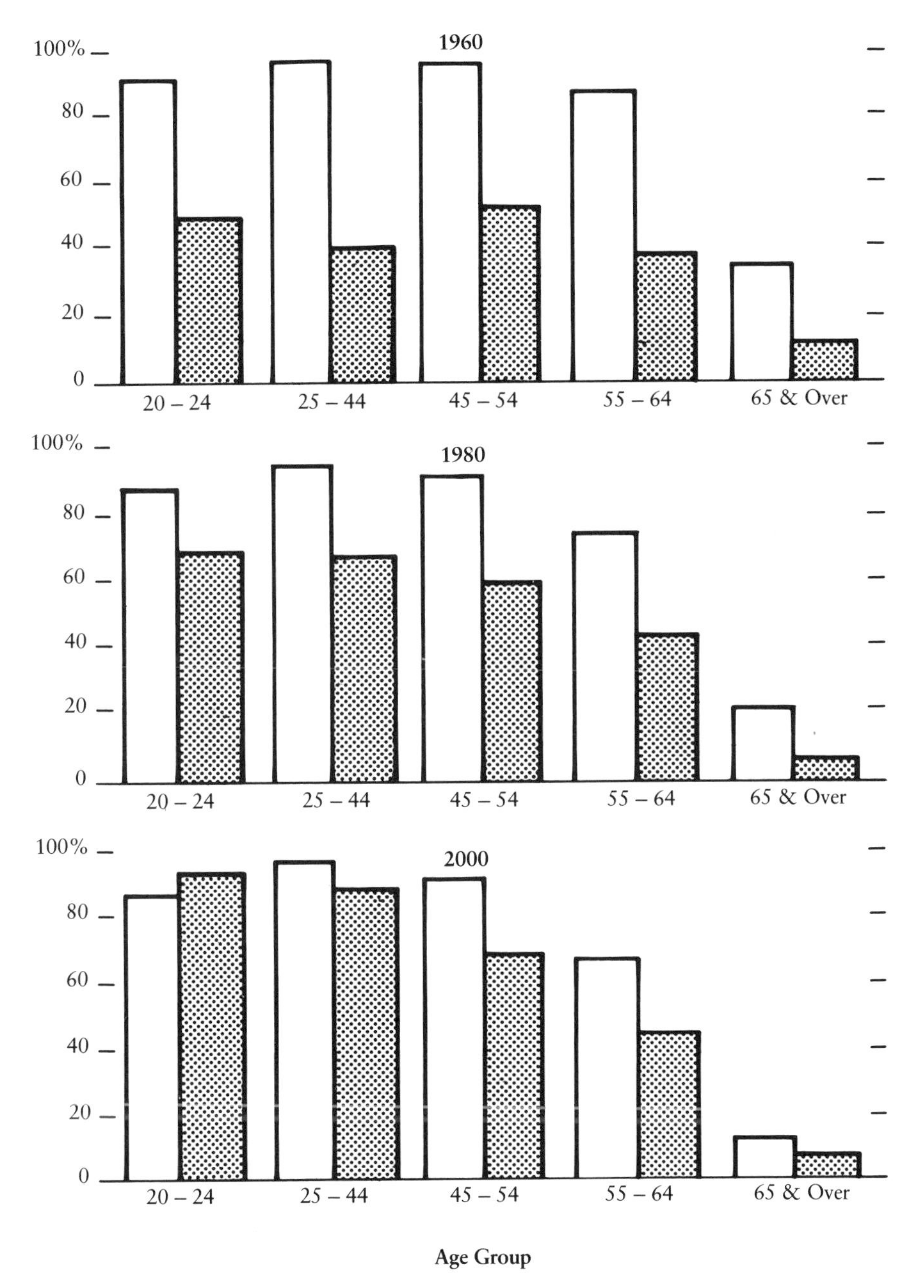

Source: U.S. Department of Labor, Bureau of Labor Statistics, From Axel, H. and Brotman, H.B., Demographics of the Mature Work Force, 1982, p. 17.

Figure 1–2. Percentage of Population in the Civilian Labor Force by Age and Sex, 1960, 1980, 2000. *(Shaded bars = Female; Non-Shaded bars = Male)*

(*USA Today* May 15, 1986). The persistence of racial problems and inequities for blacks is likely to continue, especially in unemployment and disproportionate low-level jobs. These difficulties are likely to be exacerbated by poor schooling and by immigrants taking over the lowest-paying jobs, causing an increase in black unemployment (Bezold et al. 1986).

In addition to the continuing high birth rates among blacks, immigration patterns also are contributing to racial shifts within the work force. Immigration from non-European countries generally has been lower than from other areas of the globe. Since 1940, the number of non-European immigrants has dramatically declined. In the near term, the bulk of projected immigration will come from Asian and Latin American countries. During the next ten years, Hispanics will come close to replacing blacks as the largest minority (Bezold et al. 1986). In some regions, such as the Southwest, that pattern is already apparent and is likely to escalate given political and economic disruptions in Mexico and other parts of Latin America (Lamm 1985).

A final important demographic change that is closely related to gender and racial shifts is family structure. The "typical" family (one with a husband wage earner, a wife homemaker, and two or more dependent children) now accounts for less than 10 percent of all households (Bezold et al. 1986). There has been a rapid growth over the past fifteen years in single-parent, single-person households at all ages. Between 1970 and 1982, the number of single-mother households grew by 88 percent (Segal Associates 1986). In addition from 1970 to 1980, there was a doubling in the numbers of never-marrieds among individuals in their twenties and thirties; there are 4.2 million such women now and 6.1 million men (*Wall Street Journal* May 28, 1986). Since 1980, many young adults have been doubling up in the old family nest, possibly to save money because of economic difficulties (*Washington Post* November 20, 1985). At the same time, people have tended to postpone marriage and childbearing; the median age of marriage for men is now 25.5 and for women 23.3, the highest recorded.

These household shifts are summarized: between 1970 and 1985, married-couple households declined from nearly 71 percent to 58 percent of all households, while nonfamily households increased from almost 19 percent to nearly 28 percent. Other family households, such as unmarried mothers with children, grew from 10.6 percent to 14.3 percent (*Washington Post* November 20, 1985). As the division between family and work becomes more blurred, these household shifts will continue to have major impact on the workplace.

Education and Mobility

Two other demographic characteristics require examination because of their impact on tomorrow's work force. Formal education has increased markedly. In 1970, approximately one-quarter of those in the labor force were not high school graduates; 12 percent were college graduates. By 1981, the picture had changed: 1 in 5 workers was not a high school graduate, while just under 1 in 5 had graduated from college. From 1975 to 1985, the percent of college graduates in the labor force, age 25–64, climbed by 7 percentage points to 25 percent (Segal Associates 1986). Among the baby boomers born between 1946 and 1962, one-quarter are college graduates, while just 12 percent did not graduate from high school.

This level of educational achievement bodes well in the next decade for performance and productivity of tomorrow's older workers, who will place a high premium on skill upgrading because of their prior educational experience. The levels of educational achievement of the "baby busters," the entry level workers of today and tomorrow, will be more modest. A number of experts believe that the quality of schools has declined since the time the baby busters started entering them, in part because of a decline in teachers' real income, performance, and qualifications (Greenwald 1986). Student performance has dropped significantly on Scholastic Aptitude Tests since the early baby boomers took tests (Greenwald 1986). Growing numbers of teenage pregnancies have led to higher high school dropout rates, as have larger minority and immigrant populations. Currently, 22 percent of both blacks and Spanish-speaking adults (age 20 and older) are illiterate, with highest concentrations for those between 20 and 39 and, secondarily, for those 60 and older (*Time* May 5, 1986).

The baby busters, who will be the teachers of tomorrow, are now entering college at a time when education as a profession is receiving a smaller slice of a shrinking pie of talented graduates (Griffin 1986). Despite the increase in nonwhite Americans, the racial and ethnic breakdown of undergraduate college students in 1984 was 9 percent black, 5 percent Hispanic, and 3 percent Asian (*Wall Street Journal* August 4, 1986). Thus, the baby busters will evidence greater educational discrepancies compared with the baby boomers.

A final demographic characteristic with impact on the work force is mobility. The 1980 Census shows that Americans have flocked to the Sunbelt, largely because of job availability and retirement relocation patterns (Bureau of the Census 1984; *National Newsletter* 1986). Other shifts have included urban to rural and, more recently, urban to suburban drifts as the baby boomers enter their child-rearing years.

This geographic mobility has been accompanied by job mobility that reflects redistributions of age groups in the working population and the infusion of greater numbers of women into the work force. In 1978, 2 of every 5 workers held their current jobs for 2 years or less; only 1 in 5 had been on the same job for more than 10 years (Axel and Brotman 1982). As the baby boomers age, they will have a greater tendency to stay put (because generally mobility decreases with age), but the baby busters are likely to demonstrate a greater mobility to improve their economic position (Greenwald 1986).

Career mobility will create differences between the baby boomers and baby busters. Baby boomers, because of their greater numbers and increased competition, may experience fewer promotional opportunities and more career plateauing with consequent decreased motivation. Baby busters, especially those with greater technical skills, may experience greater career mobility because of fewer numbers and lower competition.

Implications of Demographic Changes

All of these demographic changes will have substantial impact on the work force during the next decade and into the twenty-first century. The working population will be older on average. It is unclear what that may mean for productivity. This is because we tend to confuse what happens as a consequence of biological aging with the consequences of a few years of education that have rapidly grown out of date (Ryder 1986). It is clear that the educational process will need to be extended over the life span, with more involvement of business and government in education and training. This is largely because there are and will be fewer entry-level workers, many of whom will not have the higher skills required by new technology. Shortages are already occurring in low-paying service jobs and in many positions that require technical skills, resulting in pervasive and maddening labor mismatches (*Time* April 28, 1986).

The escalating labor force participation of women of all ages means that greater concerns will be raised about pay equity, sexual discrimination and harassment, and work scheduling, as well as care for children, aging spouses, and parents who will facilitate women remaining in the work force. Similarly, an increasing minority work force will bring with it different cultural values about work and work expectations, and probably greater educational and communication problems. Changing household composition and marked differences in the educational attainments of older and younger workers will have continued major effects on benefit packages, job mobility, and employee turnover.

All of these shifts will result in a vastly different and far more heterogeneous work force than today's. This more diverse work force will require greater ingenuity and more innovative management skills to increase productivity, which is especially important in view of the changing and uncertain economy.

Economic Conditions and Trends

In recent years, the economic scene in the United States and other industrialized nations has been influenced by several major trends that will continue to shape the rapidly changing nature of work. The growth of a fiercely competitive global economy in which the United States no longer enjoys unchallenged leadership plus increasing international economic problems (such as severe trade imbalances and greater numbers of debtor nations) have an unprecedented impact on the U.S. economy.

Growth in the trade and service industries, especially the knowledge industry, has been dominant, resulting in a fundamental shift away from goods-producing "smoke stack" industries. Between 1960 and 1980, manufacturing dropped from a 30 to 24 percent share of Gross National Product (GNP); there was a 25 percent drop in the number of people employed in the steel industry alone (National Council on the Future of Women in the Workplace 1984). Nine out of ten new jobs created in the 1970s were in the trade and service sectors (Joint Economic Committee 1981). These shifts resulted in changes in "collar colors" of the work force: fewer blue, more pink (as women surged into clerical and support jobs), and more white. The latter trends are continuing with a projected increase of 60 percent more white collar workers in the 1980s (Bushnell 1981). Fewer but less-skilled entry-level workers (green collar) and consequent recruiting of older (gold collar) workers by firms such as McDonald's (Berlow 1986) are turning the American work force into a veritable rainbow.

This service industry growth will continue predominantly in businesses with fewer than 50 workers. The Bureau of Labor Statistics (BLS) projects that by 1995, the ratio of service to manufacturing jobs will grow to 4.3 to 1, compared with a 1986 ratio of 3.8 to 1 (Bezold, Carlson and Peck 1986). It is projected that nearly 90 percent of the American work force will be in service industries, with about 44 percent employed in information services by the beginning of the next century (*National Newsletter* 1986). At the same time, structural unemployment in the manufacturing sector is likely to continue, resulting in "normal" unemployment levels of 6 to 7 percent, in contrast with earlier "acceptable" levels of 4 percent.

As a consequence, middle-level opportunities are declining. The fastest-growing occupations are all nonmanufacturing, nonunionized, low-wage occupations (National Council on the Future of Women in the Workplace 1984) in small businesses where there are fewer hierarchical levels. Also responsible for the decline in midlevel opportunities is a strategy to regain competitiveness through large-scale reductions in corporate work forces—"downsizing." This is largely accomplished by thinning out the ranks of middle management, often by offering early retirement incentives (Yankelovich et al. 1985). This growing bifurcation of the work force is accompanied by the movement of industries and jobs to other countries as American companies seek cheaper sources of labor.

These economic shifts are producing a lower standard of living for the American worker. While jobs in the manufacturing sector average about triple the minimum wage, many jobs in the service sector are temporary, part-time, or part-year in nature (National Council on the Future of Women in the Workplace 1984). Slightly over 20 percent of the labor force, or 24.7 million Americans, consists of part-time workers (Segal Associates 1986). Since 1978, the average worker's real wages have declined by 10 percent (Bernstein 1986). Two salaries are and will be needed for economic survival (*National Newsletter* 1986). According to the Bureau of Labor Statistics, there also is an increase in moonlighting, approximately 40 percent of which is driven by "bread and butter" motivations. Among older workers, 25 percent moonlight for personal gratification, to give vent to creative energy, and explore new careers. The 25 percent increase of "contingent workers" in the past decade translates into lower labor costs for employers. It also denotes a more tenuous employee–employer relationship and a different kind of work ethic from yesteryear's work force (*New York Times* July 9, 1986). In addition to more part-time work, shorter working hours for full-time workers also have developed. By the year 2000, it is projected that the full-time workweek will be 20 to 25 hours; productivity, however, will increase because of greater reliance on technology (*National Newsletter* 1986).

High technology consisting of computer integrated manufacturing and robotics is redesigning the factory (*Business Week* June 16, 1986). It is freeing many workers from hard physical labor and increasing the need for workers with a wide range of technical and problem-solving approaches. Researchers at the Upjohn Institute for Employment Research estimate that over one-half of all jobs created by robotic technology will require two or more years of college education (National Council on the Future of Women in the Workplace 1984) as well as additional training and retraining.

In addition to redesigning the factory work site, high technology has effected work site location. Certain regions of the country, most notably the Sunbelt South and West and the Northeast, have attracted a favorable industrial mix heavily skewed toward information processing and smaller high tech companies (Kasarda et al. 1986; Hershey 1986). The largest numbers of new jobs created in the United States by the year 2000 are predicted to be in Texas, California, Arizona, Massachusetts, the Washington, D.C., area, and Colorado (*National Newsletter* 1986).

Beyond this bicoastal disparity in job growth, high technology, especially the computer, has played a large role in the development of telework/telecommuting, such as working from home or neighborhood satellite offices in rural or suburban settings. A rising cottage industry or home work trend is developing. The U.S. Chamber of Commerce and AT&T estimate that more than 10 million Americans do all their paid work at home, while another 12 million do some of their work there (Herbers 1986). Workers separated by 500 miles collaborate on projects leading to highly decentralized, nonhierarchical work teams. Under these circumstances, a compensation system linking pay to productivity makes more sense than pay based on fixed hourly or annual salaries set without regard to actual company performance.

In a period of rapid change and uncertainty, new compensation schemes, work schedules, and job and work place restructurings will continue to pose bold challenges to workers and managers alike and mold their work expectations and preferences (Bezold et al. 1986). In an economy that is likely to grow more slowly—at an average annual rate of 2.5 percent or less in real GNP, in comparison with the more dynamic 3.1 percent rate experienced in the 1965–80 period (Technical Committee on an Age-Integrated Society 1981)—these preferences and expectations will have resounding impacts on productivity.

Expectations and Preferences

In the postindustrial society, it is clear that the values, expectations, and preferences of tomorrow's work force will not resemble those of the past. The United States has moved toward "dissensus" (a lack of consensus) and value diversity (Toffler 1985). "Demassification" (individualization) and decentralization of production, consumption, communication, family life, and other aspects of American life are encouraging wider social diversity, innovation, and greater individuality (Naisbitt 1982; Toffler 1985). At the same time, uncertain and highly competitive economic conditions and longer life spans will lead to a more sustained focus on needs for greater stability and security. Productivity and innovation are not just related to products or technologies. They are related to people. Managers will need to take into account the sometimes conflicting worker needs for autonomy, flexibility, and security; they will need to review their assumptions about how tomorrow's worker should be treated and managed.

While high tech has enhanced worker productivity, it has also increased demands for what has been characterized as "high touch" (Naisbitt 1982). Needs for more personalized work experiences, for situations in which a sense of commitment may be invested, and for intrinsic, nonmonetary rewards are being felt in the workplace. The "information" worker wants more authority and autonomy in the management of the workplace, requiring fewer layers of supervisors between workers and managers. "Consultative"—rather than top-down—management and spontaneous—rather than bureaucratic—organizational arrangements fulfill the desires for greater participation in decision making and for the workplace as a setting in which self-enhancement and many of the new "expressive" values can be experienced and sought (Toffler 1985; Bezold et al. 1986). Critical factors in the productivity of knowledge workers are attitudes, job relationships, and the design of jobs and teams, creating a need to rethink and restructure career ladders, compensation, and recognition of merit (Drucker 1986).

The changing age composition of the work force means that over the next ten to fifteen years, we will be heavily staffed with people in their "best years," with fewer promotional opportunities for younger people. Satisfaction and achievement will increasingly have to be built into the job itself (making the job richer, more demanding, and more challenging) rather than coming from rapid promotion (Drucker 1986).

Attention to worker choices is becoming more pronounced, with greater emphasis on alternative work options, such as job sharing and "cafeteria" benefits (a benefit program under which employees determine how dollars will be allocated for each type of benefit from the total amount due to them from the employer). Fringe benefits packages including pensions, stock option plans, and tuition reimbursement are increasingly being tailored to the varying needs (often age- and career-related) of a highly diverse labor force. Greater numbers of women in the work force have led to increasing use of flex-time, job-sharing, home work, and other work scheduling and workplace alternatives. In 1986, flex-time and job-sharing, which are also of interest to gold collar workers, are used by 29 percent and 17 percent of companies, compared with 22 percent and 11 percent, respectively, of companies in 1981 (Administrative Management Society 1986).

Fringe benefit packages increasingly include maternity and parenting leaves, training and retraining opportunities, care for dependents, deferred compensation, postretirement health benefits, IRAs, and financial planning. Dependent care is becoming more available for younger women in response to their need to balance family and work (Bureau of National Affairs 1986). Elder care may become the employee benefit of the 1990s in response to the greater numbers of older women in the work force who are caregivers for their spouses and older parents (Friedman 1986). Financial and career planning and preretirement counseling also indicate growing sensitivity to the different and changing needs of workers as they age.

The changes in benefit packages are becoming increasingly responsive to the needs of a more demographically diverse work force, workers' growing desire to balance work versus leisure over their whole lives, and nontraditional security needs (Spencer 1986). While retirement, medical, and capital-accumulation benefits are more in tune with traditional economic needs, the issues of skills maintenance, dependent care, and health promotion are focused on family and personal integrity and growth. Companies benefit from less absenteeism, heightened emotional well-being, and more positive attitudes.

The escalating costs of all fringe benefits, most notably for health care and pensions (especially if early-retirement bonuses are used) are personnel costs that must be offset by greater productivity of all workers. The key task of managers in achieving this greater productivity is to promote a work environment that motivates and revitalizes their employees and that avoids or diminishes burnout. This requires a better means of assessing job performance and knowledge of the impact of company policies on innovative personnel practices such as reassignment, lateral transfers, job redesign, and part-time work options. These practices can promote greater congruence of preferences, abilities, and productivity needs, regardless of age and organizational structure. To do otherwise would be less than good leadership and management practice. In the case of older workers, poor management decisions could lead to long-range losses of vital skills, experience, and an understanding of corporate history. In the short term, poor decisions can lead to lawsuits stemming from the changed legal environment brought about by recent legislation and court rulings.

Public Policy and Legislation

Since the 1960s, Congress has enacted a number of policies focused on discrimination in the workplace and on enhancement of work force participation by older workers, women and minorities. In addition, a number of retirement and pension policies have been legislated that affect workers of all ages, particularly older workers. In the latter category, the 1983 Social Security amendments raise the normal retirement age to 66 in the year 2009 and 67 in the year 2027. Neither public nor private sector employers have made changes to address this policy shift (Salisbury 1986). Within the next decade, forward-looking companies will have to examine their personnel policies in relation to this major retirement policy change.

While it may be too soon to measure the effects of that recent legislation, the impact of the Age Discrimination in Employment Act (ADEA) and its amendments is apparent. The ADEA prohibits the hiring, promotion, and termination of persons 40 years and older, based on their age. While there are some exceptions that deal with hiring and termination ages for public safety types of jobs such as bus drivers and air traffic controllers, court interpretations require that companies show an absence of age discrimination. Evidence suggests that age biases do occur in the workplace (as they do in society in general), especially in personnel and pension policies. Consequently, managers need to increase their awareness of decisions based on age factors and stereotyping rather than performance. Otherwise, morale problems will occur among older employees and even among somewhat younger workers who may anticipate similar treatment as they become older. Additionally, managers who are unaware of age biases in company policies also run the risk of increased court resolution of this discrimination.

Termination of older workers is resulting in expensive court cases because of inadequate evidence of poor performance. In addition, early-retirement incentive plans are now also being subjected to greater scrutiny for age discrimination. Charges of such discrimination filed with the Equal Employ-

Table 1–1
Major Older-Worker Legislation

Age Discrimination in Employment Act (ADEA) of 1967. Prohibits the hiring, promotion, or termination of persons 40 and older if age is used as the only criterion.

Senior Community Service Employment Program (SCSEP) of 1973. Provides part-time community service employment for low-income older persons age 55 and over.

Employee Retirement Income Security Act (ERISA). Provides for federal regulation of private pensions by the Internal Revenue Service, Department of Labor, and Pension Benefit Guaranty Corporation. Sets forth standards for reporting and disclosure of administration and investment practices as well as vesting and funding of pension funds. Amended several times.

Job Training Partnership Act (JTPA) of 1982. Provides federal funds for a state-administered program of remedial education, training, and employment assistance to low-income and unemployed youth and adults.

Social Security Act Amendments of 1983. Provide for the raising of the age of eligibility for normal retirement benefits to age 66 in the year 2009 and to age 67 by 2027.

Tax Reform Act of 1986 and *Budget Reconciliation Act* of 1986. Provide for several pension changes: lowered vesting to five years, limited integration of pension benefits with Social Security to 50 percent, expanded plan coverage, required pension-benefits accrual after age 65, and jettisoned practice of not permitting persons within five years of a plan's normal retirement age to participate in the plan.

Age Discrimination in Employment Act Amendments of 1986. Abolish mandatory retirement at any age and require employers to extend benefits to older workers regardless of age.

---

ment Opportunity Commission (EEOC) have risen markedly. In 1981, approximately 9,500 cases were filed; by 1984, this number had more than doubled to just under 22,000 filings (Equal Employment Opportunity Commission 1985). As more older workers become aware of their rights, especially when the baby boomers hit their fifties and sixties, it is likely that lawsuits will increase.

Managers need to understand the law, to examine company policies and management practices for possible violations, and to identify and resolve situations in which age discrimination plays a part before complaints are filed and litigation occurs. It is particularly important that top-level management designates the identification and resolution of age-related work problems as a prime responsibility of all managers in the organization. See table 1–1 for a summary of major older-worker legislation.

With passage of the ADEA amendments, the age of mandatory retirement was raised to 70 years. Federal legislation in 1986 barred employers from forcing retirement at *any* age, following the lead of the 14 states that had already enacted laws of this kind. Additionally, nearly all federal employers are exempted from mandatory retirement. Consequently, employers can no longer require or depend upon the customary labor force exit of employees at age 62 or 65. Both experience and projections demonstrate that many persons will not take advantage of this raised retirement provision. Nevertheless, with the impact of increasing the age for Social Security eligibility, increased Social Security credits for delayed retirement, and some inflation, individuals may delay retirement until after age 65 or 70. The 1986 legislation that prohibited the freezing of pension benefit accrual at age 65 will also act as an incentive for older workers to remain in the work force. Managers will need to develop techniques that will allow them to capitalize on the talents and experience of these older workers who choose to remain in the workplace for several additional years.

Similarly, as more women and minorities will be part of tomorrow's work force, managers also need to be aware of the provisions of the Equal Pay Act of 1963 and the Civil Rights Act of 1964. Sexual harassment is becoming an important management issue; reports have increased nearly 50 percent since the EEOC started counting in 1981, and in 1986 the Supreme Court significantly expanded the circumstances in which sexual harassment may be a violation of federal civil rights law (*Wall Street Journal* June 24, 1986). In another set of recent cases, the Court upheld affirmative action based on race. To avoid lawsuits and to enhance productivity through use of the talents of these work force members, managers will need to be sensitive to their needs and rights.

Legislation focused on enhancing labor force participation also has been introduced or passed. The Job Training Partnership Act (JTPA), the Senior Community Services Employment Program, and the Vocational Education Act of 1984 have enabled states to provide displaced homemakers, older workers, and low-income, unemployed workers with opportunities for employment and training services in the private sector. Bills requiring firms to provide parental leaves have been introduced and are gaining support. A recent law was passed requiring an extension of group-health insurance for early retirees before they are Medicare-eligible, laid-off workers between jobs, and other categories of workers and their dependents. Managers of an increasingly diverse work force need to be aware of these and similar legislative enactments that ensure work opportunities and benefits for different groups of individuals.

Implications for Management of a Changing and Older Work Force

Most managers have not been prepared to respond to new demographic and age-relevant changes in the workplace. Labor surpluses and scarcities, pension costs, new technology, skill obsolescence, and legal pressures are but a few of the age, gender, and racial factors testing organizations. In light of these changes, competent managers at all levels will need to look at company policies and workplace options to ensure they are able to attract, motivate, and retain valuable workers of *all* ages.

Managerial vision will necessarily encompass both philosophical and practical approaches to human resource management. A nonageist or age-neutral perspective will need to predominate. This will require a critical self-examination of both personal and corporate tendencies to age bias and stereotyping. Company policies must be critiqued and, if necessary, rewritten to ensure the eradication of any age discrimination. Training of managers should be undertaken to assist them in recognizing and overcoming their own age biases, including attitudes about their own aging. Employers and managers will need to develop specifically age-irrelevant personnel policies, especially concerning job performance, promotions, and compensation. They also will need to become more knowledgeable about legislation against age discrimination and to remain up-to-date about federal enactments that affect employment and training, job discrimination, and pensions for workers age 40 and older. The same approaches will need to be undertaken relative to gender and racial factors.

Conclusion

Employers and managers will need to increase the knowledge, skills, and attitudes that are necessary to develop more effective human resource management of a diverse, maturing work force. This will require a greater comprehension of the linkages among the extrinsic and intrinsic values of work, employee motivation, and productivity. Top management and human resource management personnel will play key roles in promoting awareness of how company policies and practices enable a diverse work force to perform most effectively. To do so is both humane and good business. Based on the best information and planning strategies, the most able and competent managers will be prepared to make critical decisions about managing an aging and changing work force that will benefit not only those workers, but society as a whole.

References

"A Maddening Labor Mismatch." *Time* (April 28, 1986): 48–49.

Administrative Management Society. *1986 AMS Flexible Work Survey.* New York: Administrative Management Society, 1986.

Axel, H., and Brotman, H.B. "Demographics of the Aging Work Force." In *Employment and Training of the Mature Worker: A Resource Manual,* Bauer, D., Barocas, V.S., and Ferber-Cahill, P., eds. Washington, D.C.: National Council on the Aging, 1982, pp. 14–48.

Berlow, E. "Going for the Gold-Collar Worker." *Washington Post,* June 12, 1986, p. D5.

Bernstein, H. "New Inducements May Stem Unions' Slide." *Los Angeles Times,* July 23, 1986, pp. IV-1, 4.

Bezold, C., Carlson, R.J., and Peck, J.C. *The Future of Work and Health.* Dover, Mass.: Auburn House, 1986.

Bureau of National Affairs. *Work and Family: A Changing Dynamic.* Washington, D.C.: Bureau of National Affairs, 1986.

Bureau of the Census. *Projections of the Population of the United States by Age, Sex, and Race: 1983 to 2000,* Series P-25, No. 952. Washington, D.C.: U.S. Government Printing Office, 1984.

Bushnell, D. *Workshop Brief: Workforce Productivity.* Prepared for the National Dialogue on the Business Sector, mimeo, 1981.

"Census Data Illustrates Sharp Shift in Makeup of Nation's Households." *Washington Post,* November 20, 1985, p. A13.

"College Enrollments." *Wall Street Journal,* August 4, 1986, p. 19.

Drucker, P.F. "Goodbye to the Old Personnel Department." *Wall Street Journal,* May 22, 1986, p. 30.

Equal Employment Opportunity Commission. *Compliance Report, 1975–84.* Washington, D.C.: Equal Employment Opportunity Commission, 1985.

Friedman, D.F. "Eldercare: The Employee Benefit of the 1990s?" *Across the Board* (June 1986): 45–51.

Fullerton, H.N., Jr. "The 1995 Labor Force: BLS' Latest Projections." *Monthly Labor Review,* (November 1985): 17–25.

Greenwald, M. *Beyond the Boom: How Will the "Baby Bust" Be Different?* Paper presented at Demographic Outlook '86, New York City, June 4–5, 1986.

Griffin, J.L. "Higher Pay Lures Teachers Back." *Chicago Tribune,* July 6, 1986, p. 15.

Herbers, J. "Rising Cottage Industry Stirring Concern in U.S." *New York Times,* May 13, 1986, p. A18.

Hershey, R.D., Jr., "Economic Study Cites a 'Bicoastal' Disparity." *New York Times,* July 17, 1986, p. D5.

"High Tech to the Rescue." *Business Week* (June 16, 1986): 100–108.

"Jobs and Work Styles of the Future." *National Newsletter* 5, no. 4 (Spring 1986). Association of Part-Time Professionals.

Joint Economic Committee, U.S. Congress. *The 1981 Midyear Report on Productivity.* Washington, D.C.: U.S. Government Printing Office, 1981.

Kasarda, J.D., Irwin, M.D., and Hughes, H.L. "The South is Still Rising." *American Demographics* (June 1986): 32–39, 70.

Lamm, R.D. *Megatraumas—America at the year 2000.* Boston: Houghton-Mifflin, 1985.

"Losing the War of Letters." *Time* (May 5, 1986): 68.

Menken, J.L. "Age and Fertility: How Late Can You Wait?" *Demography* (Fall 1985): 469–483.

Naisbitt, J. *Megatrends—Ten New Directions Transforming Our Lives.* New York: Warner Books, 1982.

National Council on the Future of Women in the Workplace. *The Invisible Worker in*

a Troubled Economy. Washington, D.C.: The National Federation of Business and Professional Women's Clubs, 1984.
"Nationline." *USA Today,* May 15, 1986.
"New Job Trend: Temporary Workers." *New York Times,* July 9, 1986, pp. A1, A14.
Rhine, S. *Managing Older Workers: Company Policies and Attitudes.* Report No. 860. New York: Conference Board, 1984.
Ryder, N. Statement to the Joint Economic Committee of the U.S. Congress. July 25, 1986, mimeo.
Salisbury, D.L. "Private Sector Impact of an Aging Society." Prepared for The Travelers Symposium of an Aging Workforce, February 26-28, 1986 (mimeo). Washington, D.C.: Employee Benefit Research Institute, 1986.
Segal Associates. *Compendium 1985.* New York: Martin E. Segal, 1986.
"Sexual Harassment at Work is a Cause for Growing Concern." *Wall Street Journal,* June 24, 1986, pp. 1, 17.
Spencer, B.F. "Who Should Be Responsible for Retirement?" *Employee Benefit Plan Review* (July 1986): 32–33.
"Staying Single." *Wall Street Journal,* May 28, 1986, p. 1.
Technical Committee on an Age-Integrated Society. *Economic Policy in Aging Society: A Study of the Future Impact of Public Policy Changes on the Economy and on the Elderly.* 1981 White House Conference on Aging Report. Washington, D.C.: 1981.
Toffler, A. *The Adaptive Corporation.* New York: McGraw-Hill, 1985.
USA Snapshots. *USA Today,* June 17, 1986.
Yankelovich, Skelly and White, Inc. *Workers Over 50: Old Myths, New Realities.* Washington, D.C.: American Association of Retired Persons, 1986.

Suggested Readings

Bezold, C., Carlson, R.J., and Peck, J.C. *Future of Work and Health.* Dover, Mass.: Auburn House, 1986.

This book examines the current—and sometimes conflicting—trends in work and health care. Among the issues discussed are the changing demographics of the work force, the development of increasingly flexible working arrangements and settings, the shifts to a service and information economy, the implication of extended life expectancy, increasing corporate activism in health care, and the emergence of the workplace as a dominant setting where health is pursued.

Bureau of National Affairs, Inc., *Work and Family: A Changing Dynamic.* Washington, D.C.: Bureau of National Affairs, 1986.

This special report focuses on the massive restructuring of the U.S. labor force in the last thirty years and its impact on employees who are balancing family and work. It identifies the lack of corporate response until recently and presents case studies concerning the responses by employers, unions, and government to meet employees' needs for child care and parental leave, alternative work schedules, and relocation-assistance programs.

Ragan, P.K., ed. *Work and Retirement: Policy Issues.* Los Angeles: University of Southern California Press, 1980.

Significant policy issues in the public and private sectors and the role of the older person in the labor force are presented. Specific topics include alternative work patterns, age structure of occupations, assessment for retirement, and changing work and retirement patterns.

Rhine, S. *Managing Older Workers: Company Policies and Attitudes.* Report No. 860. New York: The Conference Board, 1984.

Based primarily on a survey of 363 companies, this research report was undertaken to explore whether company policies and practices encourage or discourage early retirement. Two major issues are addressed: retirement (including delayed-retirement and early-retirement incentives) and management of older workers (including employer perceptions and attitudes, performance, and job tailoring).

Yankelovich, Skelly and White, Inc. *Workers Over 50: Old Myths, New Realities.* Washington, D.C.: American Association of Retired Persons, 1985.

This report is based on a survey of human resource decisionmakers in 400 companies—100 each in four size groupings—representing companies with 50 or more employees. Designed to document the perceptions, policies, and practices of U.S. business related to older workers, the study focuses on the perceived strengths and weaknesses of older workers, equity considerations in a new business climate, and the need to create a framework in which the objectives of both companies and older workers can be met.

Step 2: Implement the Age Discrimination in Employment Act and understand its implications for management policy and practice.

Age Discrimination: The Law and Its Underlying Policy

Martin Lyon Levine

Many modern corporations have had a variety of personnel practices that differentiate among employees or applicants based on their age—what we can call age/work practices (Levine 1980). Mandatory retirement, refusal to hire the middle-aged, and preference for promoting younger workers are among these common practices. A Congressional statute, the Age Discrimination in Employment Act (ADEA) extends the concept of discrimination to age and prohibits most of these age/work practices; a 1986 amendment to the ADEA protects older workers without any age limit.

The Age Discrimination Policy

The ADEA was first enacted in 1967; its coverage has been enlarged several times since by Congress. The statute is an outgrowth of the modern attention to discrimination; it is largely based on the 1964 Civil Rights Act primarily aimed at racial discrimination.

The purposes of the ADEA, as stated by Congress, are to promote employment of older persons based on their ability rather than age; to prohibit arbitrary age discrimination in employment; and to help employers and workers find ways of meeting problems arising from the impact of age on employment.

Age/Work Practices. It is controversial to extend the idea of discrimination to include age discrimination. Sometimes, practices based on age may be fair, because the elderly are in fact different from younger persons, and because each group of persons will be old in turn. The Supreme Court has said that the government does not violate the Equal Protection Clause of the Constitution of it chooses to treat its older workers differently from the young by maintaining an age-based mandatory retirement system (*Massachusetts* v. *Murgia* 1976; *Vance* v. *Bradley* 1979).

Prior to the ADEA, age/work practices were widely accepted in the United States as in other Western countries. Many large firms forced older workers to retire and refused to hire older job applicants. These practices are of modern origin. Before the late nineteenth century, there had not been a tradition of forcing people to retire from work at some fixed age.

The usual explanations given for these modern age/work practices really do not justify them (Levine 1987). For example, a common explanation for such practices is the supposed reduced job performance of the elderly. But, modern evidence indicates that most older workers who are healthy and want to work are able to perform satisfactorily (Doering et al. 1983). They may be slower and less strong, but they are likely to be as intelligent as ever (Schaie 1983). They also are able to approach their jobs differently so as to compensate for physical changes, particularly if their employers cooperate. For example, if older workers are able to control the moment-to-moment pacing of their job, they are likely to be able to maintain overall daily output. The evidence also undercuts the common belief that younger workers will have more years of work in which a firm's investment in training will be rewarded. Older workers are less likely to leave the firm (Doering et al. 1983).

Excluding older workers from the job market also has been supported as necessary to make available jobs for younger workers. Since most older workers choose to retire because of ill health or pension benefits (even where forced retirement is banned), the traditional mandatory retirement system at its height only opened up a small fraction of 1 percent of the nation's jobs each year (Barker and Clark 1980).

Automatic retirement often was justified on the grounds that it is cruel to decide individually which older workers deserve forced retirement. There is little or no evidence of such a problem in firms that never had age-based mandatory retirement or firms in states that outlawed the practice (Friedman 1984).

Extension of the Idea of Discrimination. Therefore, it was appropriate for the Congress to use the discrimination concept to deal with employment of the elderly (Levine 1980). The civil rights approach to age/work issues has gathered wide support. When the ADEA was first adopted in 1967, Congress acted with the support of some major employer organizations, organized labor, and associations of the elderly. By 1986, when Congress extended the ADEA to protect workers over age 70, there was unanimous support in Congress for the total prohibition of age-based mandatory retirement. Temporary exceptions were made to allow retirement at age 65 for a few types of jobs presenting special problems such as fire fighters, police, and tenured college faculty.

The ADEAs Requirements

What establishments are covered? The ADEA binds every employer with twenty or more employees that is covered by federal labor laws. The law also covers employment agencies and labor organizations, the federal government, and state and local governments.

Who is protected? The ADEA protects employees and job applicants 40 years and older with no upper age limit. Workers who are independent contractors rather than employees are not protected by the ADEA. For example, a district sales manager paid by commission who does not have to account for work time is not protected by the law.

What is prohibited? The ADEA safeguards the older worker from discrimination in favor of the younger, and it protects those over age 40 against all age-based distinctions, including age-based mandatory retirement. Age-based differentiations are prohibited in hiring, wages, discharges, reductions in force, promotions, hours worked, availability of overtime, fringe benefits, training programs, career development, vacations, and sick leave.

Examples of activity forbidden by an employer include the familiar custom of mandatory retirement at 65; advertisements directly or indirectly indicating an illegal age preference, (such as seeking boys or girls, students, or recent graduates); and any suggestion on hiring or application forms that there is a preference for certain ages. Employers also are forbidden to use employment standards based upon age of the applicant or employee, such as requiring an older worker to take and pass physical or mental tests not imposed on younger workers, using promotion standards that differ on the basis of the age of the employee, or treating the misconduct of employees differently on the basis of age. Furthermore, employers are prohibited from retaliating against individuals who complain about prohibited practices, file an ADEA charge, or testify in an ADEA case.

The ADEA in Practice

A Sample Case. One of the most famous ADEA cases involved the I. Magnin clothing store chain and its firing of Philip D. Cancellier (vice president-stores/operations) and two other middle-management executives who were all in their early fifties (Friedman 1984). There was evidence that the store's decision to fire these executives was based on age. For example, the personnel vice president had taken notes of the meeting on one of the employees that read "dead end here . . . age 50. [Reached] maximum potential" The company had been worried about the "youth market" and wanted to attract "younger customers." Company reports said there were "too many superannuated salespeople" and called for "new, younger-thinking people who can merchandise and sell in tune with the 70s." Magnin had begun recruiting "bright, young" managers. Furthermore, there was a company supplementary retirement plan that would pay extra benefits to executives who retired after a certain number of years of service. Only three employees qualified for the benefits between 1976 and 1980. The scholar who studied this case stated, "the jury no doubt suspected that Magnin was playing a dirty game; that it was double crossing its executives by getting rid of them before they could qualify for pensions" (Friedman 1984, p. 55). After a six-week trial, the jury in the case of *Cancellier* v. *Federated Department Stores* (1982) awarded the Magnin employees damages of $1.9 million dollars.

Who files cases? In fiscal 1984, older workers filed over 17,000 age discrimination charges with the EEOC; double the number filed in 1981 (*ADEA Guidebook* 1986). A study on the cases that were litigated all the way to the federal courts of appeal showed that most cases, 153 out of 190, were brought by men, usually executives and white collar workers. They included engineers, attorneys, teachers, sales managers, and airline pilots. Most cases (100) involved termination; of these, 25 involved forced retirement. Twenty-one involved failure to promote. Only a few (11) complained of failure to hire (Friedman 1984).

Who wins? In this sample of cases, most (153 out of 190) were brought by private individuals rather than the Equal Employment Opportunities Commission, suggesting that this sample consists of cases the government did not think meritorious. Even in these cases, defendants won only about half the time. In a large number of the cases studied, the employer's defense was essentially procedural or technical, such as arguing that the individuals had missed the time limits in filing their charges of discrimination. This finding is borne out by another studied that included cases that went to trial but were never appealed (Schuster 1982).

The Three Stages of an ADEA Case

If a worker, an applicant, or the government brings to court a complaint that a firm has committed age discrimination, the ultimate question is whether age was a "determining factor" in the employer's personnel decision; it is not necessary to show that age was the only factor. Consideration of the case involves in turn three issues: whether the plaintiff can establish a prima facie case, employer's defenses, and evidence of pretext.

Prima Facie Case. Plaintiffs first have to establish their basic case. According to some courts, they just have to show that the individuals (1) are over age 40, (2) were subjected to adverse personnel action, such as being rejected for a job vacancy or involuntarily retired, and (3) met the minimum basic qualifications for the opening or were doing satisfactory work on the job. Other courts also ask if the employer knew their age and if a younger worker got the job. Some courts ask for any evidence, direct or circumstantial, that supports the conclusion that the employer consciously refused to consider hiring or retaining the individual because of age or at least regarded age as a negative factor.

Employer's Defense. It is then up to the firm to answer the plaintiff's case by showing that the personnel action fits under one of the statutory defenses discussed in the next section. For example, an employer might show that in determining whom to lay off in a slow season, it used an objective system of rating performance and ability which is a "reasonable factor other than age."

Evidence of Pretext. Even if the employer produces evidence of "good cause" or some other defense recognized by the statute, plaintiff may still present evidence that the employer's supposed reasons are only a pretext for discrimination, and that in fact "age was a determining factor" in the personnel decision. There may be evidence that the employer's motivation is discriminatory. For example, there may be improper advertisements ("We seek bright young people. . . ."), entries made on an interview file about the applicant ("She's too old."), or testimony about policy ("We're trying for a younger image.") Even in the absence of evidence of bad motivation, statistics may be offered to show a pattern or practice that the employer has a disproportionate number of younger employees. Some courts will find discrimination on proof that certain policies of the employer have a disproportionate adverse impact on the elderly. For example, an establishment with budgetary problems adopted a policy of not hiring applicants with more than five years of experience. A court held the policy violated the ADEA because statistics showed a disparate impact on older workers.

There are, however, a number of employment qualifications, such as physical requirements, that are likely to have an adverse impact on older workers, but are nevertheless generally regarded as "reasonable factors other than age" rather than illegal age discrimination. These practices may hurt the job chances of older workers, but they probably will not be regarded as age discrimination as long as they are uniformly applied to all employees and if they are reasonably necessary for the performance of the particular job.

At the end of each case, a jury will weigh all the evidence to determine if age discrimination was a motivating factor in the personnel decision.

Employer's Defenses

Under the ADEA, an employer has four possible defenses. (1) The law recognizes that age may sometimes be a "bona fide occupational qualification (BFOQ) reasonably necessary to the normal operation of the particular business." (2) Adverse personnel action is allowed if based on "reasonable factors other than age." (3) Businesses are also allowed to observe the terms of bona fide seniority systems or any bona fide employee-benefit plan such as a retirement, pension, or insurance plan. (4) Finally, discharge or other discipline is permitted if taken for "good cause."

Reasonable Factors other than Age. A personnel test or other employment practice that has an adverse impact on employment of older workers can only be justified when it is a business necessity. Factors other than age that may be considered reasonable include physical fitness requirements, quantity or quality production standards, educational or apprenticeship prerequisites, use of validated tests, or insistence that employees work fulltime. Tests or evaluations that are not adequately job-related or that are not sufficiently objective, do not provide a defense.

Bona Fide Occupational Qualification. If an employer wishes to use age as a BFOQ defense, the burden of proof on the employer is almost impossible to meet; even for public safety jobs, the employer must have strong facts to back up the policy. The employer first must show that the BFOQ is "reasonably necessary to the essence" of the business. For example, requiring older pilots to retire might be necessary for an airline, but requiring older flight attendants to retire certainly is not. In addition, the employer must show that it has a "factual basis" for its beliefs about older workers. The policy may be based on the conclusion that *substantially all* persons of that age would be unable to perform the job duties safely and efficiently. Alternatively, the policy may be based on the conclusion that most persons of that age would be unable to perform, and that it is impractical to evaluate persons of that age for the job on an individual basis. Acceptance of the BFOQ defense has been very limited. It has been accepted for actors who must be of a certain age for authenticity, for spokespeople promoting products directed to a particular age group, and for pilots (which is in dispute) and bus drivers.

Although employers may believe that the relative economic costs of hiring, training, or retaining older workers should be taken into account, these will not be honored as BFOQ. Additionally, employers may not discriminate on the basis of age because of the preferences of their customers or fellow employees.

Moreover, the defense may not be based upon stereotypes of assumptions that disqualify an entire age class. For example, a strenuous job cannot be limited to younger persons on the assumptions that all older workers lack the needed strength. Even if most older persons could not do the job, where it is practicable to make decisions individually, each person must be given the opportunity to try to qualify. It makes no sense to rule out a strong older person from a job just because most other people of that age would not have the requisite strength. Declaring such practices to be discriminatory is the essence of the ADEA.

Benefit Plans. The ADEA specifically permits employers to follow "bona fide" employee retirement, pension, and insurance plans so long as they are not a "subterfuge to evade the purposes of the law." Employers must offer their employees over age 65 the same benefits that are offered to younger employees. Benefit plans may not be used as a basis for refusal to hire older persons or as a basis for mandatory retirement. As an exception, executives over age 65 may be involuntarily retired if they are entitled to immediate, nonforfeitable pension or deferred compensation of at least $44,000 per year.

Enforcement

The ADEA is enforced by state age discrimination agencies in many states and by the Equal Employment Opportunity Commission (EEOC). When private persons believe they have been subjected to age discrimination in violation of the ADEA, they must first file charges with the state agency (if their state has one) and with the EEOC (Fretz 1985). The law provides an entirely different set of procedures for federal employees.

Conciliation. The EEOC is expected to seek voluntary compliance through informal methods of conciliation, conference, and persuasion. The government should explain the alleged violations to the employer, offer it an opportunity to respond, explain the potential liability, and inform the employer that a lawsuit may be filed unless the employer complies. There is no requirement that the government bargain or compromise its position.

Time Limits. In states that have age discrimination agencies, individuals must file their charges within 300 days of the alleged discriminatory practice; in states without such agencies, the time limit is 180 days. These time limitations may be disregarded by a court on grounds of fairness.

Sixty days after the administrative charge was filed, if conciliation has not been successful, either the individual or the EEOC may bring a court action under the ADEA. If the individual wishes to file the court action, it must be done after the conciliation period and within three years of an alleged violation of the ADEA. If the alleged violation is nonwillful or accidental, the time limit is two years. If the EEOC rather than the individual is bringing the suit, these time limits may be extended an additional year to allow for conciliation. The time limits for going to court are distinct from the time limits for filing the administrative complaint.

Procedure. An individual may sue a private employer in an ADEA case in either federal or state court. If the individual is seeking lost wages from a private employer, there is a right to a jury trial.

There can also be class action lawsuits under the ADEA. Most courts require that individuals take affirmative steps ("opt in") to join the class of plaintiffs in such an ADEA suit.

Remedies. If a lawsuit is brought and the court finds that illegal age discrimination has occurred, it may compel hiring, reinstatement, or promotion. The court may also grant appropriate back pay. Several courts have awarded cash in lieu of reinstatement ("front pay"). In trying to compensate the employee, the court can also restore seniority rights, lost health benefits, insurance benefits, and sick leave. If the court decides that the firm willfully violated the law, it may assess the firm an additional amount ("liquidated damages") equal to twice the amount of actual damages. The court may not award punitive damages or damages for pain and suffering. In a suit brought by the EEOC, the court may also issue an injunction requiring that the firm give up patterns, rules, or procedures that have a widespread discriminatory impact. When an individual wins an ADEA lawsuit, the law requires the firm to pay the individual's attorney's fees and costs.

State and Foreign Law

Many states have acted to outlaw age discrimination in employment as a matter of state law; these laws cover firms that are too small to be covered by federal labor laws and are not covered by the ADEA. Thirteen states have enacted statutes specifically banning age-based mandatory retirement, without a maximum age cap for the protection, for both public and private sector employees. These states are: California, Florida, Georgia, Hawaii, Iowa, Maine, Massachusetts, Montana, New Hampshire, New Jersey, New York, Tennessee, and Wisconsin. All but three of these state laws apply to all employers. In six additional states, mandatory retirement has been prohibited under age discrimination statutes by court interpretation. These states are Alaska, Nevada, New Mexico, North Carolina, North Dakota, and Vermont. Five states have an age discrimination statute, without age cap, covering the private sector, though retaining mandatory retirement for public employees.

They are Arizona, Colorado, Connecticut, Maryland, and Michigan. Nineteen other states have age discrimination laws that protect employees' rights to work until age 70 (sometimes with a lower mandatory retirement age for the public sector). These laws exist in Arkansas, Delaware, Idaho, Illinois, Indiana, Kansas, Kentucky, Louisiana, Nebraska, Ohio, Oregon, Pennsylvania, Rhode Island, South Carolina, South Dakota, Texas, Utah, Washington, and West Virginia (U.S. House 1986).

There is also some support in other countries for the idea that age/work practices constitute discrimination. Canada's new constitution specifically prohibits age discrimination. Both its parliament and its courts are considering whether mandatory retirement should still be permitted in that country. The International Labour Organization, a conference of national management and labor organizations and governments of every country, has recommended that all nations forbid age discrimination in employment and reconsider their mandatory retirement practices. A number of European nations have laws that limit in some way personnel actions based on age (Levine 1987).

Effect of the ADEA

Has the ADEA affected employment decisions generally or has it merely caused personnel managers to keep quiet about their age-based decisions? It is hard to know the extent to which the legislative condemnations of age discrimination and the conciliation efforts of the ADEA have convinced managers that age is usually a poor proxy for performance.

There is information on management practices in response to the abolition of a retirement age. California acted before the federal government did to outlaw age-based forced retirement at any age. A survey obtained information from 17 California private employers and 4 public agencies (Friedman 1984). Most companies retained policies using the idea of a "normal" or "expected" retirement age even though it was no longer mandatory. In order to keep working past that age, 9 businesses required no special procedure and the worker just continued working. In 10 cases, the worker had only to notify a supervisor or central department, while in 2 public agencies the procedures were more complicated. Only 1 of the 21 companies used routine tests to identify incompetent older workers; several others reserved the right to test particular individuals who want to keep on working; 8 mentioned procedures including performance evaluations, physical exams, and, in 1 case, a certification of competence. Evidence from this sample suggests that outlawing mandatory retirement may be accepted by the business community without fuss.

Conclusion

Two prime rationales for applying the discrimination concept to employment practices are that age is a poor proxy for performance and that age/work practices generally have no rational business purpose. Instead, these practices seem to have grown up largely for cultural or psychological reasons (Levine 1987). The practice deserves the label "discrimination."

The fragmentary evidence available indicates that under the ADEA, employers have either shifted to individual evaluations of employee's competence or have been satisfied to allow voluntary retirement and inducements to retire to deal with those individuals where age has taken its toll on performance. As more employers have experience with the contributions of more workers of advanced years, the folk wisdom that older workers are dead wood may be forgotten, and managers may increasingly make personnel decisions based on actual productivity instead of stereotypes.

References

ADEA Guidebook. Washington, D.C.: American Association of Retired Persons, Worker Equity Department, 1986.

Age discrimination in Employment Act, as amended, 29 U.S. Code secs. 621–34.

Barker, D.T., and Clark, R.L. "Mandatory retirement and Labor-Force Participation in the Retirement History Study," *Social Security Bulletin* 41 (November 1980): 20.

Cancellier v. *Federated Department Stores,* 672 F.2d 1312 (9th Cir. 1981).

Doering, M., Rhodes, S.R., and Schuster, M.R. *The Aging Worker.* Beverly Hills: Sage, 1983.

Fretz, B.D. "Age Discrimination." In *Representing Older Persons: An Advocates Manual,* National Senior Citizens Law Center, 1985 ed. Chicago: National Clearinghouse for Legal Services, 1985.

Friedman, L.M. *Your Time Will Come: The Law of Age Discrimination and Mandatory Retirement.* New York: Russell Sage Foundation, 1984.

Levine, M.L. *Age Discrimination and the Mandatory Retirement Controversy.* Baltimore: Johns Hopkins University Press, 1987.

Levine, M.L. " 'Age Discrimination' as a Legal Concept for Analyzing Age/Work Issues." In *Work and Retirement: Policy Issues,* Ragan, P. ed. Los Angeles: University of Southern California Press, 1980.

Massachusetts Board of Retirement v. *Murgia,* 427 U.S. 307 (1976).

Schaie, W. "Age Changes in Adult Intelligence." In *Aging: Scientific Perspectives and Social Issues,* Woodruff, D.S., Birren, J.E. eds. 2nd ed. Monterey, Calif.: Brooks-Cole, 1983.

Schuster, M. H. "Analyzing Age Discrimination Act Cases," *Law and Policy Quarterly* 4 (1982): 339.

U.S. House of Representatives, Select Committee on Aging. *Eliminating Mandatory Retirement*, Comm. pub. no. 99-561. 99th Cong., 2nd sess., 1986.

Vance v. *Bradley*, 449 U.S. 93 (1979).

Suggested Readings

Eglit, H.C. *Age Discrimination Law*, vol. 2. Colorado Springs, Colo: Shepards/McGraw-Hill, 1981 (with looseleaf updates).

This comprehensive discussion of the subject of age discrimination devotes an entire volume to ADEA law. A firm's lawyer would use this book to research detailed points.

Player, M.A. *Federal Law of Employment Discrimination in a Nutshell*. 2nd ed. St. Paul, Minn.: West, 1981.

This pocket-size book, published as a review for law students, devotes forty pages to a summary of the Age Discrimination in Employment Act. It is a good first place to look and will probably be sufficient for the needs of an employer seeking to understand the act. Note that since the book's preparation, the ADEA has been amended to cover workers over age 70 and that court interpretations on several points may have changed.

Levine, M.L. *Age Discrimination and the Mandatory Retirement Controversy*. Baltimore: Johns Hopkins University Press, 1987.

It evaluates the explanations and justifications offered for mandatory retirement plus arguments used to support applying the discrimination concept to age-differentiation. It reviews the historical, economic, psychological, and biological evidence on mandatory retirement and the older worker.

Ruzicho, A.J., and Jacobs, L.A. *Litigating Age Discrimination Cases*. Wilmette, Ill.: Callaghan, 1986.

Attempting to be a complete guide to age discrimination law, this work is organized as a lawyer's practice pointer. Thus, in addition to discussion of the statute and cases, it includes chapters on the steps of pretrial, trial, and appeal process in an ADEA lawsuit.

Step 3: Know the facts about the normal aging process.

The Physiological Aspects of Aging

Roger B. McDonald

> Aging is not disease because it is not contrary to nature.
> —Aristotle (384–322 B.C.)

From conception to death, our bodies go through many transformations collectively called aging. Inevitably, everyone experiences aging, but when does one really become "old"? Unlike some other physiological processes, growing old has no definitive boundaries. Aging cannot be easily defined because it is an ongoing process that begins at birth and continues, with great individual variation, throughout the life cycle. This chapter describes some theories of aging and the physiological changes associated with that aging process.

There has been a dramatic shift in the number of older people in this country. Since 1900, there has been a fivefold increase in the population of the United States. During this same period, the number of individuals over 65 years of age has increased 8 times. In 1982, there were 26,824,000 persons over the age of 65 years, representing approximately 11.7 percent of the total U.S. population (Metropolitan Life 1984). By the year 2025, when the baby boomers become the aged population, those over the age of 65 will represent 19.5 percent of the population with numbers totalling 63,000,000 (Metropolitan Life 1984). In addition, the fastest-growing age segment of the population is the over—85-year-old group. Within this age segment, women outnumber men approximately 3 to 2.

These numbers are supported by the fact that there has been a major increase in the life expectancy in the United States. Life expectancy today is slightly greater than 74.6 years, while in 1900, life expectancy was 49.2 years (Metropolitan Life 1985). This gain reflects the progress made during this century in medicine, sanitation, and public health education. Two particular reasons for the gain in life expectancy are prominent. First, infant mortality was close to 15 percent at the turn of the century. Today, infant mortality is less than 1 percent. Second, the development of antibiotic drugs in the 1940s significantly decreased the number of people dying of infectious disease, once a major cause of death among the elderly.

In response to the growing number of elderly, two separate fields have emerged that relate to the study of aging—gerontology and geriatrics. Gerontology is the study of the life span, while geriatrics is the medical science that studies the diseases of old age. This chapter will deal primarily with gerontology and the normal physiological losses that are associated with aging, but not the diseases.

Theories of Aging

What causes aging? Why is it that simply the passage of time must lead to decreased function? Four such theories are discussed: the wear-and-tear theory, the autoimmune theory, the error theory, and the free radical theory. It should be noted that none of these theories has been sufficiently tested to be accepted as fact.

Wear-and-Tear Theory. As the name implies, this theory assumes that a body "wears out" when exposed to extended use or stress, somewhat like the tires on a car. Support for the wear-and-tear theory has come from the work of Selye (1966), who has suggested that old age results in the loss of the resistance to stress, causing a greater risk of disease and death. On the surface, the wear-and-tear theory would seem reasonable since mechanical objects wear out with use and old age results in a significant loss in physiological function. However, nature has endowed living tissue with two distinctive properties that separate us from nonliving objects. First, humans have the capability of self-repair—the healing process. Although this process may be slowed during old age (Kligman et al. 1985), it is always present. Second, the human species can improve itself through specific intervention. For example, exercise lessens the risk of heart attack. The wear-and-tear theory once enjoyed wide acceptance. Its popularity has waned in recent years with the arrival of more sophisticated theories.

Autoimmune Theory. The immune system of an organism can prevent sickness by identifying and destroying viral, bacterial, and other harmful organisms. In essence, the human body manufactures substances known as antibodies that have the ability to differentiate between the body's own cells and those that do not belong. The ability to differentiate between self and nonself is referred to as self-tolerance. As one ages, there appears to be a loss in the discriminating ability of this system and it fails to recognize the difference between friend and foe (Roberts-Thompson et al. 1974). The failure in the immune system with age creates at least two conditions that may hasten aging. First, the aged have an increased rate of contracting infectious diseases (Hausman and Weksler 1985). The immune system fails to destroy invading viruses or bacteria that can cause disease. Without proper medical attention, these diseases may lead to premature death. Second, some evidence suggests that certain immune compounds, known as autoantibodies, increase with age (Hallgren et al. 1973). Autoantibodies destroy normal healthy cells, causing the immune system to lose its capacity for self-tolerance.

The Error Theory. Ever since Watson and Crick (1953) revealed the structure of DNA (*d*eoxyribo*n*ucleic *a*cid), scientists have continued to study this molecule in hope of better understanding the complex nature of life. DNA not only determines genetic traits (such as eye color, height, and shoe size), but also provides for growth, tissue repair, and all other bodily processes throughout a lifetime. It is not surprising, therefore, that some gerontobiologists have implicated "errors" in the structure of DNA as the possible cause of aging.

How would an error in the structure of DNA cause the aging process? Physiological processes can be carried out only if DNA supplies the proper information for making proteins. If a section of the DNA molecule develops an error, an event known to occur in aging animals (Reiss and Gershon 1976), improper proteins will result and normal body functions could be disrupted. The accumulation of these miscoded proteins, known as mutants, could slowly produce changes associated with aging. Examples of these changes include loss in antibody production, slow healing process, and loss of skin elasticity.

Free Radical Theory. In order to carry out normal biological functions, the human body uses dietary fuels, mainly fats and carbohydrates. During this process, these fuels are converted into energy, water, and carbon dioxide—each either is used to power the cell (energy) or is harmlessly discarded as waste product (water and carbon dioxide). The process that turns food into energy also generates free radicals, a class of chemicals that possess an extra electron and are highly reactive. The most notable free radical is the superoxide radical (O_2^-). The superoxide radical reacts with and attacks the protective fat layer that surrounds each cell. If the superoxide radicals are allowed to react with the fat membrane, the cell will eventually become damaged and cease to function properly. It is also possible that free radicals can attack and mutate DNA. Free radical attack on DNA results in miscoded and nonfunctional proteins. Fortunately, the normal human body has developed mechanisms that convert the superoxide radical into harmless compounds which are carried out of the cell. However, it is still possible that some of the superoxide radicals produced during normal metabolism elude conversion and react with the fat lining of the cell. Although the damage done to any one cell is small, the accumulation of this damage over many years could prove detrimental to the organism.

Physical Changes during Aging

Determining the changes to our bodies that can be attributed solely to aging presents a great challenge to researchers. Changes in personal appearance such as graying of hair, wrinkling of skin, and loss of hearing and visual acuity can easily be attributed to aging. In some cases, the effects of aging on the human body cannot be easily separated from voluntary action. Although genetics may play the principal role in determining the rate of aging, many years of inactivity, poor diet, and a stressful life-style can hasten the aging process. Regardless, there are at least two parameters that definitely can be characterized as part of the normal aging process: functional loss and declining homeostasis.

Functional Loss. As one ages, the body loses the ability to operate at its optimum level or functional capacity. Functional capacity can best be described as an ability to perform some physical task or involuntary physiological process, such as lifting a weight or having one's heart beat at a maximal rate. For example, during the years between ages 30 and 65, one loses 40 percent of the maximal breathing capacity, 20 percent of the nerve conduction velocity, and 25 percent of cardiac function (Strehler 1977). At age 30, the normal disease-free male would have a maximal heart rate of about 190 to 200 beats per minute. By the age of 70, this same male would only be able to achieve a maximal heart rate of 150 to 160 beats per minute (Sidney and Shephard 1977).

Many other functional capacities are age-dependent. These include bone volume, reaction time, and muscle strength. It is important to note that the observed age-related losses in functional ability greatly vary between any two individuals. Therefore, people must be viewed individually in order to determine their abilities. Further, the age-related loss in functional capacity should be distinguished from a decline in function resulting from specific disease or ill health. Disease is common to all age groups. A loss in functional capacity is strictly an aging phenomenon.

Decline in Homeostasis. In the strictest sense, homeostasis is the ability of the human body to maintain normal operation regardless of the environmental challenges presented. An example of a physiological homeostatic control system is the regulation of body temperature. Humans and all homeothermals (animals that maintain a constant internal temperature) have developed a complex system that maintains a constant internal temperature regardless of the surrounding environmental conditions. When placed in a hot room, the body cools itself by sweating. Conversely, in a cold room, the body maintains heat by shivering. The loss in thermoregulation may be a common feature of the aging process. This loss in the elderly is well documented by their higher mortality during heat waves and cold temperatures as compared to younger individuals (Collins et al. 1977; Ellis 1972).

Some diseases that are especially likely to affect the elderly can be viewed as stemming from a loss in normal homeostatic control. In particular, adult onset diabetes is of interest. Although diabetes is a serious and complex disease, the primary symptom is high blood glucose, a type of sugar, resulting from insufficient production of the hormone insulin by the pancreas. Insulin facilitates the entry of blood glucose into the cell. Without it, blood glucose concentration increases and the cells starve for fuel or glucose. Without this fuel, the cells will become damaged. The production of insulin is regulated by the level of glucose in the blood. This type of regulation is known as a homeostatic feedback loop. If the blood glucose becomes too low, insulin production is stopped until the level increases. If blood glucose becomes too high, insulin production increases to facilitate the removal of the sugar into the cell. In the elderly, blood glucose is elevated above normal level compared to younger subjects (Hayner et al. 1965). Although increased blood glucose of the elderly can be distinguished from the disease diabetes, it is evident that both represent a loss in homeostatic control of glucose regulation.

Cardiovascular Alterations and Age. Most research indicates that the heart and vascular system undergo dramatic age-related changes. The resting heart rate drops from an average of 72 beats per minute at age 25 down to 50 beats per minute by the age of 65. Both systolic and diastolic blood pressure rise, suggesting an increased risk of hypertension by those people over the age of 60 (National Center for Health Statistics 1976). Further, the cardiac output (the amount of blood pumped out of the heart per beat) decreases 1 percent per year in mature adults (Brandfonbrener et al. 1955). The veins and arteries also change with age. In normal young adults, the arteries have extreme elasticity which allows them to expand or contract depending on the amount of blood flow. In the elderly, there is a marked reduction in the ability of the veins to expand during periods of increased blood flow or volume. The loss of elasticity in the veins and arteries of the elderly increases the risk of hypertension and stroke (Kohn 1977). Arteriosclerosis, a general term for thickening and hardening of the arterial wall, increases with age (Bierman 1985). The causes of arteriosclerosis are multifactoral but are generally associated with increased fat deposits on the walls of blood vessels. As the artery narrows from an accumulation of fatty deposits, blood pressure rises and the risk of heart attack (coronary artery disease) and stroke (cerebral vascular accident) increases.

Skin Changes. Looking in the mirror and finding a wrinkle under one's chin may be the first encounter with the reality of aging. Many changes occur in the skin during aging. The wrinkling of skin is caused by two major factors. First, the protective lining of fat just below the skin decreases with age. Because the skin does not shrink, a wrinkle will form in place of the fat. Second, too much sunlight (in particular, the ultraviolet rays of the sun) over many years causes a loss in the elasticity of the skin. Therefore, the skin's ability to stretch is decreased. The skin of the elderly becomes drier with age. This is caused by a loss in the secretion of sweat and oil glands located within the skin. In the elderly, skin appears to take a longer time to heal after a wound or surgery compared to younger persons (Kligman et al. 1985).

Hearing and Aging. Hearing loss among the elderly accounts for the largest number of all sensory loss disorders. Although many elderly lose the ability to hear low-volume sounds, the majority of the elderly suffering from hearing disorders lose the ability to hear high-pitched sounds, including the consonant sounds of *z, s, g, f,* and *t.* Since speech is a mixture of high- and low-pitched sounds, the loss of any sound range can lead to problems in understanding the spoken word. Older adults frequently require an increase in volume to hear properly and have difficulty filtering out extraneous noise.

Gastrointestinal Changes. The normal aging process will result in many changes to the gastrointestinal tract that can lead to improper nutrition. The loss of teeth can result in the inability to chew hard or coarse food, causing many older persons to omit foods essential to good nutrition. Further, taste acuity diminishes with age; in some cases, eating may become less enjoyable, causing some elderly to skip meals. The ability of the stomach and intestinal tract to properly digest food decreases with age. The emptying time of the stomach increases with age (Bhanthumnavin and Schuster 1977), resulting in a greater incidence of gastritis or heart burn. In the small intestine, there is a loss of ability to absorb nutrients (Gallagher et al. 1979). As a result, the elderly may need greater quantities of food or vitamin and mineral supplements in order to meet their recommended daily allowance for nutrients. In the large intestine (colon), there is a decrease in muscle tone and motor function. This may cause the transit time of fecal material to increase. Thus, the incidence of constipation may increase with advancing age (Shklar 1972).

The previous paragraph outlines the physical changes of the gastrointestinal tract that may lead to nutritional problems in the elderly. Also important is the social aspect of eating. In American society, the dinner table has developed as a primary meeting place for lovers, friends, and companions. As one ages and loses loved ones and companions, eating alone can be a barrier to good nutrition because of the decreased interest in food, leading to serious nutritional problems. Further, for the frail elderly, shopping for food becomes hard and, in some cases, impossible. Although many physical changes occur during aging that can lead to poor nutrition, one should not underestimate the importance of nutritional problems associated with the social aspects of eating.

Body Composition Changes. Between the ages of 30 and 65, the composition of the human body goes through many changes. The most notable change is the increase in the amount of body fat. At age 30, a normal male will have approximately 10–15 percent body fat; a female will have 15–25 percent body fat. By the age of 60, these figures will have increased by approximately 40 percent (Shephard 1978). In addition, the amount of muscle tissue, also known as lean body mass, will decline by as much as 20 percent. The increase in fat content is related to the loss of lean body mass and the decrease in physical activity with age. It has been well documented that the amount of energy required to maintain normal body function decreases with age (Tzankoff and Norris 1977). The rate known as basal metabolic rate (BMR) is directly related to the loss in lean body mass. During rest, muscle tissue uses many more calories than fat tissue. The loss of this muscle tissue with age results in fewer calories burned. Because the elderly do not exercise as hard or as often as younger persons, they will not use more calories as a result of physical activity. Therefore, it is important that the elderly decrease food intake (calories) to match the loss of physical activity. Most people do not decrease the amount of calories consumed, causing an excess of calories stored as fat. Although there is much evidence that fat tissue increases with age, extreme obesity (greater than 50 percent ideal body weight) is not a major problem in the elderly. The most obvious reason is that people who are morbidly obese die from related diseases before reaching old age. In fact, the very old, those greater than 90 years of age, actually begin to lose fat tissue.

By the age of 70, an individual loses an average of one to two inches in height. This may be the result of years of bad posture or a compression of the spinal column due to a loss of calcium in the vertebrae. The loss of bone calcium, the major component of bone, appears to be a normal process in aging (Garn et al. 1967). Abnormally large losses of bone calcium can often lead to the development of osteoporosis, a bone disorder characterized by an increased risk of fracture. More than 37 percent of persons over the age of 65 develop osteoporosis (Avioli 1984). Four out of five of these people are women. Although the exact cause of osteoporosis is not known, inactivity, low calcium intake, and a loss in estrogen production in postmenopausal women may all play a role in this disorder.

Health and Well Being

Throughout the ages, the thought of growing old has sent the human species on a relentless search for immortality. Can life be extended far beyond the present limits? The maximal life span of the human is currently 115 to 120 years. From all available evidence, this has not changed over the last 300 years. During this time period, biomedical technological advances have done much to eliminate many diseases that curtailed the average life span. In fact, if the two major current causes of death (cancer and heart disease) were eliminated, probably life expectancy would only be extended by ten to fifteen years, suggesting that maximal life span may have some genetically predetermined limit. With this thought in mind, efforts to improve the condition of life should be directed at improving the quality of life rather than the length. The question becomes what can be done during youth and old age that can significantly improve one's chances of leading a normal healthy existence into the ninth and tenth decades of life?

Contrary to popular belief, all elderly are not sick. At any given time, 95 percent of adults over the age of 65 live outside nursing homes and are active participants in life's daily activities. This does not suggest that the elderly do not suffer from a greater incidence of minor health problems such as influenza, common colds, and digestive problems. The incidence of minor diseases increases with age (Hausman and Weksler, 1985). It is not clear whether the greater incidence of minor health problems is a phenomenon of aging or a result of improper health maintenance throughout a lifetime. Although there is limited knowledge about ways preventive health measures will affect the life span, research on diet and exercise suggests health can improve during old age.

Diet

For centuries, people have tried to manipulate their diet in hopes of extending life. The bookshelves of America are laden with volumes that claim to have the secret Ponce de Leon overlooked. However, scientific knowledge of the nutritional needs of the elderly is limited. In fact, the basic daily requirements for protein and vitamins in those over 65 have not even been established.

This is evident by the U.S. recommended dietary allowances (RDA) for nutrients (Food and Nutrition Board 1980) that are divided into only two adult categories—21 to 50 years and greater than 50 years. Clearly, an 80–year-old will have different needs from the 50–year-old.

In 1935, C.M. McCay and others (1935) found that chronic restriction of food intake in the rat resulted in an increase in the animals' maximal life span compared to animals given unlimited food. Since that time, many investigators have repeated McCay's experiments with similar results. They found that dietary restriction of laboratory rats lends to decreased incidence of cancer, heart disease, and kidney failure (Berg et al. 1962; Ross and Bras 1971). The implication from these studies is clear: eat less, stay slim, and live long. The question is whether data from studies of laboratory rodents during dietary restriction provide sufficient information directly applicable to the human. The human, unlike the laboratory rodent, is not confined to a small cage and given constant access to unlimited food. It would appear that these studies may be a better model for human overindulgence (obesity). In fact, epidemiological study of the survival of humans shows that those who are just slightly overweight (5 to 10 percent greater than ideal body weight) tend to live the longest.

Although our knowledge of nutritional needs of the elderly is limited, there are a few disorders that can be improved by nutritional intervention. The bone disorder osteoporosis appears to be directly related to the insufficient intake of calcium throughout a lifetime. Increasing the amount of calcium in the diet has been shown to decrease the loss of bone calcium (Recker et al. 1977). Further, the elderly may need more calcium in the diet because the absorption of calcium decreases with age (Armbrecht et al. 1980). Some have suggested that postmenopausal women need 1200 to 1500 mg of calcium daily in order to maintain positive calcium balance (calcium intake greater than the amount excreted) (Recker et al. 1977). This amount is 400 to 700 mg. greater than the current RDA of 800 mg. Other possible problems related to diet include iron-deficiency anemia, rickets (lack of vitamin D), and high blood pressure (excess of sodium intake). The greatest dietary risk to the elderly may not be a deficiency at all, but one of too much food—obesity. Obesity is the most common nutritional problem of public health concern in the United States. Gross obesity is rare in the elderly, as previously mentioned, because grossly obese people often die before they reach old age. Obesity above 50 percent of ideal weight can lead to disability and disease. Excess weight can cause diabetes, heart disease, gall stones, hernias, and gout. The primary cause of obesity in the elderly comes from a decrease in the level of physical activity without a decrease in caloric intake. Consequently, the elderly must be aware to keep activity and caloric intake in close balance.

Exercise and the Elderly

Although exercise will not extend the life span, it will improve the functional capacity of the elderly. First, regular exercise training will improve maximal aerobic capacity, which is the best measure of one's cardiovascular fitness level. Although a decline in aerobic capacity is an age-related phenomenon, it is possible for the elderly to improve this value with regular exercise. The improvement in aerobic capacity in the aged can be of a magnitude similar to that seen in young people. Second, exercise in the elderly can reduce the risk of heart disease, the number one cause of death for those over the age of 65. This can be accomplished in a number of ways. Exercise can reduce the risk of fatty accumulation in the arteries by lowering the blood cholesterol level. This is accomplished by increasing the circulating high-density lipoproteins (HDL) that remove cholesterol from the blood (Wood and Haskell 1979). Exercise may improve the circulation in the arms and legs (Sanne and Sivertsson 1968). The enhancement of peripheral blood flow decreases resistance in the arteries and thus lessens the work of the heart. These improvements will add up to a healthier cardiovascular system.

In recent years, there has been a significant amount of research performed on the benefits of exercise on bone. Since the turn of the century, it has been known that bone will develop according to the stress placed on it. In 1941, F. Albright (Albright et al. 1941) reported a greater incidence of osteoporosis in women who had been bedridden compared to active women. It was not until the 1980s that Everett Smith at the University of Wisconsin was able to show that a regular exercise program in the elderly would result in stronger bones (Smith et al. 1981). It is now widely accepted that exercise (especially exercise performed against gravity, such as jogging, aerobics, and biking) is a preventive measure as well as a treatment of osteoporosis. Not so easily measured, but nonetheless real, is an overall improvement in the vigor and general outlook on life that exercise can provide the older adult. It is often said that exercise may not add years to one's life, but it will surely add life to one's years.

Conclusion

Aging will affect everyone in some manner. The loss in abilities that occurs with aging are real and, unfortunately, cannot be reversed. The normal changes that occur with aging need not affect one's productivity, life-style, or role in society. After all, it is society—not nature—that has placed the elderly into the role of nonparticipation. Although it is true that aging results in a loss of certain functional capacities, there is no physiological reason why the elderly cannot remain active and vital throughout a lifetime. By living a life that maximizes healthful practices, such as not smoking, not consuming alcohol in excess, participation in regular physical exercise, wearing a safety belt while driving, getting proper nutrition, and reducing stress, the vast majority of elderly can expect to lead healthy, productive lives well into their seventies.

References

Albright, R., Smith, P.H., and Richardson, A.M. "Postmenopausal Osteoporosis." *Journal of the American Medical Association* 116 (1941): 2465–74.

Armbrecht H.J., Zenser, T.V., Bruns, M.E.H., and Davis, B.B. "Effect of age on intestinal calcium and phosphorus restriction changes with age." *American Journal of Physiology* 239 (1980): E322–27.

Avioli, L.V. "Calcium Supplementation and Osteoporosis." In *Nutritional Intervention in the Aging Process,* Armbrecht, H.J., Prendergast, J. M., and Coe, R.M., eds. New York: Springer-Verlag, 1984.

Berg, B.N., Wolf, A., and Simms, H.S. "Nutrition and Longevity in the Rat. IV. Food Restriction and Radiculoneuropathy of Aging Rats." *Journal of Nutrition* 77 (1962): 439–47.

Bhanthumnavin, K., and Schuster, M. "Aging and Gastrointestinal Function." In *Handbook of the Biology of Aging,* Finch, C., and Hayflick, L., eds. New York: Van Nostrand Reinhold, 1977.

Bierman, E. L. "Arteriosclerosis and Aging." In *Handbook of The Biology of Aging,* Finch, C.E., and Schneider, E.L., eds. 2nd ed. New York: Van Nostrand Reinhold, 1985.

Brandfonbrener, M., Landowne, M., and Shock, N.W. "Changes in Cardiac Output with Age." *Circulation* 12 (1955): 557–76.

Collins, K.J., Dore, C., Exton-Smith, A.N., Fox, R.H., MacDonald, I.C., and Woodward, P.M. "Accidental Hypothermia and Impaired Temperature Homeostasis in the Elderly." *British Medical Journal* 1 (1977): 353–56.

Ellis, F. P. "Mortality from Heat Illness and Heat-aggravated Illness in the United States." *Environmental Research* 5 (1972): 1–58.

Food and Nutrition Board, National Research Council. *Recommended Dietary Allowances.* 9th ed. Washington, D.C.: National Academy of Sciences, 1980.

Gallagher, J.C., Riggs, B.L., Eisman, J., Hamstra, A., Arnaud, S.B., and Deluca, H.R. "Intestinal Calcium Absorption and Serum Vitamin D Metabolites in Normal Subjects and Osteoporotic Patients." *Journal of Clinical Investigation* 64 (1979): 729–36.

Garn, S.M., Rohmann, C.G., and Wagner, B. "Bone Loss as a General Phenomenon in Man." *Federation Proceedings* 26 (1967): 1729–36.

Hallgren, H.M., Buckley, C.E., Gilberstsen, V.A., and Yunis, E.J. "Lymphocyte Phytohemagglutinin Responsiveness, Immunoglobulins and Autoantibodies in Aging Humans." *Journal of Immunology* 111 (1973): 1101–7.

Hausman, P.D., and Weksler, M.E. "Changes in the Immune Response with Age." In *Handbook of The Biology of Aging*. Finch, C.E., and Schneider, E.L., eds. 2nd ed. New York: Van Nostrand Reinhold, 1985.

Hayner, N.S., Kjelsber, M.O., Epstein, F.H., and Francis, T., Jr. "Carbohydrate Tolerance and Diabetes in a Total Community, Tecumseh, Michigan." *Diabetes* 14 (1965): 413–23.

Kligman, A.M., Grove, G.L., and Balin, A.K. "Aging of Human Skin." In *Handbook of the Biology of Aging*, Finch, C.E., and Schneider, E.L. eds. 2nd ed. New York: Van Nostrand Reinhold, 1985.

Kohn, R.R. "Heart and Cardiovascular System." In *Handbook of the Biology of Aging*, Finch, C.E., and Hayflick, L., eds. New York: Van Nostrand Reinhold, 1977.

McCay, C.M., Crowell, C.M., and Maynard, L.A. "The Effect of Retarded Growth Upon the Length of Life-span and Upon Ultimate Body Size." *Journal of Nutrition* 10 (1935): 63–79.

Metropolitan Life. "Gains in U.S. Life Expectancy." *Statistical Bulletin* 66 (1985): 18–23.

Metropolitan Life. "United States Population Outlook." *Statistical Bulletin* 65 (1984): 16–19.

National Center for Health Statistics, "Blood Pressure of Persons 6–74 Years of Age in the United States." *Vital and Health Statistics*, No. 1. Washington, D.C.: U.S. Public Health Service, 1976.

Recker, R.R., Saville, P.D., and Heaney, R.P. "Effects of Estrogen and Calcium Carbonate on Bone Loss in Postmenopausal Women." *Annals of Internal Medicine* 87 (1977): 649–55.

Reiss, U., and Gershon, D. "Rat-liver Superoxide Dismutase." *European Journal of Biochemistry* 63 (1976): 617–23.

Roberts-Thompson, I.C., Whittingham, S., Youngchaiyud, U., and Mackay, I.R. "Ageing, Immune Response, and Mortality." *Lancet* 2 (1974): 368–70.

Ross, M.H., and Bras, G. "Lasting Influence of Early Caloric Restrictions on Prevalence of Neoplasms in the Rat." *Journal of the National Cancer Institute* 47 (1971): 1095–113.

Sanne, H., and Sivertsson, R. "The Effect of Exercise on the Development of Collateral Circulation After Experimental Occlusion of the Femoral Artery in the Cat." *Acta Physiologica Scandinavica* 73 (1968): 257–63.

Selye, H. *The Stress of Life*. 2nd ed. New York: McGraw-Hill, 1966.

Shephard, R.J. *Physical Activity and Aging*. London: Croom Helm, 1978.

Shklar, M. "Functional Bowel Distress and Constipation in the Aged." *Geriatrics* 27 (1972): 79–83.

Sidney, K.H., and Shephard, R.J. "Maximum and Submaximum Exercise Tests in Men and Women in the Seventh, Eight and Ninth Decades of Life." *Journal of Applied Physiology* 43 (1977): 280–87.

Smith, E.L., Jr., Reddan, W., and Smith, P.E. "Physical Activity and Calcium Modalities for Bone Mineral Increase in Aged Women." *Medicine and Science in Sports and Exercise* 13 (1981): 60–64.

Strehler, B.L. *Time, Cells, and Aging*. 2nd ed. New York: Academic Press, 1977.

Tzankoff, S.P., and Norris, A.H. "Effect of Muscle Mass Decrease on Age-related BMR Changes." *Journal of Applied Physiology* 43 (1977): 1001–6.

Watson, J.D., and Crick, F.H.C. "Molecular Structure of Nucleic Acid. A Structure for Deoxyribose Nucleic Acid." *Nature* 1717 (1953): 737–38.
Wood, P., and Haskell, W.L. "The Effect of Exercise on Plasma High Density Lipoproteins." *Lipids* 14 (1979): 417–27.

Suggested Readings

Burnet, M. *Endurance of Life.* Melbourne: Cambridge University Press, 1980.

Macfarlane Burnet, a Nobel laureate, presents a theory of aging in terms of genetics. From this, he goes on to discuss the genetic factors that, moderated by the environment, produce intelligence, temperament, and behavior. Although the content may be somewhat controversial, this is an informative treatise based on scientific observation.

Comfort, Alex. *A Good Age.* New York: Crown, 1976.

In this light-reading book, Alex Comfort discusses the positive side of growing old. Topics as varied as physiology, pets, and "officials and the runaround" are presented. In addition, short descriptions of people successful during old age are given periodically throughout this most enjoyable and valuable book.

Finch, C.E., and Schneider, E.L., eds. *Handbook of the Biology of Aging.* New York: Van Nostrand Reinhold, 1985.

A highly technical book covering a wide range of topics concerning the biology and physiology of aging. Although the reading may prove difficult in some cases, this book is the best source for factual information on the biology of aging.

Shephard, R.J. *Physical Activity and Aging.* London: Croom Helm, 1978.

Although technical, this is the best comprehensive publication on the topic of exercise and aging. It includes a brief chapter on guidelines for exercise in the elderly population.

Walford, R.L. *Maximum Life Span.* New York: W.W. Norton, 1983.

A noted immunologist, Dr. Walford presents his original theory of aging based on dietary restriction. In this book, Dr. Walford suggests that maximum life span may be extended far beyond the present limits. While his approach to increasing the human life span may have its critics, the book presents an excellent description of the theories of aging.

Step 4: Prevent work-induced stress detrimental to older workers and encourage effective stress management.

Stress and the Older Worker

Robert M. Tager

Stress affects people of all ages; no one is immune. Although some stress is necessary for people to be productive and creative, unrecognized and unmanaged stress that exceeds the level needed for maximum productivity frequently results in decreased performance. It is at this point that the adverse effects of stress begin. Additionally, unmanaged stress contributes to illness, accidents, absenteeism, and job dissatisfaction (Warshaw 1979).

Physical And Emotional Responses to Stress

According to Selye, stress is the "non-specific response of the body to any demand made upon it" (1975, p. 14). This definition points out that stress is a *response*—something within the individual—not the events that produce the response. These events causing the stress are called stressors. The definition also emphasizes that the response is *nonspecific* and can come from a variety of causes.

Stress from multiple causes is additive and leads to greater stress responses. Regardless of whether the stress-producing events are positive or negative for the individual, real or only perceived as real, the effects on the individual are the same.

A number of physiological changes occur in the stress response (Farquhar 1978). The response includes focused attention, elevated blood pressure, increased pulse, and breathing rates, increased muscle tension, clammy hands, tightened abdominal muscles, and a flushed forehead. The physiological response is the same for a dangerous or exciting situation. For example, an individual will experience the same response in a near-miss automobile accident or a roller coaster ride. The emotional response varies according to whether the stress is acute or chronic. Typically, acute stress produces fear and anxiety, while chronic stress causes depression.

Stress produces diverse effects that vary according to the situation. In the case of a danger situation, the stress response mobilizes the individual for self-protection or escape. This "fight or flight" response was described near the turn of the century. In the case of an exciting recreational situation, the response contributes to the overall thrill and enjoyment.

A well-managed stress response frequently mobilizes an individual to perform an efficient and productive day's work (Warshaw 1979). In a deadline situation, the stress response is usually intense, producing a high degree of mobilization and productivity. In all of these situation—danger, recreation, and work—the stress response provides a benefit in the form of protection, enjoyment, or productivity.

Unfortunately, other causes of stress that produce a prolonged stress response eventually result in physiological or psychological harm. Conditions such as high blood pressure, headaches, gastrointestinal symptoms, and a variety of musculoskeletal symptoms often result. Also, underlying medical conditions such as diabetes, high blood pressure, or gout not caused by stress can become more symptomatic under stressful situations (Tager 1980).

Causes of Stress

Common employment-related stressors include heavy work loads, time pressures, unrealistic deadlines, responsibility without authority, office politics, and lack of feedback from supervisors. A lack of feedback often is more stressful than constructive criticism or information about errors. Problems involving interpersonal relationships are another example of stressors that affect anyone in the work force. These problems occur internally, between coworkers and supervisors, and occur externally with customers or clients.

Although causes of stress in the workplace affect workers of all ages, these universal sources of stress have more of an effect on older workers for at least two reasons. First, as individuals age, their ability to recover from stress is impaired (Zarit 1980). The physiological responses that provide balance, or homeostasis, become slower with age. Second, older workers are affected by more stress-related illnesses than the average younger worker (Cooper 1984). Of course, not all older workers have difficulty adapting to stressful situations. Different coping mechanisms can be accounted for by differences in life events experienced by the older person (Siegler and George 1984). However, some workers who have reached their limits for advancement, have declined from a previous performance peak and have been experiencing a large number of stressors, may exceed their ability to cope effectively with these events.

Older workers, especially in the more advanced years, are likely to suffer a large number of stressful events both on and off the job. Older workers are likely to be experiencing illnesses of family members, deaths of family or friends, and a decreased availability of previously supportive people in their lives due to relocation, retirement, and other factors. Therefore, older workers are subject to serious stressors, with a cumulative effect occurring over the years.

Stressors and the Older Worker

Myths about Aging. Myths about aging can produce a stressful environment for older workers. Although progress has been made, negative stereotypes, myths, and prejudices about aging persist that directly or indirectly affect older workers' feelings of self-worth and capability. Such prejudices are based on common myths such as older persons being less capable, less efficient, or less productive than their younger counterparts (Stagner 1985).

Non promotability. The sources of stress for older workers are diverse. Some older workers who leave the work force and then reenter find they need to update their skills to adapt to the changing environment. This is especially common for women who stopped working to raise a family and reentered their labor force years later. In such a situation, workers may find that the promotions were given to younger workers.

Skill obsolescence is a problem for some older workers who have a continuous employment history. The lack of up-to-date skills may interfere with promotional opportunities.

Some older workers who stay on the job face the problem of the Peter principle—advancing beyond the level at which they are competent and remaining there. This makes the older worker more subject to some of the stressors previously discussed, such as excessive work load, time pressures, or even loss of a job. Older workers who leave their jobs and start a second career often find they have to start at the bottom again, where advancement may be difficult. Limited advancement because of an irregular employment history, skill obsolescence, the Peter principle, or any other reason is stressful.

Younger supervisors. Another source of stress for older workers involves working for younger supervisors. In situations where older workers have not advanced to higher supervisory, management, or professional levels, their supervisors are likely to be younger. Such a situation can provide a background for misunderstandings and potential conflicts. The sources of such potential conflicts are with the older worker, the younger manager, or both.

Younger managers may cause stress when they avoid discussing a performance problem with an older employee. The reluctance to address performance problems and provide constructive feedback to older workers may occur because supervisors believe that older workers cannot change or that they will retire soon. Younger supervisors may be hesitant to confront older workers about performance issues because they associate a positive or negative parental image with the older worker. The younger supervisor with older parents often draws analogies or parallels, consciously or unconsciously, to the child–parent relationship. Supervisors who had negative experiences with older relatives are sometimes prejudiced against the capabilities of older workers.

From the point of view of an older worker, interpersonal problems with younger supervisors occur for a variety of related reasons. For example, the worker feels that the younger supervisor is inexperienced and unqualified to be in a position of authority. They may resent a more advanced education level of a young manager and feel that only experience should bring organizational advancement. Holdovers from parent–child relationships may also affect older employees who find it difficult to receive instructions and constructive criticism and to be evaluated by someone younger than themselves.

Lack of Finances or Personal Rewards. In some cases, the older worker experiences a real or perceived lack of financial or personal rewards in the workplace. These feelings are more intense for an older employee who does not anticipate the opportunity for future years of growth as would a younger individual. Although any worker is subject to the problem of burnout, the older person who spent more years doing the same job is more prone to this problem. Boredom sets in, and the person becomes sensitized to repeated events or conditions that produce a stress response.

Competition. Older workers compete with younger employees whose training is more recent and who may have more up-to-date education. Such older persons also observe and have to work with younger workers and supervisors who are striving for advancements that may not be forthcoming to the older worker. Whether this is actually the case or is merely perceived to be the case makes no difference because the stress response to the situation will be the same. The threat of potential or actual loss of job position or loss of employment itself due to early retirement or layoffs is a major source of stress.

Fewer opportunities are available to older workers, especially for those with limited education, training, and experience (Cooper 1984). The risk of layoff and demotion is greater for those who have lower levels of training, less recent training, and lower seniority. This is the case for a person who has a gap in employment or who has started a second career.

Responses and Effects. Individuals can respond differently to the same situation. Some will be more prone to a loss of efficiency and productivity over time; others will be less prone to these changes. Unfortunately, there are no specific ways to identify which individual is likely to have a problem with stress. However, observation and awareness can identify such people as the process is occurring, and preventive measures can be taken.

Stressors tend to have a cumulative effect. As people live longer, there is more chance for negative life events to have occurred. These include nonemployment factors such as death of a loved one, divorce, or illness. They also include employment-related factors such as being passed over for a promotion, unwanted transfers of location or job task, and reaching a limit on salary advancements. Stressful events in an older employee's personal life along with such events in their work can compound to produce a strong effect.

Management of Stress

The general principles of stress management that apply to older workers are basically the same as those for younger adults. One obvious difference is the type of exercise recommended for older and younger persons (Tager 1981b). Certain aspects of nutrition may also need modification in the older age group, especially in the case of an individual with a chronic health problem. Although there are some differences in the content of stress management information for older and younger adults, it is possible to provide adequate information for everyone in a group with a broad age range.

Recognition

The first and most important step in management of stress is its recognition (McLean 1979). Improvement is only possible if individuals recognize the presence of an excess level of stress and the need to do something about it. Some of the signs of excess stress are fairly obvious, but others are subtle. An increasing level of irritability is often an early sign that stress is not being managed well. This may appear as an unusual snapping at other workers during conversation or the occurrence of arguments that seem unwarranted. Irritability can spread from worker to worker. An early identification of the cause may help avoid a significantly larger problem later.

The stress response may cause a person to worry unnecessarily over personal matters or about work problems. Efficiency in problem solving drops off after stress rises to an excessive level, and otherwise readily solvable problems may appear insurmountable when the stress level rises too high (Tager 1984). People under stress may begin to complain about minor physical problems or various symptoms that are bothering them. Increasing absenteeism or arriving late from breaks may also indicate an unmanaged stress problem. It is important to recognize these symptoms early and investigate the cause.

There has been an increasing incidence of stress-related disability claims in the workers' compensation system (*CWCI Bulletin* 1985). Early identification and management of stress-related problems may result in a significant cost savings as well as a decrease in absenteeism and employee dissatisfaction.

Increased alcohol consumption is common in chronic stressful situations and is a real danger sign. Many companies have employee-assistance programs that can help with problems of this type. Again, early intervention is of paramount importance. Increasing smoking can be a similar sign that is easy to detect. Increased alcohol consumption or smoking is a sigh of unmanaged stress that can have a direct, adverse effect on health and is related to increased absenteeism and illness (Cooper 1984).

Although increased coffee consumption does not produce nearly as great a health risk as increased alcohol intake or smoking, it may be a sign of a higher stress level. The stimulating effect of caffeine may also contribute to stress-related symptoms such as irritability. Taking tranquilizers is another sign of stress. Although the use of tranquilizers is very common in American society, they are not appropriate for use in the management of day-to-day stress.

Unmanaged stress may cause decreased productivity, increased errors, missing reasonable deadlines, unusual lack of neatness in work, and changes in social behavior. An example of the latter is the employee who is friendly with many coworkers and then becomes withdrawn. In the case of long-term stress, depression results along with its characteristic appearance of sadness and decreased activity.

Communication

After the recognition of unmanaged stress, the next step is open communication. This is best done privately and in a nonintrusive manner. It is important for a manager not to appear threatening and, at the same time, to show genuine concern for the employee's well-being. The conversation might begin something like this: "I notice that you have seemed irritable lately, and I'm concerned that something might be wrong." Such a statement does not accuse and gives the employee a variety of methods of answering. Such an opening conversation works best if it is held promptly after the recognition of poorly managed stress and is most effective if there is already a basis for open communication from previous conversations on business or on nonbusiness-related topics. During this communication, it is important to keep in mind common fears that affect older workers (such as loss of job position, potential loss of employment, and decreased self-esteem) both on an employment basis and on a personal basis.

After communication is open, a manager can proceed in a variety of ways. If the stress-producing events are directly work-related, the manager may be able to assess the condition that is causing the stress. If that is not possible, the manager should counsel the employee on how to handle the situation better. In the case of interpersonal employee differences, it often is helpful to talk to each employee separately and, after gaining a basic understanding of the situation, have a discussion with the two or more employees involved to reach an equitable solution to the problem. The opening of discussion is therapeutic in itself. When people openly discuss what is bothering them, the doors open for communication and resolution of problems. In such a group situation, part of the manager's role is to maintain a reasonable level of comfort in the discussion, avoiding accusations and nonproductive arguments.

Referrals

A referral is appropriate if the problem is not work-related or if it is producing a greater response than the manager comfortably can handle. A referral can be directed to a company doctor, nurse, psychologist, social worker, or qualified person in the personnel department. Companies with employee-assistance programs usually have either appropriate counselors available within the company or, in the case of smaller organizations, referral sources in the community. For non–work-related problems, referral sources include the employee's personal physician, community agencies, and clergy if the employee has a religious affiliation.

In some communities, consultants offer stress management programs to companies and other organizations. In hiring such an individual or group as employees, as consultants, or for workshops, it is important to be aware of their credentials. Some individuals offering stress management programs are very well trained. They might be physicians or nurses who have taken special training in the field, health educators with a masters degree in health education or related fields, or licensed clinical social workers. A degree or credential does not guarantee quality, but it does establish a level of education, training, and supervised experience. At the other end of the spectrum are individuals who have taken a weekend stress management workshop and then propose to teach the subject. As part of the selection process, it is important to ask for documented experience in the field and references.

The management of employee stress situations is very important. However, a more important goal is to prevent situations from getting to the point where an employee is suffering personally and work efficiency is deteriorating (Tager 1984). This again requires the recognition of stress in an employee or in a group of employees and an early investigation of the source of the problem. This process can help educate and train people to manage their stress so that it does not take a personal or organizational toll.

Stress Management Programs

Some of the components commonly included in stress management programs are communication techniques, exercise appropriate for a person's age, nutrition, and deep relaxation methods. Each of these components has a potential for helping manage the stress response; used together, they can provide an effective program. Major elements of such a program can help promote general employee health at the same time. If stress is unmanaged, it can manifest itself with poor health, job dissatisfaction, apathy, absenteeism, and labor turnover (Cooper 1984).

Communication Techniques. Open communication is an effective technique in reducing the effects of psychological stressors that produce fear, anxiety, and depression. Communication can be used in a number of different ways. Discussions between managers and employees are only part of a spectrum. It is beneficial for employees to talk with peers and non–work-related friends and relatives. Talking about a problem to a nonthreatening listener is very helpful as a problem-solving technique. The listener need not solve the problem, but rather should allow individuals to express themselves and reach their own solutions. Problem resolution frequently is more difficult when an individual ponders a problem in isolation; in fact, this isolation can cause the situation to become worse. When a problem has continued for some time or is producing fairly marked personal or organizational symptoms, professional help is indicated.

Exercise. Exercise is one of the most individualized components of a stress management system. Individuals should check with their physicians before undertaking an exercise program. Although jogging has received much publicity, it is not the best exercise for everyone, particularly for older individuals who are prone to musculoskeletal problems and who have cardiovascular or respiratory conditions. In general, I recommend walking as the best general exercise for older people. Walking does not require any special equipment, other than a good pair of shoes; it can be done almost anywhere and rarely produces the aches and pains that sometimes occur with more vigorous exercises. Also, with a doctor's approval, walking is a good exercise for people with a variety of medical conditions such as heart disease or diabetes. A wide variety of exercises including swimming and cycling are available, but these need to be tailored to the individual.

Cooper (1970) compares many different exercises and discusses gradual ways of getting involved in an exercise program. The variety of exercises available allows an individual to select one or more that fit their level of health, past experience, interests, living location, and economic status. Individuals should be consistent with a modest amount of exercise rather than vigorously pursue an extensive program that will later be dropped. It is important to provide for a warm-up period before exercising and a cool-down period afterward in order to allow the heart and lungs time to adapt to the change and as an aid in avoiding muscle cramps and aches. Stretching may also be appropriate, but is best learned on an individual basis.

Exercise has a variety of positive effects. Although moderate exercise does not burn a great deal of calories, the amount of calories used is additive over time and can aid in maintaining weight. People who are well exercised also tend to have lower resting blood pressures and pulse rates and more efficient breathing abilities. Exercise can also help an individual generally feel better both physically and psychologically.

Nutrition. Stress has been directly or indirectly linked to a number of disease states that can be prevented or modified by proper nutrition (Brody 1981). Such conditions include high blood pressure, heart disease, gastrointestinal problems, and certain types of cancers. Except in people with specific disease states, nutrition can be more generally applied than exercise, which needs to be more individualized. Nutrition is a subject area in which there are many different and strongly held beliefs (Tager 1981a). However, there are some basic factors that if adhered to, have a significant positive effect on health. Seven basic rules are well described in the *Dietary Guidelines for Americans* (1985) published by the U.S. Department of Agriculture. These guidelines are based on scientific evidence, are logical, and are easy to follow.

1. *Eat a variety of foods.* This can provide the necessary vitamins, minerals, proteins, carbohydrates, and other nutrients that may not be sufficiently present in a diet with a limited number of foods. People under stress often eat poorly, which makes them more subject ot illness (Brody 1981).

2. *Maintain desirable weight.* This means consuming an adequate, but not excessive amount of calories to maintain one's weight within the desirable body weight range for the individual. The desirable ranges are fairly broad and allow for reasonable individual differences. Some persons under stress eat excessively and gain excess weight. This, along with stress, can contribute to heart disease and musculoskeletal problems.

3. *Avoid too much fat, saturated fat, and cholesterol.* Excesses of these contribute to the risk of heart attacks. Avoiding these nutritional excesses can have a protective effect against the adverse effects of stress on the cardiovascular system.

4. *Eat foods with adequate starch and fiber.* This provides for sufficient consumption of calories, and the fiber aids digestion and decreases problems with the gastrointestinal tract. Stress-related gastrointestinal disorders can be aided by a diet with a proper carbohydrate balance.

5. *Avoid too much sugar.* In addition to being a major factor in tooth decay, sugars add calories, but little else in the way of nutrients. People under stress sometimes increase their consumption of sweets.

6. *Avoid too much sodium.* Sodium, as is present in table salt and MSG, has been implicated in the problems of high blood pressure, a major risk factor in causing heart attacks and strokes. Since one of the stress responses is an increase in blood pressure, limiting sodium intake may have a

protective effect and help reduce the incidence of high blood pressure and its complications.

7. *If you drink alcoholic beverages, do so in moderation.* Alcohol, like sugar, is high in calories and low in nutrients, and excesses can produce obvious problems. Increased alcohol consumption is a common result of unmanaged stress and can lead to many problems including liver disease and damaged interpersonal relationships.

Deep Relaxation. The word *relaxation* is commonly used to refer to activities such as watching television, fishing, reading, knitting, and going to a ball game. *Deep relaxation* refers to a state where an individual is profoundly relaxed and calm, and is aware of a minimum of external stimuli. This is a healthful, rejuvenating state in which the body's repair processes function best. There are a wide variety of deep relaxation techniques as there are with exercises.

A number of physiological changes occur when the techniques are practiced. Deep relaxation tends to lower an individual's blood pressure, pulse rate, and breathing rate and also can help to produce a feeling of well-being. Benson (1976) demonstrated a decrease in resting blood pressure with the regular practice of meditation. Some techniques, such as meditation, are ancient, while others are modern, such as biofeedback (which requires electronic instrumentation). Techniques such as progressive relaxation, where muscle groups are sequentially tightened and then relaxed, can be accomplished by listening to instructions on a tape player. Other techniques include self-hypnosis, autogenic training (a specialized form of self-hypnosis using suggestions such as heaviness and warmth) and various forms of yoga (Schultz and Luthe 1959). The variety is helpful in that individuals can select methods consistent with their general physical condition, the time they wish to spend, and their beliefs.

Deep relaxation techniques can be learned in many ways. Formal instruction is generally preferable, although self-teaching tools such as books and tapes are helpful. Although individual instruction is available, most techniques are taught in groups. Instruction is provided by many community colleges through courses or workshops in which techniques can be learned, by private groups or individuals who provide training, and by some organizations which use existing employees or outside consultants as instructors.

Conclusion

Older workers have some of the same problems and sources of stress as younger workers. They also have some specialized problems to address. When older workers have some assistance in managing the stress that they are experiencing, their value to an organization can further increase and they will find their work more personally fulfilling.

Communication skills, exercise, nutrition, and deep relaxation are major factors in the management of stress. They can be helpful individually and collectively, providing a framework for comprehensive stress management and general health promotion. When stress is well managed, its manifestations can be limited or reversed. Such manifestations include poor health, job dissatisfaction, apathy, absenteeism, and labor turnover (Cooper 1984). Stress management programs usually include voluntary physical activity. This can do much to counter adverse health effects and provide self-fulfillment (Shephard 1984).

References

Benson, H. *The Relaxation Response.* New York: Avon, 1976.

Brody, J. *Jane Brody's Nutrition Book.* New York: Norton, 1981.

California Workers' Compensation Institute Bulletin. No. 85–7. San Francisco: September 4, 1985.

Cooper, C.L. "Sources of Occupational Stress Among Older Workers." In *Aging and Technological Advances,* Robinson, P.K., Livingston, J., and Birren, J.E., eds. New York: Plenum Press, 1984.

Cooper, K.H. *The New Aerobics.* New York: Bantam, 1970.

Farquhar, J.W. *The American Way of Life Need Not be Hazardous To Your Health.* New York: W.W. Norton, 1978.

McLean, A. *Work Stress.* Reading, Mass.: Addison-Wesley, 1979.

Schultz, J., and Luthe, W. *Autogenic Training: A Psychophysiological Approach To Psychotherapy.* New York: Grune and Stratton, 1959.

Selye, H. *Stress Without Distress.* New York: Signet, 1975.

Shephard, R. J. "Technological Change and the Aging of Working Capacity." In *Aging and Technological Advances,* Robinson, P.K., Livingston, J., and Birren, J. E., eds. New York: Plenum Press, 1984.

Siegler, I.C., and George, L.K. "Aging, Health, Stress and Technology in the Work Context: Concepts and Issues." In *Aging and Technological Advances,* Robinson, P.K., Livingston, J., and Birren, J.E., eds. New York: Plenum Press, 1984.

Stagner, R. "Aging in Industry." In *Handbook of the Psychology of Aging,* Birren, J.E., and Schaie, K.W., eds. 2nd ed. New York: Van Nostrand Reinhold, 1985.

Tager, R.M. "Physical Assessment." In *Aging and Mental Disorders,* Zarit, S.H., Ed. New York: Free Press, 1980.

Tager, R.M. "Physical Health Realities—A Medical View." In *Aging: Prospects and Issues,* Davis, R.H., ed. 3rd ed. Lexington, Mass.: Lexington Books, 1981a.

Tager, R.M. "Achieving Higher Level Wellness In The Older Population." *Health Values: Achieving High Level Wellness* 5 (1981b): 73–80.

Tager, R.M. "Health Promotion." In *Retirement Preparation,* Dennis, H. ed. Lexington, Mass.: Lexington Books, 1984.

U.S. Department of Agriculture, U.S. Department of Health and Human Services. *Dietary Guidelines for Americans*. Home and Garden Bulletin No. 232, Washington, D.C. U.S. Government Printing Office, 1985.
Warshaw, L. J. *Managing Stress*. Reading, Mass.: Addison-Wesley, 1979.
Zarit, S.H. *Aging and Mental Disorders: Psychological Approaches to Assessment and Treatment*. New York: The Free Press, 1980.

Suggested Readings

Benson, H. *The Relaxation Response*. New York: Avon, 1976.

This book describes relaxation as it relates to stress management and gives a readable description of meditation in Western terms.

Brody, J. *Jane Brody's Nutrition Book*. New York: Norton, 1981.

This comprehensive and understandable review of sound nutritional practices is based on scientific data.

Cooper, K.H. *The New Aerobics*. New York: Bantam, 1970.

This well-written and quantitative book concerns exercise and how to develop a personal exercise program.

Selye, H. *Stress Without Distress*. New York: Signet, 1975.

This lucid description of stress and the stress response is by the person who defined the word *stress* and did much of the early work leading to our present knowledge of the subject.

Tager, R.M. "Physical Health Realities—A Medical View." In *Prospects and Issues,* Davis, R.H., ed. 3rd ed. Lexington, Mass.: Lexington Books, 1981.

This book gives an organized approach toward looking at major factors regarding health and independent living in the later years.

Step 5: Know the health-related cost/benefit issues of older workers and use cost-management strategies.

Health Care Issues and the Older Worker

Carol A. Cronin

Aging of the U.S. population will affect all sectors of American society. Accommodation to the demographics of aging is already apparent as evidenced by institutional change currently underway. Universities are upgrading their continuing education curriculum, marketing departments are studying the needs and buying habits of older consumers, and the mass media are designing entertainment programs based around older characters.

U.S. business will be affected by the aging of the population. Older workers (defined under the Federal Age Discrimination in Employment Act as those 40 years and older) currently comprise a large segment of the American labor force. The 1984 labor force median age of 35.2 is projected to grow to 37.6 by the year 1995 with the aging of the baby boom generation (Fullerton 1985). As employers (as funders of retiree income and health programs) and community citizens face the needs of a graying population, business will need to develop new strategies to address current and future change.

A concurrent trend of great importance to U.S. business is the cost of health care provided to employees, dependents, and retirees. Statistics from the 1984 annual U.S. Chamber of Commerce employee-benefits survey indicate the dramatic increase in insurance payments. In 1951, employers paid an average of $47 per hourly employee for insurance, with 88 percent of this insurance cost covering health insurance. The average yearly outlay per employee in 1984 was $1,581 (U.S. Chamber of Commerce 1985).

In addition, the cost of federally funded health programs also has increased dramatically. Medicare, which provides health services to those over 65, has experienced a 19.9 percent annual increase in inpatient hospital-benefit payments from 1974 to 1982 (Guterman and Dobson 1986). Despite this growth, Medicare beneficiaries still pay 15 percent of their health costs out-of-pocket—an equivalent amount to what they paid prior to the enactment of Medicare in 1965 (U.S. Senate Special Committee on Aging 1985–86).

Several factors are responsible for the rapid increase in private and public spending for health care. Health policy analysts point to the costs associated with the growth of new health care procedures and technologies such as transplants, implants, and magnetic resonance imaging systems. Reimbursement policies for private and public health care have also contributed to escalating costs. Physicians, hospitals, and other health care providers have traditionally been paid for their services retrospectively, with fees based on stated costs incurred. This fee-for-service system of reimbursement offered no incentives for controlling costs given that bills were simply paid as presented to Medicare or to insurers. In addition, health care consumers were often insulated from the costs of their health care given that employer-based insurance or Medicare paid for a majority of hospital and physician services.

Health care incentives changed dramatically with the introduction of new reimbursement policies. In 1983, Congress passed a law that shifted Medicare from a fee-for-service system to a prospective payment system (PPS). Under PPS, hospitals are reimbursed a fixed per-case payment based on one of 468 diagnoses-related groups (DRGs). For example, hospitals admitting a patient classified under DRG #127 (heart failure and shock) will receive a fixed amount for that case. Cost overruns or cost savings based on that fixed amount will be absorbed by the hospital.

Corporate Cost-Management Strategies

In response to escalating health care bills, many employers have introduced a wide range of strategies that better manage the cost and utilization of their health care plans. Some cost-management strategies, such as health maintenance organizations (HMOs), offer a comprehensive alternative deliver system on a prepaid basis. Other strategies seek to move patient care to less expensive settings. These include home health care and incentives to use outpatient or ambulatory health centers. Second-opinion programs and preadmission certification requirements before entering a hospital are additional attempts to control health care utilization. Finally, preferred provider organizations (PPOs) offer health care services from a limited group of providers who have discounted prices.

A survey conducted in early 1985 indicated that over 70 percent of employers report that they had changed their health care plans a great deal or somewhat over the past three years (Harris and Associates 1985). The survey indicated that the most frequent corporate changes included introducing second-opinion programs (54 percent), increasing deductibles (50 percent), adding new program features designed to reduce unnecessary hospitalization (47 percent), and offering employees an HMO option (34 percent).

Two other corporate health-cost–management trends of increased importance are collecting employer-specific data on health care costs and utilization and communicating with employees about the importance of properly using the health care system. Collecting data allows employee-benefit decisionmakers to profile their employees' use of health care, identify inappropriate use of health care services, and note the incidence of high-cost cases. Armed with this information, communication strategies can be targeted to particular segments of the work force based on their incidence of illness and use of health services. The ability to target health-cost–management strategies, together with the growing awareness of the aging of the population, has increased corporate interest in health care issues as they relate to older workers.

Older-Worker Health Issues

Illness

Many of the diseases experienced by workers over 40 are related to life-style choices and therefore are modifiable. The three major causes of death for adults—heart disease, cancer, and stroke—are related to risk factors such as smoking, hypertension, exercise, and weight reduction. Though scientists are still researching the exact linkage between health habits and improved health, all agree that encouraging a healthy life-style is worthwhile.

The type of illnesses experienced by adults changes with age. Acute conditions such as respiratory and digestive conditions generally decline with age, while the prevalence of chronic conditions such as arthritis, hypertension, and heart disease increase with age (U.S. Senate 1985). Different health-care–utilization patterns accompany the changing nature of illness in middle and old age. Except for women in child-bearing years, the number of hospital discharges per thousand population increases consistently with each older age group, as indicated in data from the National Center for Health Statistics in table 5–1. Days of hospital care also increase with age, with adults age 35 to 44 utilizing 8.9 percent of the total days compared to 14.4 percent for adults age 55 to 64 in 1983. Finally, length of stay in hospitals increases with age. Adults age 35 to 44 were slightly under the national average of 6.9 days in 1983, while adults between the ages of 55 and 64 registered an average 8 days of hospital care per episode.

Work Disability

Work disability also increases with age. The average age of the working-age disabled is 50, while the average non disabled employee is 34 years of age (Bowe 1985). Health problems affecting work increase gradually as people grow older. Only small differences in health status usually are found between adjacent age groups, and the vast majority (84 percent) of persons over age 45 report no work disabilities (U.S. Senate 1985). Self-perception of health

Table 5–1
Number, Percentage Distribution, and Rate of Patients Discharged from Short-Stay Hospitals with Days of Care and Average Length of Stay by Age Group, 1983

	Discharged patients			*Days of Care*			
	Number (thousands)	*Percent Distribution*	*Rate per 1,000 Population*	*Number (thousands)*	*Percent Distribution*	*Rate per 1,000 Population*	*Average Length of Stay (days)*
All ages	38,783	100.0	167.0	268,337	100.0	1,155.2	6.9
Under 15 years	3,654	9.4	70.8	16,682	6.2	323.4	4.6
Under 1 year	936	2.4	255.8	6,164	2.3	1,684.0	6.6
1–4 years	1,146	3.0	80.9	4,203	1.6	296.7	3.7
5–14 years	1,572	4.1	46.6	6,316	2.4	187.1	4.0
15–44 years	15,269	39.4	140.3	76,971	28.7	707.5	5.0
15–19 years	2,012	5.2	106.0	9,251	3.4	487.5	4.6
20–24 years	3,155	8.1	149.9	13,415	5.0	637.2	4.3
25–34 years	6,279	16.2	158.7	30,554	11.4	772.1	4.9
35–44 years	3,823	9.9	131.0	23,751	8.9	813.7	6.2
45–64 years	8,558	22.1	192.2	65,029	24.2	1,460.6	7.6
45–54 years	3,725	9.6	167.0	26,299	9.8	1,179.2	7.1
55–64 years	4,833	12.5	217.5	38,731	14.4	1,743.2	8.0
65 years and over	11,302	29.1	412.7	109,655	40.9	4,004.3	9.7
65–74 years	5,468	14.1	334.2	50,222	18.7	3,069.5	9.2
75–84 years	4,295	11.1	504.2	42,416	15.8	4,979.6	9.9
85 years and over	1,539	4.0	614.8	17,016	6.3	6,798.4	11.1
Under 17 years	4,243	10.9	72.2	19,670	7.3	334.5	4.6
17–69 years	25,923	66.8	167.1	162,889	60.7	1,050.1	6.3
70 years and over	8,617	22.2	469.0	85,778	32.0	4,668.9	10.0

Source: National Center for Health Statistics. *Utilization of Short-Stay Hospitals,* unpublished data, 1983, p. 19.
Note: Measures discharges from nonfederal hospitals. Excludes newborn infants.
Percentages do not always total 100 percent due to rounding.

Table 5–2
Average Claims per Employee by Age and Plan Type

Age Group	*Plan A $1,600**	*Plan B $2,000**	*Plan C $2,400**	*Plan D $2,800**
Under 45	1,280	1,600	1,920	2,240
45–49	1,600	2,000	2,400	2,800
50–54	1,800	2,240	2,700	3,150
55–59	2,000	2,500	3,000	3,500
60–64	2,560	3,200	3,840	4,480
65–69	3,600	4,500	5,400	6,300

Source: U.S. Senate Special Committee on Aging. *The Costs of Employing Older Workers*, 1984, p. 45.
*Per employee average claim cost that includes dependent care.

status has been found to be highly correlated with an individual's health care utilization. Data indicate that 84 percent of those age 45 to 54 and 75 percent of those between 55 and 64 perceive their health as excellent, very good, or good, a significant factor affecting health care costs (National Center for Health Statistics 1983).

Aging, Health, and Employee Benefits

How do these health issues affect corporate employee-benefit–plan utilization and costs? Little research has been conducted on health-benefit costs by age, though an increasing number of employers are now integrating age into the data reports requested from insurers. A U.S. Senate Special Committee on Aging report, *The Costs of Employing Older Workers* (1984), established index numbers appropriate for attributing claim costs by age with the 45–49 age group set to equal 100 percent. As indicated in table 5–2, the average per-employee claims costs can be estimated for different age groups and different plans. The data indicate the steady rise in claims costs with each successive age group.

Research conducted in four companies studied by the Andrus Gerontology Center at the University of Southern California found that the total cost of employee health insurance claims paid was higher for workers aged 50 and older than for workers under age 50 (Paul 1984). When the factor of employee sex was taken into account, research findings indicated that male workers aged 50 and older were more expensive in their health insurance claims than male workers under age 50. In contrast, female employees over

50 were less expensive with reference to health insurance claims than female employees under age 50, due primarily to the high costs associated with child bearing.

Health issues associated with older workers have taken on added significance with the passage of successive Congressional provisions shifting primary coverage of workers over 65 and their dependents from Medicare to employer plans. Most recently, the Consolidated Omnibus Budget Reconciliation Act of 1985 (COBRA) mandated that employers must offer the same group health plan to all employees over 65 as that offered to employees under 65. Where employees elect such coverage, Medicare (rather than the employer's group health plan) then becomes the secondary payer. Though workers over 65 comprise a relatively small percentage of the current labor force, some experts predict a gradual increase in their numbers, given legislation raising the Medicare eligibility age to 66 by 2005.

Another factor accounting for increased interest in older-worker health-benefit issues is growing recognition of the health costs associated with retirement. Surveys indicate that anywhere from 61 percent to 95 percent of medium-size and large firms offer health benefits both to their early retirees and to retirees receiving Medicare. Employers who have investigated their outlays for retiree health benefits are discovering that: (1)costs for early retirees are high given that the employer plan bears the full cost of adults beginning to experience chronic diseases and (2) post-65 retiree costs are also growing rapidly given that many employer plans are based around a Medicare plan that is escalating in cost. A survey conducted by the Washington Business Group on Health (1985) indicated that many employers have extended a variety of cost-management strategies to their retirees including preadmission testing programs, incentives for using outpatient surgery facilities, and other utilization-control mechanisms. The survey also found that few employers fully take advantage of the opportunity to shape health care attitudes and utilization patterns of older workers prior to retirement. For example, most companies discussed only corporate health benefits and Medicare in the health component of retirement-planning programs. Information on health care consumerism, nutrition, exercise, and community health resources is largely missing from many retirement-planning sessions.

The importance of the retiree health-benefit issues will escalate given the current legal and financial accounting environment. Some courts have upheld a retiree's right to receive postretirement medical benefits for life when a company has sought to alter or terminate those benefits. In addition, the Financial Accounting Standards Board (FASB), a policy-making board for the accounting profession, is studying whether employers should be required to recognize and prefund the liability associated with retiree health benefits. FASB has already required corporations to disclose some retiree benefit information in their 1984 financial statements.

A final issue affecting employer interest in health and aging is a growing awareness that many older workers are assuming responsibility for care of elderly and chronically disabled dependents. A recent survey by the Travelers Insurance Company found that 28 percent of workers over 30 were providing an average of 10.2 hours of care per week to an older relative (The Travelers 1985). Over half of the respondents indicated that care-giving responsibilities created stress and interfered with their social and emotional needs.

Older Workers' Attitudes toward Health-Cost–Management Strategies

The health care sector has changed dramatically over the past 25 years, resulting in generational differences in attitudes and knowledge about health. Employees now ages 40 to 65 were born and raised between 1922 and 1947 in a health care environment dominated by physicians and hospitals. A 55–year-old worker today faces a health care arena comprised of HMOs, PPOs, urgicenters, and other new forms of health care delivery.

Focus group research conducted for the American Association of Retired Persons (AARP) revealed that older workers had questions and concerns about new forms of health care that would affect their proper utilization of services (Needham 1985). The focus groups, conducted with workers over age 50, found that participants did have a choice of traditional and nontraditional health plans through their employer. The majority had chosen traditional plans based on: the desire to keep their own physician, perceptions of more personalized care in the traditional plans, geographic flexibility regarding emergency care, and the perceived lower cost of the plan.

Focus group participants had the following concerns about cost-management strategies:

Preferred Provider Organizations. Many of the older employees had never heard of PPOs and immediately questioned the caliber of doctors who would be attracted to such a practice. They worried about increased patient volume and "discount" care.

Health Maintenance Organizations. Most of the participants were familiar with the concept of HMOs. They felt that they would not join an HMO unless their own physician were on staff. They also questioned the quality of HMO physicians.

Second Surgical Opinions. This strategy was viewed as an effective means of providing useful information to the patient. Participants were concerned about how second-opinion programs would work in an emergency and registered confusion about whether their insurance plans would cover the cost of the second opinion.

A national study of consumer health care knowledge and utilization conducted by the National Research Corporation also discovered some age-related differences (Jensen 1986). The study found that older consumers were somewhat less likely to know about outpatient services. While 80 percent of consumers aged 18 to 54 were aware of outpatient services available at hospitals, only 70 percent of those aged 55 and older knew about them. In addition, the telephone survey found that those most likely to be involved in a wellness or health education program were ages 25 to 44. Only 18 percent of the population age 45 to 54, 16 percent of the population age 55 to 64, and 15 percent of the population over 65 had ever taken part in a wellness program.

Corporate Response

Corporate response to the issue of targeting health-cost–management strategies to older workers has taken a variety of forms. Many companies do not have the resources to direct a health care campaign specifically to older workers. Indeed, some companies philosophically oppose the concept of singling out older workers for special treatment given their concern with reinforcing existing stereotypes. In many cases, it is less a matter of stereotyping older workers than a case of ignoring their concerns and needs in health communication vehicles. For example, until recently, few employee-benefit and health information materials included pictures of older workers or examples of how benefits would apply in a case relevant to them. Health education articles appearing in in-house newspapers are now starting to include articles relevant to older workers on topics such as arthritis, osteoporosis, and heart disease.

Health-Promotion Activities. Revamping health promotion activities is another area where companies are starting to address older workers' health concerns. Campbell's Soup, Tenneco, and Kimberly Clark are companies that have modified exercise programs to attract older workers. John Hancock, a financial services company in Boston, sponsors a walkers' club and screening classes on cancer, blood pressure, and diabetes. The System Development Corporation, a division of Burroughs Sperry Corporation, has introduced several innovative health-screening programs relevant to older workers including in-house carotid duplex scanning and blood pressure monitoring.

Data Collection. Collecting data on health care expenditures and utilization by age is another strategy employed by some companies. Of particular concern to some employers is data indicating that older workers tend to stay in traditional indemnity insurance plans, while younger workers are more likely to join HMOs. Adverse selection can have direct cost implications for employers, given that the average cost of the indemnity plan will increase to reflect the generally higher health costs of older workers. Targeting communication strategies to increase older workers' understanding of HMOs or negotiating age-adjusted HMO premiums are two strategies conducted by some employers who have identified the problem. Employers also are using data to identify high-cost health claims in order to better manage utilization in those cases. A recent survey by the Washington Business Group on Health (WBGH) revealed that 68 percent of the large corporate respondents track high-cost health care claims (Schwartz 1986). The survey also indicated that many of the illnesses accounting for high costs are associated with middle-aged and older workers. They include heart disease, cancer, muscular-skeletal conditions, strokes, respiratory problems, and transplants.

The value of extending case management techniques to chronic-disease cases is not yet recognized. Simply stated, case management refers to the organization and sequence of services and resources to respond to an individual's health care problem. The process usually involves stabilizing medical conditions, providing optimal independence, and managing health care costs. The WBGH survey found that only 22 percent of surveyed companies have some type of program to help employees cope with and manage chronic illness. Few companies recognize that the costs of not attending to chronic disease or not attempting to prevent it can become equivalent to the costs of catastrophic illness.

Health Education. Another corporate response to aging and health issues is a reevaluation of the health sessions of preretirement and postretirement programs. Companies are starting to incorporate information in their health modules on health care consumerism (how to talk to your doctor, how to use alternative delivery systems, and the importance of second opinions), wellness activities (concerning nutrition, exercise, and proper drug use), and community resources particularly relevant to the aging. Health information about these topics also is increasingly available through retiree club meetings, retiree newsletters, and toll-free health care information numbers for retirees.

Linkages to Aging Organizations. Linkage with community-based aging organizations is another strategy underway in some companies, particularly in response to employer involvement in providing information to workers caring for aging parents. After identifying the dimensions of the care-giving issue in its work force, the Travelers held a resource fair which included representatives from more than twenty agencies with expertise on home health care, adult day care, nursing homes, legal and financial help, and coping with stress.

Wang Laboratories in Lowell, Massachusetts, also was involved in a care-giving project with local aging organizations. In addition to surveying the firm's female employees to determine the effect of care giving on work, the project involved placing twenty elders cared for by Wang employees in adult day care. A study will be conducted to determine the impact of offering adult day care as a employee benefit on worker absenteeism and productivity.

Future Issues Affecting Aging and Health

Aging issues have reached the agendas of many corporate decisionmakers. Coverage of aging in both the general press and the business media has created a contextual understanding of the issue. In addition, the universality of aging insures that corporate decisionmakers often are facing the issue personally within their own families. The following future issues will shape current corporate health-benefit decisions.

Long-Term Care

The financing and delivery of long-term–care services present a challenge to public and private organizations as well as to individuals and their families. Currently, 52 percent of nursing home care is paid for by older adults themselves, with the vast majority paid out-of-pocket. The government, primarily through state Medicaid programs, picks up the other 48 percent of nursing home costs (U.S. Senate 1985).

As employee-benefit directors increase their communication with retirees through retiree clubs, employee-benefit hotlines, and newsletters, there is an increased awareness on their part of the gaps in current health benefits in the area of long-term care. Some employers and health policy makers are beginning to investigate the possibility of prefunding long-term–care benefits over the working life of an employee through a medical IRA vehicle, a flexible benefit approach, or some type of group longterm–care benefit. These efforts will be enhanced or slowed based on the direction of retiree health-benefit policy and Medicare.

Growth in Part-Time Employment

Studies have indicated the increasing use of part-time and temporary workers in many work sites nationwide. Many employers cite lower labor costs as one of the most attractive reasons for hiring part-time or temporary workers. In addition, those workers can help meet peak production demands and can often be hired quickly without the need for extensive training. Critics of the trend toward part-time work stress that increasing part-time work weakens the tie between worker and employer, promises little stability for employees, and may result in long-range societal costs based on uncompensated health care costs and the inability of part-timers to gain access to pension coverage.

Surveys of the total working public indicate that many would like to continue some type of paid part-time work after retirement (Harris and Associates 1981). In many cases, it can be expected that older adults interested in part-time work have health coverage available from another source such as Medicare or a spouse's employer's health-benefit program. Public policy makers are becoming increasingly concerned with the number of Americans who have no health insurance coverage. Of particular concern is the fact that data from the 1977 National Medicare Care Expenditure Survey indicate that over half the uninsured were employed for all or part of the year (Shanks 1984).

Research by the Small Business Administration indicates that workers in firms with fewer than 500 employees have only slightly better than a 50 percent chance of receiving health benefits from their employer (U.S. Small Business Administration 1985). In addition, there is some indication that older workers are more likely than younger workers to work for smaller or medium-sized firms. Data from Medicare indicate that in 1983, 80 percent of all workers over age 65 worked in firms with under 500 employees (U.S. Small Business Administration 1985). The high number of part-time jobs with small and medium-sized employers also accounts for the lack of health insurance.

Federal and state health policy makers have begun to address the issue of uncompensated health care. Solutions discussed have included the implementation of state risk pools for those unable to access health insurance; continuation of health insurance coverage for workers who had access to employer-based health insurance after they are laid off, terminated, widowed, or divorced; benefits for part-time workers; or making the provision of health benefits a mandatory condition of employment for any size employer. The employer role in contributing to the solution of the uncompensated care problem will affect future benefit decisions affecting older workers.

Technology and Ethics

The rapidly changing nature of technology is a third factor affecting the future of health and aging. In addition to the cost of new health care technologies, each new advance intensifies the debate over who should receive treatment, who should pay, and who should decide. Increasingly, it is employee-benefit managers who are addressing these questions, given their involvement in corporate reimbursement policies.

Current discussion about transplants is a good case in point. Employee-benefit directors are more than ever faced with questions such as the following: Should a company pay for a transplant that costs up to $240,000, but keeps most adult recipients alive for less than a year? What about the cost of antirejection drugs that could amount to $18,000 a year per patient? Medicare has recently decided to pay for heart transplants at government-approved transplant facilities nationwide. Medicare payment, however, is limited to patients no older than 55 and in otherwise good health. Given that Medicare policy decisions often drive employer health-benefit decisions, it can be assumed that corporations will soon begin to directly address whether age will directly or indirectly become a factor in their reimbursement policies for health care.

Telecommunication advances will also shape the future of health and aging. Some employers are already experimenting with computer-based health-benefit systems that provide information on benefit eligibility and resources. Future older workers may have online access to multiple data bases providing information on health consumerism, cost and quality of local hospitals and other health care providers, and community resources helpful in caring for elderly parents. The rapidity of change within the health care arena may make access to health information a future employee benefit in its own right.

Conclusion

Examining health-benefit issues relating to older workers must be done in the context of overall employer productivity concerns. Survey research conducted by Yankelovich, Skelly and White (1985) for the American Association of Retired Persons indicated that an overwhelming majority of employer respondents (90 percent) felt that the cost of older workers is justified when you consider their value to the company. In addition, 62 percent of those surveyed felt that the extra cost of health insurance for older employees was insignificant compared to total company health care costs.

Forward-looking companies are beginning to implement management education programs about aging, while others are instituting interdepartmental approaches to aging issues that involve corporate medical, employee-benefit, legal, employee assistance, human resources, and public affairs staff. These efforts, and others like them, will enable employers to proactively respond to both an aging America and the health and well-being of their current and future retirees.

References

Bowe, F. *Disabled Adults in America.* The President's Committee on Employment of the Handicapped. Washington, D.C.: 1985.

Fullerton, H. "The 1995 Labor Force: BLS' Latest Projections." *Monthly Labor Review* 198, no. 11 (1985):23.
Guterman, S., and Dobson, A. "Impact of the Prospective Payment System for Hospitals." *Health Care Financing Review* 7, no. 3 (Spring 1986): 111.
Harris, L., and Associates. *Aging in the Eighties.* The National Council on the Aging. Washington, D.C.: November 1981.
Harris, L., and Associates. *Corporate Initiatives and Employee Attitudes on Cost Containment.* The Equitable Life Assurance Society of the United States. New York: Equitable Life Assurance Society, February and March 1985.
Jensen, J. "Health Care Alternatives." *American Demographics.* 8, no. 3 (March 1986): 36–38.
National Center for Health Statistics. *Utilization of Short Stay Hospitals.* DHHS Pub. No. (PHS) 85-1744, Public Health Service. Washington, D.C.: U.S. Government Printing Office, May 1985.
National Center for Health Statistics, unpublished data, 1983.
Needham, P. *Report of Older Worker Focus Groups on Perceptions of Health Benefits.* Washington, D.C.: American Association of Retired Persons, June, 1985.
Paul, C. *Age and Health Care Costs.* Prepared for the Administration on Aging. Grant No. 90AP002/03. Los Angeles: Ethel Percy Andrus Gerontology Center, University of Southern California, April 1984.
Schwartz, G. *State of the Art: Corporate Behavior in Disability Management.* Washington, D.C.: Washington Business Group on Health, July 1986.
Shanks, N. *What Legislators Need to Know about Uncompensated Care.* National Conference of State Legislators, Denver, Colo.: 1984.
The Travelers Companies. *The Travelers Employee Caregiver Survey.* Hartford, Conn.: The Travelers, June 1985.
U.S. Chamber of Commerce. *1984 Employee Benefits.* Washington, D.C.: 1985.
U.S. Senate Special Committee on Aging. *The Costs of Employing Older Workers.* Washington, D.C.: U.S. Government Printing Office, September 1984.
U.S. Senate Special Committee on Aging. *Aging America.* Washington, D.C.: U.S. Government Printing Office, 1985-86.
U.S. Senate Special Committee on Aging. *Health and Extended Worklife.* Washington, D.C.: U.S. Government Printing Office, February 1985.
U.S. Small Business Administration. *The State of Small Business.* Washington, D.C., U.S. Government Printing Office, May 1985.
Washington Business Group on Health. *Post-Retirement Medical Benefits Survey Report.* Washington, D.C.: Washington Business Group on Health, June 1985.
Yankelovich, Skelly and White. *Workers Over 50: Old Myths, New Realities.* Washington, D.C.: American Association of Retired Persons, 1985.

Suggested Readings

Fox, P., Goldbeck, W., and Spies, J. *Health Care Cost Management: Private Sector Initiatives.* Ann Arbor, Mich.: Health Administration Press, 1984.

The book offers a comprehensive overview of private sector cost-management strategies including chapters on plan design, alternative health care delivery systems, utilization review, health care coalitions, work site wellness programs, and overall cost-containment strategies. Though the authors do not specifically address older-worker or retiree issues, the work provides the background on cost management needed before targeting efforts to older adults.

U.S. Senate Committee on Finance. *Health Promotion—Disease Prevention.* Hearings before the Subcommittee on Health of the Senate Committee on Finance. Washington, D.C.: U.S. Government Printing Office, June 14, 1985.

This collection of papers presented as testimony offers an overview of current knowledge about the relevance of health promotion and disease prevention for older adults. Those testifying or submitting material for the record included health care providers, employers, insurers, and researchers. The benefits of preventive measures for older adults in the areas of heart disease, stroke, cancer, accidents, and infectious diseases are discussed. Private sector initiatives in health promotion and disease prevention are presented.

U.S. Senate Special Committee on Aging. *The Costs of Employing Older Workers.* Washington, D.C.: U.S. Government Printing Office, September 1984.

Reviewed and examined in this committee report are the factors that affect employment-related costs including factors that may be related to age. Age-related statistical data is presented to the extent available. The report deals with direct compensation, employee benefits, turnover, training, performance, and productivity.

U.S. Senate Special Committee on Aging. *Health and Extended Worklife.* Washington, D.C.: U.S. Government Printing Office, February 1985.

This paper presents comprehensive information about aging, health, and work. Included are sections on the health status of older adults as defined by functional impairment and disability, utilization of medical services, and self-rated health. Information is presented in easy-to-read graphs. The report concludes by identifying research needs.

Washington Business Group on Health. *Post-Retirement Medical Benefits Survey Report.* Washington, D.C.: Washington Business Group on Health, June 1985.

Based on a survey of 131 Fortune 500 companies by the Institute on Aging, Work and Health, the report provides information on retiree health benefits. In addition to survey results on the types, costs, and funding of such benefits, the report provides background information on why these benefits have become an important topic in policy discussion. Information on pre-retirement planning, health-promotion activities, and retiree cost-management strategies make up the balance of the report.

Step 6: Use objective performance appraisals.

Performance Appraisal of the Older Worker

Harvey L. Sterns
Ralph A. Alexander

The Importance of Performance Appraisal

The accurate evaluation of each employee's job performance is a centrally important part of the supervisor's job. It is only by the conscientious attention to this important function that employees receive the necessary information to improve their job performance and are assured of receiving equitable treatment in personnel decisions. Equally important, accurate performance appraisals affect the long-range financial health of the organization. Not only will employee performance and morale be effected, but accurate and timely appraisals of job performance will help assure a better match between the position held by an employee, that person's wages, and the employee's value to the organization (Cascio 1982).

Performance appraisal is used by supervisors to serve three specific purposes: (1) to determine which individuals will be selected for promotion, training, transfer, demotion, or layoff, (2) to make salary decisions, and (3) to provide feedback to employees for improving job performance. Such judgments are often made by a supervisor in the form of ratings. Performance appraisals are designed for evaluation of past performance, for administrative decisions, and for providing important information regarding future career planning and development. The decisions made and feedback to employees that come from such appraisals will only be useful if the appraisals themselves are well done.

The three R's of performance appraisal are *reasonable, relevant,* and *reliable.* Reasonable means that the appraisal approach is clear, comprehensive, and acceptable to those who are involved. Relevant means that it concerns only those aspects of the job that are important. Clear statements of job requirements in terms of knowledge, skills, and abilities will assure a more accurate appraisal. The focus should be on how well employees perform their jobs. Reliable means that the appraisal system is applied consistently when carried out by different raters or at different times within the organization. The three Rs are important for the assessment of workers of all age groups and organizational levels.

Most managers are aware of the fact that the race or sex of the worker cannot be used when making personnel decisions. The Age Discrimination in Employment Act (ADEA) of 1967, 1978, and 1986 extends protection to those age 40 and above. This legislation was designed to prohibit discrimination based on age in hiring, job rotation, compensation, and other terms and conditions of employment. The law is designed to promote employment of older workers (those over 40) based upon their ability, not their age. This is becoming an important issue to managers and organizations for a number of reasons. The 300 percent increase since 1978 in number of complaints alleging age discrimination (American Association of Retired Persons); the need to recognize the potential of workers who happen to be older; the need to consider ways of effectively utilizing employees who may want to work well beyond what used to be considered retirement age; and the elimination of mandatory retirement for most employees (Sterns and Alexander, in press).

There are several major issues to consider when conducting performance appraisals of older workers. The performance appraisal should be designed to allow for relevant, reasonable, and reliable appraisals. A second major issue is the problem of rater error and the training of raters to minimize bias against the older worker. A third consideration which is very important is the type of information used to make personnel decisions. It is becoming apparent, based upon court decisions, that different kinds of performance appraisal information is needed for termination, layoff, and promotion (Walker and Lupton 1978). Finally, accurate feedback to employees regarding their performance is essential.

Bias against Older Workers in Performance Appraisals

In the past several years, we have seen increased research attention devoted to evaluating age-bias in supervisors' appraisals of employee job performance. While there is no evidence of systematic or pervasive bias against older workers, there is convincing evidence that there is a potential for such bias and a widespread belief that such biases exist.

There are a number of general stereotypes about older workers. It is often felt, for example, that they are more difficult to train (the "you can't teach an old dog new tricks" bias), are resistant to change, are more likely to have accidents or illness, and are less motivated. On the positive side, beliefs that they are more loyal, dependable, conscientious, and cooperative are common (Doering et al. 1983). To the degree that supervisors allow such beliefs to enter into their evaluations of employee performance, the performance appraisals will be biased.

Recent national surveys have shown that as much as 80 percent of the working population believe that organizations' personnel systems are generally biased against older workers (U.S. House 1982). This gives a strong indication that the supervisor is in a situation where people almost automatically expect that performance appraisals will not be fair. Such an atmosphere makes it difficult for the supervisor to have appraisals accepted as fair and accurate reflections of the individual's job performance. This will not only undermine much of the positive benefit of performance appraisals but can affect employee morale and good working relations between supervisors and their subordinates.

Since there are both the possibility and expectation of age bias, it is particularly important for performance appraisals to be carried out in an accurate, fair, and age-neutral manner. The supervisor needs to make every effort to project an unbiased, open, and objective demeanor to each employee when evaluating job performance.

Designing a Performance Appraisal System

Well-designed performance appraisal systems tend to have the following characteristics (Cascio 1982; Schuster and Miller 1981):

The performance appraisal is based on a carefully conducted job analysis.

Supervisors are trained on the appraisal procedures.

Clear, written instructions are given to evaluators.

Specific performance standards are used.

Appraisals are conducted on a regular basis.

Feedback is given to employees with the opportunity to review and comment on the results.

The program is administered systematically and consistently from one evaluation period to the next.

Good records assure support for personnel decisions and aid in documenting a decision when faced with a lawsuit. Written performance appraisals should be conducted at least once per year. The appraisal might include critical incidents and/or statistics on job performance. These records should be kept for a period of three years.

Job Analysis and Performance Standards

It is difficult to overemphasize the importance of a thoroughly and competently conducted job analysis. Without such a job analysis, performance appraisal can become an almost useless exercise and accurate appraisals are next to impossible (Cascio 1982).

Job analysis involves systematically defining the job in terms of specific tasks to be performed and the duties and responsibilities expected of the person performing that job. The result of this kind of analysis is a clear description of the job so that both the employee and supervisor share a common set of expectations. In addition, such an analysis will provide the basis for a set of job standards and performance objectives against which the employee's actual job performance will be evaluated.

Such a job analysis and standards-setting process will help assure that the performance evaluation covers all relevant aspects of job performance, that irrelevancies are eliminated, that feedback to the employee will be accurate and helpful, and that personnel decisions based on these appraisals will add to the effectiveness of the organization.

Issues in Rating Employees

When evaluating employee performance, there are three general categories of measures: direct measures, proficiency testing, and subjective measures.

Direct measures include measures such as number of units produced per unit time, unexcused absenteeism, and number of accidents. Proficiency testing in the form of standardized work sample measures (for example, a typing test) also is occasionally used when measure of skill level rather than actual on-the-job performance is needed.

The most commonly used performance evaluations, and those that are most susceptible to problems, are subjective measures. The subjective performance measures such as rating scales, checklists, employee comparisons, critical incident techniques, group appraisals, and essay evaluations are more susceptible to various types of human errors in judgment. The manager may knowingly or unknowingly introduce bias into a subjective appraisal responding to non–job-related issues such as the employee's age.

Stereotypes about aging may influence the subjective appraisal of an older worker and not accurately reflect that worker's actual job performance. Studies in industry comparing older and younger workers using performance appraisal techniques have shown that many older workers perform as well as or better than younger workers on actual job performance. Aging bias can interact with other common evaluation errors which are well known in the performance appraisal literature.

Some managers are reluctant to give extremely high or low scores and continuously use the center point on rating scales, which is referred to as the *central tendency error.* Even though large differences in proficiency may exist, it is not apparent from the evaluations. Some managers tend to concentrate their rating on the upper end of the scale, which is the *strictness error.* Another well-known error is the *halo effect.* This is the tendency to rate an employee either high or low on many factors because the manager feels the employee is high or low on a single factor. There is also a tendency for people to allow a few noteworthy events, either exceptionally positive or negative, to affect all their judgments about that person. For example, an employee who is thought to relate exceptionally well to people may be rated higher on many other job characteristics, which may not be the case. It is not unusual for some people to form strong *first impressions* of others. When this happens, there is a tendency for the supervisor to continue to hold this opinion even in the face of contrary evidence.

A rating issue emerges when younger supervisors and older supervisors rate the same older worker differently. Age stereotypes are fairly common and these may be more prevalent among younger people. Older workers are often believed to be less able or willing to learn new skills or to adapt to change in work assignments or technology. On the other hand, some supervisors may believe that older workers have better judgment and that their extensive experience automatically makes them more trustworthy. Such *personal beliefs* have no place in performance appraisals. There appears to be less opportunity for these errors in situations where objective evaluations of behavior can be conducted and where job performance measures are clear. The issue of age has become a major concern because of the ADEA; however, the research literature in industrial settings has indicated an employee's physical attractiveness, race, sex, ethnic background, seniority, level of education, social standing, and personality also can distort a manager's rating. To minimize rating errors:

Use written instructions that can be easily followed.

Make the raters aware of possible bias.

Train the raters.

Allow raters to practice the use of the rating scale so they are more accurate and reliable.

Provide feedback following evaluation of practice cases.

Feedback to the Employee

Providing feedback to the employee as a part of the performance appraisal process serves two important personnel functions. First, it gives employees the opportunity to review the appraisal and to know the reasons for the evaluations they receive. Second, it gives employees important information about what is expected in the performance of a job and what must be done to improve job performance.

Many supervisors are especially reluctant to give negative feedback to older employees, particularly if the supervisor is considerably younger. This is an unwarranted form of hidden age bias in and of itself. It is important that the supervisor treat all employees equitably. Failure to give negative feedback to older workers deprives them of the information they may need to improve their performance. In addition to that, the supervisor who fails to tell older employees that they are failing to meet performance standards is likely to run the risk of a charge of age discrimination if they later demote, fail to promote, or fire such employees.

Use of Performance Appraisal Information

The issue of what type of information to use when making a decision based on performance appraisal data varies depending upon the decision to be made. For some negative decisions such as failure to promote, layoff, and discharge, care in the use of information is particularly important. In the *failure to promote* decision, the critical issue is the employee's performance relative to other workers. It is not enough to show the ability to perform the current job; there must be evidence that a person can perform the job at the next level. When making a decision on the *layoff* of an employee, the critical issue is performance in relation to other workers and what jobs are needed. For the layoff situation, the employer must justify the action (for example, due to economic conditions) to assure that it is not a subterfuge to avoid compliance with the ADEA. If a manager wishes to use performance appraisal information to *fire* an employee, the appraisal should show a failure of the employee to perform the job adequately at the minimum allowable level.

Conclusion

When evaluating the older worker, the manager must use actual job performance. The appraisal system cannot be based upon the assumption that the performance declines with age. This assumption has been repeatedly refuted when examining older workers' job performances (Rhodes 1983; Rosen and Jerdee 1985; Waldman and Avolio 1986). Managers should be cautious so that age discrimination does not exist behind the mask of a formal performance appraisal system, which might occur if workers are rated on the assumption that performance declines with age. When evaluating the performance of the older worker, the manager or supervisor should remember:

1. Job performance cannot be assumed to decline with age. On speed and skills tasks, older workers may perform as well as or better than younger workers.
2. The older worker is often a valuable asset to the organization due to accumulated knowledge, skill, and experience, as well as low absenteeism, turnover, and accident rates.
3. The purpose of the ADEA is to ensure older workers (age 40 and older) equal opportunity in human-resource–allocation decisions based upon job performance, not age.
4. The performance appraisal is an important administrative process which must be conducted in a way that is fair and equitable to the employee.
5. The performance appraisal should be relevant, reliable, and reasonable.
6. When making a decision using performance appraisal information, consider only relevant job-performance data. If an older worker is being evaluated, remember these points:

    In a promotion decision, the information to consider is the worker's ability to perform the new job.

    In a layoff decision, consider how well the worker performs the job relative to other workers.

    In a termination decision, the information to consider is whether or not the worker performs the job at the minimally acceptable level.

References

American Association of Retired Persons. *Working Age* 1, no. 6 (May/June) 1986.

Cascio, W.F. *Applied Psychology in Personnel Management*. Reston, Va.: Reston Publishing Co., 1982.

Doering, M., Rhodes, S.R., and Schuster, M., eds. *The Aging Worker.* Beverly Hills, Calif.: Sage, 1983.

Rhodes, S.R. "Age-related Differences in Work Attitudes and Behavior: A Review and Conceptual Analysis." *Phychological Bulletin* 93 (1983): 328–67.

Rosen, B., and Jerdee, T.H. *Older Employees: New Roles for Valued Resources.* Homewood, Ill.: Dow Jones-Irwin, 1985.

Schuster, M.H., and Miller, C.S. "Evaluating the Older Worker: Use of Employer Appraisal Systems in Age Discrimination Litigation." *Aging and Work* 4 (1981): 229–43.

Sterns, H.L., and Alexander, R.A. "Industrial Gerontology: The Aging Individual and Work." In *Annual Review of Gerontology and Geriatrics*, vol. 7, K. W. Schaie, ed. New York: Springer (in press).

U.S. House, Select Committee on Aging. *Age Discrimination in Employment: A Growing Problem in Employment.* Washington, D.C.: U.S. Government Printing Office, 1982.

Waldman, D.A., and Avolio, B.J. "A Meta-analysis of Age Differences in Job Performance." *Journal of Applied Psychology* 71 (1986): 33–38.

Walker, J.W., and Lupton, D.E. "Performance Appraisal Programs and Age Discrimination Law: *Aging and Work* 1 (1978): 73-83.

Suggested Readings

Bass, B., and Barrett, G. *People, Work, and Organization.* Boston: Allyn & Bacon, 1981.

The chapter on performance appraisal covers many basic issues in this excellent text on industrial organizational psychology.

Cascio, W.F. *Applied Psychology in Personnel Management.* Reston, Va.: Reston Publishing, 1982.

The book integrates psychological theory, tools, and methods into the practice of personnel procedures. This is an in-depth examination of the components of an evaluation decision covering job analysis, human resource planning systems, criterion problems and concepts, the validation of measures, and fairness issues. A chapter is devoted to performance appraisal. Appendices contain legal guidelines.

Rosen, B., and Jerdee, T.H. *Older Employees: New Roles for Valued Resources.* Homewood, Ill.: Dow Jones–Irwin.

An excellent book on issues of aging and work. Chapter 6 focuses on assessing performance, characteristics of assessment systems, and rater training.

Schuster, M.H., and Miller, C.S. "Evaluating the Older Worker: Use of Employer Appraisal Systems in Age Discrimination Litigation." *Aging and Work* 4 (1981): 229–43.

A review article of the use of performance evaluations and their use in age discrimination claims of older workers. They detail major court decisions as examples of what is expected of a performance evaluation system.

Walker, J.W., and Lupton, D.E. "Performance Appraisal Programs and Age Discrimination Law." *Aging and Work* 1 (1978): 73–83.

This basic review article discusses the Age Discrimination in Employment Act, examines principle techniques of performance appraisal, and encourages the design and implementation of reasonable, relevant, reliable systems. Guidelines are given for job-relevant performance appraisal.

Step 7: Offer well-designed retraining programs and encourage older workers to participate.

Training and Developing the Older Worker: Implications for Human Resource Management

Harvey L. Sterns
Dennis Doverspike

In the past thirty years, several trends within the field of training have influenced attitudes toward investing in the growth and development of the older worker. The first trend has been the growing awareness, now well documented, that older workers can be trained and retrained. This awareness was accompanied by the development of training principles and methods that recognized the unique attributes of the older worker. The second and more recent trend has involved a recognition that adults go through developmental or career stages and that the employer's management practices could have an impact on the progression through and management of these career stages. The third trend, really an integration of the first two, has been the gradual evolution of the training field into the field of human resource management. Through a systems perspective, the field of human resource management now seeks to integrate the training and development of the adult worker with the human resource goals of the organization.

In this chapter, we will attempt to show how the expanding research and knowledge base accumulated over the past thirty years regarding the older worker is relevant to the growing field of human resource management. In order to meet this goal, our discussion will cover both traditional topics in the training of older workers and newer topics in the area of career development and management. While these topics will be discussed separately, the two topics also will be shown to be interrelated as suggested by the human resource management perspective.

Age, Employment, and Training

The Age Discrimination in Employment Act of 1967, 1978, and 1986 defines older workers as individuals age 40 and above. Most adult workers fall into this category. By law, individuals age 40 and older cannot be limited, segregated, or classified in any way that would restrict their employment opportunities or otherwise adversely affect their status as employees (Faley et al.

1984). Thus, adult and older workers should not be deprived of the opportunity to participate in training programs, meetings, or innovative assignments. The law requires management to be sensitive to selecting individuals based on ability, past performance, and future potential, not age.

A major finding in industrial settings is that employers remain reluctant (1) to hire persons over 40 and offer them training and (2) to retrain those already employed (Rosen and Jerdee 1985; Sonnenfeld 1978). This reluctance persists even though older workers have developed fine records indicating that they are healthy, dependable, and productive, and have low accident rates. However, negative beliefs about aging influence employers' decisions to overlook good, available workers who happen to be older (Meier and Kerr 1976).

Older workers themselves also contribute to this situation. They often are reluctant to volunteer for training or retraining because they feel inadequate about their ability to succeed in a training program or fear competition with younger individuals. This also may be due to the expectation that supervisors would encourage them if they felt it was appropriate.

Highly productive older workers run the risk of being excluded from training opportunities. Their involvement in important ongoing projects makes supervisors reluctant to spare these workers for training and retraining. The problem faced by workers of any age is that if they do not engage in retraining, they grow farther and farther out of touch with new information, technology, and processes. Life-long retraining is necessary so that one can continue to build on previous knowledge and experience (*The Future of Older Workers in America: New Options for an Extended Working Life* 1980).

The notion that one must inevitably become obsolete is obsolete thinking. Rapid technological change creates obsolescence of knowledge among all age groups. Middle-aged and older workers may need updating, but today, the need for retraining is shared by people in their twenties, thirties, forties, fifties, sixties, seventies, and beyond if they choose to continue in the workplace (Sterns 1986).

Characteristics of the Older Worker

As previously mentioned, the Age Discrimination in Employment Act of 1967, 1978, and 1986 defines older workers as individuals 40 and above. Although many early studies on older workers concentrated on blue collar workers, the older worker can fall into any category—clerical, technical, professional, or managerial. In fact, obsolescence can create serious retraining needs for many professional and technical workers. Thus, the category of older workers contains a very heterogeneous group of individuals. As a result, any statement about the characteristics of older workers will be inaccurate for a large proportion of such individuals and presents at best the average individual.

Specialists in the field of androgogy, the art and science of helping adults learn, identify four characteristics of older workers that should be taken into account in designing training and development activities (Knowles and Associates 1984). First, older adults frequently suffer some decline in physiological functioning. As a result, the physical design of the training facility increases in importance. This includes the physical arrangement of the room, noise levels, and light. In addition, issues such as the size of print on blackboards and flipcharts becomes more critical. Second, for most older workers, twenty years have passed since they have been in a traditional, school-type environment. Thus, schoollike methods, such as the lecture, will be less familiar and more anxiety-provoking to this age group. Third, older workers have acquired extensive job and life experience that must be recognized in developing effective training programs. Fourth, older adults are going through changing career and life stages. These career stages will effect their motivation to learn.

Another important characteristic of older adults is that they can learn—and do learn effectively. In fact, research in industrial settings on the training and performance of older workers has found that their performance equals or surpasses the average performance of younger workers (Rhodes 1983). There is now a considerable amount of information on how to maximize the success of training programs through appropriate design.

Designing the Training Program

Designing an effective training program for the older worker is really not much different from the principles for effectively designing any training program. In general, an effective training program for older workers will be effective for all workers.

Needs Analysis

The design of any training program should begin with a needs analysis (Wexley and Latham 1981).

Organization Analysis. The first step in a needs analysis is an organization analysis. The purpose is to assess where training is needed within the organization and if it makes sense from a utility or cost-benefit standpoint. It may be based on surveys or interviews.

Job Analysis. The second step is the job analysis, which identifies what should be included in the training. The job analysis may be based on interviews or questionnaires (McCormick 1979). It generates a job description that identifies the relevant tasks performed and the knowledge, skills, and abilities necessary to perform the job.

Person Analysis. The third step is the person analysis. This step identifies who should be trained. This analysis may be conducted through performance appraisal or testing. Numerous articles and books provide guidance on the proper use of performance appraisal (see Latham and Wexley 1981). But, traditional tests (like training methods) may prove to be inappropriate for the older worker. One alternative testing method developed by Robertson and Downs (1979) is trainability testing. This method consists of three steps: (1) an instructor teaches the training applicant a standard task, (2) the applicant performs the task, and (3) the instructor rates the applicant's trainability. For simple tasks, this method provides an alternative to paper-and-pencil tests for assessing trainability. For more complex occupations, other simulation methods (such as those done in an assessment center) may be used as a substitute for traditional paper-and-pencil testing.

Assessment centers are popular with managerial personnel and can be applied to many occupations. An assessment center is a standardized off-the-job simulation. There, the assessees complete a number of exercises with other participants over a period of one to several days. A group of assessors then prepares a report on the participants' performance, including recommended developmental actions (Wexley and Latham 1981).

Results of the Needs Analysis. The results of the needs analysis should be a list of training requirements. Based on the training requirements, both course objectives and course proficiency items can be identified. These objectives are used to define the training strategy and, finally, to prepare the training material (Ribler 1983).

Training Programs for Older Workers

The adult and older-adult training and retraining literature has documented a number of dimensions for successful training programs. Five major areas emerge that should be considered when designing training programs. These include motivation, structure, familiarity, organization, and time.

Motivation. The issue of motivation in any training situation is not new; however, the concerns are slightly different for the older trainee. For all trainees, the desire to participate and learn is important, but for the older trainee, the desire may be masked by a fear of failure or the fear of an inability to compete against younger, better educated trainees. The trainer must encourage the older worker to alleviate fears developed in previous educational experiences. For those who have been out of school for many years and/or have had little formal education, the motivational and self-concept aspects can influence participation in a program and the results.

Once trainees have been motivated to enroll in training or retraining, they should be repeatedly encouraged to continue and complete the program. The trainer should keep trainees informed of their progress using positive feedback and aid them in understanding what they are working to accomplish. As with all training programs, it is important to examine the physical setting for maximum learning enhancement, taking into consideration human factors in design issues such as lighting, noise, temperature, setting, and rest periods (Belbin and Belbin 1972).

Structure. The training situation should be structured so that the material appears relevant, gives positive feedback, and encourages self-confidence for the trainee. This should aid in eliminating the fear of failure. The actual training material should be based on a job analysis.

It has been found that an effective training procedure is to arrange the training sequence according to increasing complexity. This must be based on a very careful task analysis. The task or material to be learned is then carefully introduced. Easier aspects should be presented first. After mastery of the basic skills, more difficult aspects are then introduced until the task or material is mastered. Past work on training intervention has led to the conclusion that older adult learning can be improved, while a reliance on task analysis appears to be a strong predictor of the success of the training program, especially for complex tasks. A critical feature for training is the assurance of task mastery of each component prior to the introduction of the next one. This allows learners to build self-confidence in their ability to complete the training. The program structure also should allow for the varying amount of time needed for individual trainees. The elimination of paced or time-pressure situations is beneficial to the older adult (Wexley and Latham 1981).

Familiarity. It is important to use familiar elements in the training program whenever possible. Industrial training efforts emphasize the use of elements from former skills on the new task when possible. The training program should be built on past skills, knowledge, and abilities when possible, using relevant, meaningful material from the perspective of the trainee. If the material must be abstract, explain to trainees the rationale so that it becomes meaningful to them. Emphasize the transferability of previous training and experience to the learning of the new material (Mullen and Gorman 1972).

Organization. Previous industrial training has found that many older workers had difficulty organizing information adequately. At a different level, research on memory has examined organizational processes in depth and has found that older adults could improve performance by the use of appropriate learning strategies and the organization of material on memory tasks.

The implication is that information within the training program should be organized so that the knowledge can be built upon at each step in the program; however, this organized structure also should assure comprehension and retention. The older-adult trainee must be instructed in the use of the organized information as well as memory techniques (Belbin and Belbin 1972).

Time. Older workers often take longer than younger workers to learn a new task; however, when given sufficient time, older adults perform as well as younger adults. Older adults may need a slower presentation rate and longer periods of study as well as instructions on the efficient use of this time. The longer training time may be tied to the need for organization and memory strategy training. At a physical level, the older adults may also show slower reaction times for new tasks, although well-practiced tasks may not show this decrement.

The training program should be designed to allow for variability in the time needed to complete the training segment. Longer training times are not effective if the older worker has not been trained in efficient use of that time. Strategies for retention, recall, and application of the information are an important part of any training program for the older worker

Many of the recommendations made in this section are principles that apply to well-designed training at any age. However, there are a number of special issues that must be considered when designing training programs for older workers. It is always important to keep in mind the individual differences that we find among young, middle-age, and older workers. Often, these differences are greater within an age group than between age groups. Well-designed training will give individuals at all ages an equal opportunity to experience successful completion of the program (Belbin and Belbin 1972).

Use of Active Participation

While older workers have extensive experience, they also may feel alienated from the traditional schoollike setting. As a result, they may experience difficulty in a standard lecture and/or rote memorization type of training program. Instead, training for the older worker should involve active participation.

Learning Strategies

Training on the subject of learning strategies is a fairly new and rapidly developing area. The rationale behind learning-strategies training is that we expect people to learn, but infrequently show them how to learn (Weinstein and Mayer 1982). Adults may need training in learning strategies because either they never developed them or they have forgotten them through lack of use. Examples of learning strategies include simple tasks such as rehearsal strategies (for example, repeating the names of things to memorize). An example of a complex strategy is outlining or creating categories. An example of a motivational strategy is overcoming computer, test, or math anxiety (Weinstein and Mayer 1982).

A well-designed training program will motivate the employee during the training process itself. By following the principles of effective design, a training environment will be created that encourages feelings of success rather than fear of failure and that promotes the feeling that learning is job-relevant. Motivation to learn within the training program is necessary but not sufficient. Clearly, the older trainee must feel motivated to participate and learn and must also be willing to transfer the newly learned skills back to the job.

Attracting Potential Trainees

Even the best-designed training program will have little impact unless the program can attract potential trainees. A training program will be attractive to trainees to the extent that they will obtain positive or valued results. That is, the employee must be able to answer yes to two questions. The first question is, "Can I do well in the training program?" The second question is, "If I do well, will that lead to valuable outcomes such as better performance, higher satisfaction, pay raises, and promotions?" If trainees believe that they can do well in training and that this will lead to valued outcomes, then they will be motivated to enter the training program. Whether employees perceive that they can be successful will depend on the design of the program and the organizational climate. Whether employees perceive that training will lead to valued outcomes will depend again on the organizational structure, the organizational climate, the employee's career goals, and objectives.

An employee's supervisor can obviously exert a great deal of influence over an older worker's willingness and motivation to participate in training. Supervisors can create a positive climate for training by being aware of and eliminating potential barriers to participants in training. Supervisors should assess their own attitudes and ensure that they have a positive attitude. They also should encourage the training of older workers. While training may interfere with current projects, older workers should be permitted adequate opportunities to pursue training activities. Supervisors should realize that, like younger workers, older workers desire and require developmental activities and feedback.

Transferring New Skills and Knowledge to the Job

While a positive attitude toward training is important, it is also critical that newly developed and learned skills be transferred back to and reinforced on the job. The successful transfer of training may be the most difficult task in the field of human resource management. One way to ensure transfer is to create an organization where supervisors and peers encourage and reinforce the older worker. As previously mentioned, this positive climate also is critical for motivation to enter training. To develop this positive environment, one must encourage the development of appropriate attitudes in trainers, supervisors, and leaders in the organization.

Establishing a Positive Climate

One such program aimed at creating a positive climate for the older workers is the national training program "Age Issues in Management" (University of Southern California). This program has been designed to sensitize human resource personnel and supervisors to the effective use of older workers. The training materials include exercises, slide and tape presentations, and case studies designed to heighten awareness of attitudes toward aging (in general and in the workplace) and increase knowledge about aging and work. (See Chapter 10.) Other examples of recent training programs include "Significant Segment—Handbook I: Employment and Training of the Mature Worker: A Resource Manual" (Bauer et al. 1982) and "Handbook II—Employment and Training of the Mature Worker: A Training Design" (Barocas 1982).

Other Methods

In addition to creating a positive climate, a number of other methods are available for ensuring transfer. Marx (1982) has developed a relapse-prevention model based on an analysis of treatment for addictive behaviors. Consisting of both behavioral and cognition components, relapse strategies can be included in the training process. These strategies focus on establishing an awareness of the relapse process, identifying high-risk situations, developing coping strategies, developing self-efficacy, understanding returns to pretraining behaviors, and practicing returns to pretraining behaviors. Goal setting provides another method of encouraging transfer (Locke and Latham 1982).

After completing training, trainees should be assigned hard, specific goals and given feedback on progress toward these goals. One of the best methods of ensuring transfer is to design the training itself to incorporate the factors underlying transfer (Goldstein and Musicante 1986). Traditional principles of transfer are to maximize similarity between the training and on-the-job environments; provide adequate opportunities for practice during training; present a variety of practice and training situations; label and identify important features; and teach general principles.

Finally, for individuals to transfer their newly learned skills back to the job, they must see their newly learned skills as leading to valued outcomes. In part, this will depend on their career goals and objectives.

Career-Development Management

The topic of career-development management is a fairly new one in the training field. The topic is constantly being redefined and expanded. A limited number of topics will be presented including career development and retirement planning.

Career Development

While theories of vocational development (Holland 1959; Osipow 1983) and adult life stages (Levinson et al. 1978) have existed for many years, management researchers only recently have looked extensively at adult vocational choices and career stages. The Bell Companies were pioneers in the study of managerial career stages; their work and research continue. Manuel London of American Telephone and Telegraph has developed a theory of career motivation (London 1983) and expanded this work into specific suggestions for managing one's own and other's careers (London and Stumph 1982). A major characteristic of London's model is that career motivation is a complex process involving individual characteristics, career decisions and behaviors, and situational conditions. London's theory also reflects a trend toward looking at the career decision-making process.

Two equally complex models of this process have been proposed recently by Rhodes and Doering (1983) and Sterns and Patchett (1984). The model proposed by Rhodes and Doering draws on a well-accepted model of turnover as well as the expectancy theory, which is important in the training-motivation process.

Sterns and Patchett (1984) and Patchett and Sterns (1984) have developed a model of adult and older-adult career development. This is a non–age-specific model that assumes transitions in work life may occur many times throughout a career. The model emphasizes that the decision to seek additional training, apply for new positions within one's company, and change jobs or leave the system are directly influenced by attitudes toward mobility and success or failure in previous career-development activities.

Attitudes toward career-development activities and mobility relate to such factors as current employment, tenure or stage in career, need for achievement, and need for growth. In addition, fear of stagnation, marketability perceptions, job market conditions, and chance encounters may play a role in decisionmaking.

The model conceptualizes career planning from a goal-setting perspective and incorporates Hall's (1971) model of career growth. A career goal decision, such as the decision to engage in training or retraining, should lead to identity growth and enhanced self-esteem. This enhanced self-esteem may lead to greater commitment to future career-development goals. Goal attainment enhances self-esteem, which may increase perceptions of self-efficacy and future commitment to career-development activities.

Older adults with low self-esteem and doubt about their abilities need encouragement and support from trainers and supervisors. Success early in the program is critical to sustain the effort. Failure could easily lead to a decision to drop out of a training program and jeopardize future career-growth opportunities and decisions. Decisions to change jobs or careers as well as decisions to engage in career-development activities may come about as a result of changes within the individual, the environment, or a combination of both.

Adults make multiple career transitions throughout the life span. There are older adults who are interested in working past traditional retirement age and who continue to be interested in changing jobs and further developing their careers. Past discussions of aging and work have almost exclusively focused on the decision to retire. More attention needs to be given to multiple career transitions which may occur within a working life.

Tools for Human Resource Management

Various methods are used to assist older workers in career development and transition. They include human resource information systems, revitalization programs, and retirement-planning programs.

Human Resource Information Systems. Any discussion of the career stage and career decision-making process would be incomplete without a discussion of the potential importance of the human resource information system (HRIS) (Beatty et al. 1985). An HRIS is a computer program or set of computer programs based on the personnel data base and designed to aid in the making of human resource management decisions including designing career ladders and offering career counseling. The HRIS may have an impact on the older worker in several ways. First, the HRIS may be used to identify possible discrimination in promotion or training against older workers. Second, the HRIS must be based on some assumptions about typical career progressions in organizations. As a result, it may also operate to discriminate against the older worker. Thus, it will be necessary in the future to evaluate the assumptions underlying the HRIS to ensure against an adverse effect on the training and promotional opportunities available to older workers. The future development of the HRIS also would seem to depend upon the development of more refined models of career processes.

Revitalization Programs. Many different types of career planning and guidance may be offered to the older worker (Cairo 1983). One of the most innovative programs described in the literature is the revitalization program for plateaued employees at Lawrence Livermore Laboratory (Brewer and Dubnicki 1983). In this program, participants moved through a five-phase process involving group discussions, supervisors groups, development of achievement-motivation patterns, action planning, and implementation. This innovative program is an excellent example of what an organization can do to aid a worker whose career has plateaued. For an expanded discussion of plateaued workers, see the recent book by Bardwick (1986).

Retirement-Planning Programs. Retirement-planning programs have always represented an important career intervention (Cairo 1983; Dennis 1984). In all likelihood, the elimination of the mandatory retirement age will increase the importance of well-managed retirement-planning programs (Beutell 1983). Although many programs focus on financial matters (Odenwood 1986), effective retirement-planning programs should deal with attitudes toward retirement, career development, and information about retirement issues. These programs can create an open atmosphere concerning career and retirement that leads to favorable employee attitudes plus valuable information for the organization (Roth 1983).

Conclusion

The middle-aged and older worker will play a greater role in organizations as we approach the next century. Adult and older workers have much to offer the modern organization and our knowledge base has grown. We now can offer firm guidelines on how to train and develop the older worker. By following these guidelines, we can maximize outcomes for both individuals and organizations. Five principles to ensure effective training and development of older workers are listed.

1. Older workers can learn and develop.
2. Supervisors need to realize that they may consciously or unconsciously exclude older workers from training opportunities due to unwarranted negative attitudes.
3. For a training program to be effective for older workers, attention must be paid to motivation, structure, familiarity, organization, and time.
4. The organizational climate must reward entry into training and transfer of skills back to the job.
5. Training must be considered within an integrated career perspective.

References

Bardwick, J.M. *The Plateauing Trap*. New York: American Management Association, 1986

Barocas, V.S. *Handbook II—Employment and Training of the Mature Worker: A Training Design*. Washington, D.C.: National Council on the Aging, 1982.

Bauer, D., Barocas, V.S., and Ferber-Cahill, P., eds. *Significant Segment—Handbook I: Employment and Training of the Mature Worker: Resource Manual*. Washington, D.C.: National Council on the Aging, 1982.

Beatty, R., Montogno, R., and Montgomery, D., eds. *Human Resource Information System Sourcebook*. Amherst, Mass.: Human Resource Development Press, 1985.

Belbin, E., and Belbin, R.M. *Problems in Adult Retraining*. London: Heinemann Educational Books, 1972.

Beutell, N.J. "Managing the Older Worker." *Personnel Administrator* 28 (1983): 31–38.

Brewer, J., and Dubnicki, C. "Revitalizing the Fires With an Employee Revitalization Program." *Personnel Journal* 62 (1983): 812–18.

Cairo, P.C. "Counseling in industry: A selected review of the literature." *Personnel Psychology* 36 (1983): 1–18.

Dennis, H., ed. *Retirement Preparation*. Lexington, Mass.: Lexington Books, 1984.

Faley, R.H., Kleiman, L.S., and Lengnick-Hall, M.L. "Age Discrimination and Personnel Psychology: A Review and Synthesis of the Legal Literature With Implications for Future Research." *Personnel Psychology* 37 (1984): 261–76.

Goldstein, I.L., and Musicante, G.R. "The Applicability of Training Transfer Model to Issues Concerning Later Training." In *Generalizing from Laboratory to Field Settings*, E.A. Locke, ed. Lexington, Mass.: Lexington Books, 1986.

Hall, D.T. "Potential Career Growth." In *Personnel Administration*34 (1971): 18-30.

Holland, J.L. "A Theory of Vocational Choice." *Journal of Counseling Psychology* 6 (1959): 43–44.

Hunt, D.M., and Michael C. "Mentorship: A Career Training and Development Tool." *Academy of Management Review* 8 (1983): 475–85.
Knowles, M.S., and Associates. *Androgogy in Action.* San Francisco: Jossey-Bass, 1984.
Kram, K.E. "Phases of the Mentor Relationship." *Academy of Management Journal* 26 (1983): 608–25.
Levinson, D.J., Darrow, C., Klein, E., Levinson, M., and McKee, B. *The Seasons of a Man's Life.* New York: Knopf, 1978.
Locke, E.A., and Latham, G.P. *Goal Setting: A Motivational Technique That Works.* Englewood Cliffs, N.J.: Prentice-Hall, 1982.
London, M. "Toward a Theory of Career Motivation." *Academy of Management Review* 4 (1983): 620–30.
London, M. and Stumpf, S.A. *Managing Careers.* Reading, MA.: Addison-Wesley, 1982.
Marx, R.D. "Relapse Prevention for Managerial Training: A Model for Maintenance of Behavior Change." *Academy of Management Review* 7 (1982): 433–41.
McCormick, E.J. *Job Analysis: Methods and Applications.* New York: AMACOM, 1979.
Meier, E.L., and Kerr, E.A. "Capabilities of Middle-Aged and Older Workers: A Survey of the Literature." *Industrial Gerontology* 3 (1976): 147–56.
Mullen, C., and Gorman, L. "Facilitating Adaptation to Change: A Case Study in Retraining Middle-aged and Older Workers at Aer Lingus. *Industrial Psychology* 15 (1972): 23–29.
Odenwood, S. "Preretirement Planning Gathers Steam." *Training and Development Journal* 40 (1986): 62–65.
Osipow, S.H. *Theories of Career Development.* Englewood Cliffs, N.J.: Prentice-Hall, 1983.
Patchett, M.B., and Sterns, H.L. "Career Progression in Middle and Later Adulthood." Paper presented at Tenth Annual Meeting of the Association for Gerontology in Higher Education, Indianapolis, February 1984.
Rhodes, S.R. "Age Related Differences in Work Attitudes and Behavior: A Review and Conceptual Analysis." *Psychological Bulletin* 93 (1983): 328–67.
Rhodes, S.R., and Doering, M. "An Integrated Model of Career Motivation." *Academy of Management Review* 8 (1983): 631–39.
Ribler, R.I. *Training Development Guide.* Reston, VA.: Reston, 1983.
Robertson, I., and Downs, S. "Learning and Predictability of Performance: Development of Transferability Testing in the United Kingdom." *Journal of Applied Psychology* (1979): 42–50.
Rosen, B., and Jerdee, T.H. *Older Employees: New Roles for Valued Resources.* Homewood, Ill.: Down Jones-Irwin, 1985.
Roth, D.F. "Why Sponsor a Preretirement Program?" *Personnel Journal* 62 (1983): 720–22.
Sonnenfeld, J. "Dealing with the aging work force." *Harvard Business Review* 56 (1978): 80–90.
Sterns, H.L. "Training and Retraining Adult and Older Adult Workers." In *Age, Health and Employment,* Birren, J.E., Robinson, P.K., and Livingston, J.E., eds. Englewood Cliffs, N.J.: Prentice-Hall, pp. 93–113, 1986.

Sterns, H.L., and Patchett, M. "Technology and the Aging Adult: Career Development and Training." In *Aging and Technological Advances,* Robinson, P.K., Livingston, J.E., and Birren, J.E., eds. New York: Plenum Press, 1984, pp. 261–77.

Sterns, H.L., and Valasek, D.L. "Training the Older Worker." In *Managing an Aging Workforce.* Los Angeles: Andrus Gerontology Center, 1984.

The Future of Older Workers in America: New Options for an Extended Working Life. New York: Work in America Institute, 1980.

Weinstein, C.E., and Mayer, R.E. "The Teaching of Learning Strategies." In *Handbook of Research in Teaching,* Wittrock, M.C., ed. 3rd ed. New York: Macmillan, 1982.

Wexley, K.N., and Latham, G.P. *Developing and Training Human Resources in Organizations.* Glenview, Ill.: Scott, Foresman, 1981.

Suggested Readings

Belbin, E., and Belbin, R.M. *Problems in Adult Retraining.* London: Heinemann Educational Books, 1972.

A classic and valuable source in the design of training programs for the older worker, this major review of training and retraining of the adult and older worker involves research from the forties, fifties, and sixties in England.

Mullen, C., and Gorman, L. "Facilitating Adaptation to Change: A Case Study in Retraining Middle-Aged and Older Workers at Aer Lingus. *Industrial Gerontology* 15 (1972): 20–39.

This research article covers one of the best examples of a well-designed and -executed training program for adult and older workers in an industrial setting utilizing a systems approach.

Sterns, H.L. "Training and Retraining Adult and Older Workers." In *Age, Health, and Employment,* Birren, J. E., and Livingston, J., eds. Englewood Cliffs, N.J.: Prentice-Hall, 1981.

This chapter focuses on education, training, and career development issues for adult and older workers. Past history, training approaches, and current issues in training are discussed.

Wexley, K.N. and Latham, G.P. *Developing and Training Human Resources in Organizations.* Glenview, Ill.: Scott, Foresman, 1981.

This book is an excellent basic source on issues surrounding the design, evaluation, and implementation of training and development programs.

Step 8: Implement alternative work schedules.

Implementing Alternative Work Arrangements for Older Workers

Carolyn E. Paul

Work Arrangements Useful to Older Workers and Their Employers

As workers approach retirement age, employers may find it useful to offer them a choice of work arrangements that represent alternatives to the jobs they have been in over a period of years. A choice in work arrangements for older workers may permit those experiencing health problems or skill obsolescence to work more productively; it can also assist those who are "burned out" to more quickly move into retirement by allowing them to reduce their hours on the job. Older employees and management can mutually benefit from this personnel practice.

Research in industrial gerontology has pointed to six different job arrangements that can be used to effectively accommodate the work needs and preferences of middle-aged and older workers (Paul 1987). These arrangements fall within two broad categories: part-time work schedules and job modifications for full-time older employees.

Part-Time Work Schedules

In recent years, a sizable number of employers in the United States have been experimenting with innovative forms of part-time employment. Part-time arrangements that have been most frequently offered to older personnel include job-sharing and phased retirement programs. Part-time reemployment of retirees is also used in some firms.

Job Sharing. Job sharing usually involves the sharing of one full-time job by two part-time workers. A number of public school districts, for example, offer older teachers the opportunity to share a job with young teachers until their retirement. This permits older instructors to reduce their teaching time in the classroom, while at the same time, they can serve as mentors to new teachers entering the profession.

Phased Retirement. Phased retirement is an employment option for full-time employees who are two or three years away from retirement. These employees are permitted to reduce their work week from forty hours to thirty hours usually and then later to twenty hours until retirement. The concept underlying the use of phased retirement is that workers can "phase" into retirement gradually rather than work full-time until the day they retire. At the same time, this arrangement gives their organization lead time to train replacement workers during the "off-time" hours. Phased retirement has been particularly popular among public schools, universities, and manufacturing industries (Paul 1987).

Reemployment of Retirees. In addition to job-sharing and phased ret irement, the reemployment of retired workers on a part-time basis has become widely used in banks, insurance companies, and the fast-food industry (Paul 1987). In most instances, the retiree is retained as a consultant in a professional capacity or is rehired on a temporary basis to fill a clerical position. Companies employing retirees frequently create "retiree job banks" that contain computerized listings of retirees available for work. These listings also identify retirees' job skills and how they may be contacted quickly.

With regard to the three current available part-time schedule arrangements, a national survey of more than four hundred randomly selected employers using Dun and Bradstreet services was conducted (Paul 1983). The survey indicated that approximately one-fourth of these organizations had job-sharing programs and another one-fourth had phased-retirement programs (Paul 1985). Nearly one half of the sample organizations were reemploying their retirees. Clearly, these part-time arrangements are being tested and permanently used with older workers by a number of public and private sector employers. In so doing, these work options represent valuable tools for effectively utilizing retirement-age personnel.

Job Modifications for Full-Time Older Employees

In contrast to the relative popularity of part-time job alternatives, presently only a small number of organizations are making changes in the actual work performed by older staff in an effort to accommodate their work needs. Essentially, this is because job modifications are more difficult and more expensive to arrange than are part-time employment options. To date, it has been the manufacturing industry that has been most willing to make job modifications for American workers. These modifications are usually made for workers assembling heavy machinery or building small, very detailed machine parts.

Three kinds of job modifications are typically used with older personnel. These include job redesign, job transfer, and job retraining. These options are best discussed through illustrations of their use in industry.

Job Redesign. When a job is redesigned, it involves either the restructuring of the work to be performed or a reshaping of the physical environment surrounding the worker. One manufacturing firm has become nationally known for redesigning the jobs of middle-aged and older workers who have health problems that limit their ability to work. For example, special chairs have been built for workers who need to stand all day; magnifying glasses have been developed for employees whose eyesight is failing, but who want to continue working in jobs that require close work with small objects. Management has stated that the organization has saved money in offering this work arrangement by helping employees remain working who would otherwise take disability leave or disability retirement.

Job Transfer. The transfer of an older worker to a less physically or mentally demanding job is another option that can be helpful to both retirement-age personnel and management. A lateral transfer, as opposed to a downward transfer, is the preferred alternative so the compensation rate of the transferred employee is not altered.

One example of this arrangement for older personnel is an office machines manufacturer that makes available a job-transfer program to its older employees who begin to experience difficulty in lifting heavy objects in the company's plants. Upon demonstrating inability to handle certain objects, a worker age 55 or older may request a transfer and be placed in less demanding positions. If a new job is at a salary classification lower than that of the previous job, a transferred employee receives a salary equivalent to the average of the two job salaries.

Job Retraining. The retraining of older, experienced employees usually involves the updating of their job skills to keep pace with the changing technology of their field. It is unusual for older workers to be trained for jobs that they have never performed. In other words, older employees are not usually trained for a second career.

A good example of job retraining for older staff occurred in an engineering firm that retrains its older engineers to acquaint them with the latest equipment released by manufacturers. In recent years, the firm has experienced difficulty in recruiting engineers from other parts of the country because of the harsh weather conditions of the region in which it is located. Consequently, it has found that by retraining its middle-aged and retirement-age professionals, some of these workers have become motivated to defer retirement and continue working.

In sum, the growth of the part-time work schedules has far exceeded the development of job-alteration programs. There are two primary reasons for the greater availability of the part-time options for older personnel. First, through the media, employers are becoming aware of the interest of older persons in part-time work. Illustrative of this is a recent Louis Harris poll conducted for the National Council on the Aging. It revealed that 79 percent of the persons surveyed who were age 55 to 64 and 73 percent of the individuals age 65 and older indicated a preference for working part-time rather than retiring (Harris 1981). The second reason relates to reports from some managers that the part-time alternatives are simply easier to implement than the job-modification alternatives. Given this, the job-alteration options may continue to remain few in number in the near future.

Factors to Consider in Implementing Alternative Work Schedules

It is important for management to weigh the benefits and costs associated with the various work schedules in considering their adoption. A review of their major advantages and disadvantages may prove helpful.

Advantages of the Work Schedules

In a study of employers using part-time work arrangements, the most frequently cited benefits derived from their availability involved the ability of management to attract skilled older workers to their organizations and retain productive retirement-age workers (Paul 1983). These arrangements were perceived as a means of offering new recruits creative ways to work, while at the same time providing a mechanism for full-time older workers to reduce their work schedules and remain productive. Part-time work arrangements were described as easy to implement, useful in maintaining or increasing worker productivity, and cost-effective.

Given the limited utilization of the job-modification options, less is known about their specific advantages to employers. However, as already indicated, these work alternatives provide managers an avenue for retaining physically impaired workers who might otherwise be inclined to use disability leave or take disability retirement. They tend to be more individually tailored to the needs and abilities of workers than the part-time arrangements and thereby hold greater potential for upgrading the productivity of the workers who use them than do the part-time alternatives.

Disadvantages of the Work Schedules

Problems often reported by employers who have used the part-time schedules include the following: coordinating the work tasks of two part-time workers who are sharing one full-time position in job-sharing arrangements; scheduling the reduction in hours for workers "phasing out" in the phased-retirement programs; and coping with the high turnover of retirees in the retiree-re-employment programs.

Also, in relation to the part-time arrangements, some managers have expressed concern about incurring additional fringe-benefit costs when employee benefits are prorated. Over two thirds of the organizations in one survey indicated that they did not find it more costly to employ people part-time in this regard (Paul 1983). This was principally because either they did not offer employee benefits to part-time personnel or, when they did, the benefit package was not at a par with the benefits provided full-time staff.

The job-alteration programs have been described as difficult and expensive to develop and implement. Lengthy "up-front" time is sometimes required to put them into place. In the cases of job redesign and job retraining, new equipment and materials frequently are needed to carry out these programs. In situations in which workers with health problems or limitations are involved, close supervision of their work may become necessary, at least more than is usually required.

Additional Management Considerations

In addition to identifying the advantages and disadvantages attached to the work schedules, four factors are important for management to take into account before implementing them. First, the culture of the organization should be considered. For example, top management should be supportive of the work arrangements in order for them to be accepted by workers. Also, the particular job alternatives used in an organization should fit the image of the organization for management to be supportive of them. For example, if management wants to project an organizational image of schedule flexibility for its employees, part-time options would be particularly useful to promote.

Second, whether or not a specific need exists for a particular arrangement within an organization must be examined. For example, if a particular department could increase its productivity by offering one of the arrangements to its employees, then there is a potential need for it. This is important to know, for if a need does not exist, then the arrangement(s) being considered will not work well for the employee or employer.

Third, the large majority of the organizations in the United States that offer part-time work arrangements are not unionized. Unions have traditionally opposed the offering of part-time employment to older workers because of the attitude that retirement-age workers want to take early retirement and, if they do continue to work, they rob young employees of job opportunities. Therefore, the presence of unions and their attitudes toward the different work alternatives should be studied.

And finally, business conditions within a firm may dictate whether or not it is cost-effective for management to offer one or more of the work schedules. For example, some companies during the 1981 recession made the decision to cease the reemployment of retirees when reductions in force were necessary. At the same time, other companies began using job-sharing and phased-retirement programs as mechanisms for reducing the work hours of employees who would have been laid off. So it becomes important to understand how the work arrangements can fit into the financial climate of the user organization.

Work Alternatives for Older Employees Only or for All Employees?

One may think that alternative work schedules, once introduced within an organization, should be made exclusively available to retirement-age employees. This should not be the case. These work arrangements can also be useful to other employees who have a real need for flexibility in their work schedules while working for their organizations. Employees with small children or frail elderly dependents can certainly benefit from the part-time work arrangements. Disabled workers of any age can profit by the job-redesign, job-retraining, and job-transfer alternatives. These are only a few examples of how the availability of the different work options can jointly benefit employees and management when specific work force needs arise. Middle-aged and older employees therefore represent only one important employee group that can be well served by their availability.

The Future of Work Alternatives for Older Americans

Today, many older workers, when offered the opportunity to take advantage of one of the work alternatives described in this chapter, express little interest in doing so (Paul 1987). Why is this? There are two main reasons for such lack of interest. First, some older employees simply want to retire rather than consider other ways of continuing to work for their employers; they want to live out the American dream of early retirement. Second, and most important, a number of older workers do not feel comfortable working in part-time jobs; these particular workers remember the stigma attached to part-time employment during the years of the Depression.

However, what is true now may not be so in the future. When the baby-boom generation enters retirement age, employee interest in all the work alternatives will swell. This group is already accustomed to creative work arrangements and will demand greater availability of these arrangements as they grow older. The older employee of tomorrow will be a very different type of worker than the older employee of today. It is important for management to be aware of this and to plan for it.

Conclusion

In conclusion, part-time work schedules and special job modifications represent important options available to manager who are interested in using their older employees more effectively. Older workers may need to be encouraged to take advantage of these options, since most older employees are not familiar with the benefits of using them. Management and older personnel will mutually gain when these alternatives work arrangements become a regular part of their work lives.

References

Harris, L. *Aging in the Eighties: America in Transition.* Washington, D.C.: National Council on the Aging, 1981.

Paul C.E. *Expanding Part-Time Work Options For Older Americans: A Feasibility Study.* An unpublished report prepared for The Travelers Insurance Companies. Los Angeles: The Andrus Gerontology Center, University of Southern California, 1983.

Paul, C.E. "A Human Resource Management Perspective on Work Alternatives for Older Americans." In *The Problem Isn't Age: Work and Older Americans,* Sandell, S., ed. New York: Praeger, 1987.

Paul, C.E. *Late Retirement Incentive Programs of Employers: Implementation, Success, and Potential.* An unpublished report prepared for the U.S. Social Security Administration. Los Angeles: The Andrus Gerontology Center, University of Southern California, 1985.

Suggested Readings

Jacobson, B. *Young Programs for Older Workers.* New York: Van Nostrand Reinhold, 1980.

This book describes innovative personnel policies and practices used by managers to accomodate the work interests of older workers and retirees. It also includes a discussion of performance evaluation and preretirement issues as they relate to the different personnel policies discussed.

Nollen, S. *New Work Schedules in Practice.* New York: Van Nostrand Reinhold, 1981.

This book outlines the major management issues involved in the implementation of part-time work schedules. The book does not deal with the value of part-time work schedules for older employees, but rather implies their value for all employees.

Step 9: Use knowledge of life stages for job assignments and team building.

Using Life Stage Theory to Manage Work Relationships

John A. Davis
Renato Tagiuri

Throughout history, people have been aware that a human life goes through stages. Writers of antiquity, theologians, the great philosophers, Confucius, Dante, and Shakespeare, all comment on the changing phases of a person's life. While interest in the life cycle is as old as man, it is only recently that many scientific studies have appeared on this topic. These works constitute the field called *life stage theory.*

This chapter identifies the basic assumptions of life stage theory and describes the life patterns found in four studies of adults by Erik Erikson, George Vaillant, Daniel Levinson, and Wendy Stewart. Building on this foundation, it presents two aspects of life stage theory: the effect of two persons' respective life stages on their work relationship and the application of life stage theory to building successful work relationships with older workers.

Principles of Life Stage Theory

Life stage theory has a few basic assumptions. The first and fundamental one is that the period between birth and death can be divided into age-related periods or life stages. Each period or life stage has distinguishing life issues and challenges that give rise to distinctive behaviors, attitudes, and life styles. For instance, between the ages of 17 and 22, a man typically faces different issues and lives differently than he does between the ages of 50 to 60. In short, the way one lives changes with age. Therefore, some aspects of life style, behavior, and attitudes can be predicted by a person's age.

Second, the ages that define these life stages are approximate because these periods of life overlap. Life stage theorists claim that the ages they attach to the life stages fit the "average" individual; they concede that many people differ from the predicted pattern at one time or another.

Third, the stages have a fixed sequence—an individual must pass through them in order. The skills gained by successfully dealing with the current life stage issues help the individual deal with the issues of the next stage. In adolescence, individuals try to establish their own identity. If *successful* at this life task, one will have an easier time developing deep long-term relationships, an important life task in later life.

If persons are *unsuccessful* in dealing with their current life issues, such as feeling competent at work or in matters of love, they may lack confidence and be confused in dealing with the issues of the next life stage. Worse yet, individuals may never get beyond a particular stage and keep focusing on its tasks. Some people in their thirties still wrestle with adolescent issues; they are stuck in adolescence. People who become seriously stuck in earlier stages have significant problems managing the life challenges of current and later life because they are distracted by the earlier issues and are missing some key life skills.

It is evident that age would not be a good predictor of a person's concerns, behaviors, and life style if that person were seriously mired in an earlier stage. Most people probably get through some life stages a little ahead of schedule (as defined by the theorists) and take a little longer than predicted on some others. On the average, according to the life stage theorists, individuals move through life stages at the ages identified in their studies.

Theories of Adult Life Stages

This section reviews four prominent theories of adult life stages. The first three theories (developed by Erikson, Vaillant, and Levinson, respectively) focus on male adult development. Stewart examines female adult development. These theories have much in common. They all propose that life is divided into periods linked to chronological age. Within each of these periods, a person must cope with particular configurations of situational demands. Development according to these theories can be thought of as growing in ways to make one more appropriate to one's age. Moving from one period of life to the next, individuals adjust to changes in both physical makeup and the world. Each theorist recognizes that development is an interactive process between individual and environment.

Erik Erikson's Stage Theory

Erik Erikson (1950) is considered the father of modern adult life stage theory even though earlier psychologists, including Carl Jung, accounted for life stage influences on behavior in their work. Erikson's theory divides adult life into very long age periods, and does not discuss the more frequent changes in adult life recognized by later psychologists. His suggestion of a predominant life issue in each stage and his discovery of emergent character traits that result from the successful or unsuccessful resolution of each life issue give his theory a simple, elegant structure. Erikson's insightful work is still the best known and most taught life stage theory in psychology. While he proposes it as a universal stage theory, it is based predominantly on males and so should be considered a male life stage theory.

Erik Erikson's theory of the male life cycle defines four stages in adolescence and adulthood.

Identity versus Identity Confusion: Ages 13 to 20. In adolescence, the teenager must work at the life task of deciding who he is and what he will do later in life or else he will fall into "identity confusion." By "finding himself," the adolescent prepares himself to develop a relationship with another person in young adulthood. If successful at this task, he develops the ability to be faithful to others, including organizations.

Intimacy versus Isolation: Ages 20 to 40. Once a person has a firm sense of identity, he must test it among his peers, especially in an intimate relationship. If he can maintain his sense of identity in close relation to others, he learns to be intimate and develops the ability to love. Otherwise, he will feel alone and isolated.

Generativity versus Self-Absorption: Ages 40 to 60. In this age period, the person must learn to extend the caring and concern found within the family to the welfare of the next generation. The widening of the love learned in the intimate relationship of the previous stage produces what Erikson calls generativity. If a man is unable to expand his ability to care, he becomes self-absorbed and stagnates.

Integrity versus Despair: Age 60 and Over. In the final stage of life, a man must look back on his life, improve what he can, and make sense of it in general. If he can look back with deep feelings of satisfaction, then senses of integrity and wisdom result. If not, the outcome is despair.

George Vaillant's Stage Theory

Vaillant's research (1977) confirms the adult life patterns outlined by Erickson and supports his belief that these stages must be passed through in sequence. Aware that Erikson's stages of development were not capturing important issues of men in the thirties and fifties, Vaillant and his colleagues defined two additional stages. The first they label "career consolidation." In this period beginning in the early thirties, men become too busy succeeding and mastering, ascending prescribed career ladders to reflect upon their lives. According to Vaillant, men in this period become "colorless individuals."

As is true of most life stage studies, Vaillant's stops at age 50. His subjects, however, describe another phase of life after the generativity–versus–self-absorption stage and before Erikson's final stage of integrity-versus-despair. Vaillant calls this intermediate stage, occurring during the fifties "keeping the meaning versus rigidity." Having weathered their childrens' and their own second coming of age in their forties, men in their fifties become more tranquil, but try to insure that their generation's culture is carried on rather than replaced. If bitterness is to be avoided, the promises and dreams they had in their forties must be replaced by reality. The challenge in this period of life is to avoid becoming too rigid about one's views of the world while trying to pass on what is useful about one's way of life.

Daniel Levinson's Stage Theory

Levinson's stage theory gives a very detailed description of the issues or developmental tasks of adult men and how they behave in each life stage.

According to Levinson (1978), the lives of all men are thought to follow a common underlying pattern. It is possible to speed up or slow down slightly the rate of maturation, but the sequence remains the same. While biological or career development may vary significantly among men of the same age, the total pictures of their lives do not. The act of aging moves a man from one chronological period to another, but for him to "mature" from one developmental period to the next, he must recognize and accept the changes that have occurred in the world and in himself. He must also work to reflect these changes in the way he lives. The developmental tasks and behaviors in adult male life, which Levinson describes up to age 50, follow a pattern of stability-transition-stability and occur in six stages.

Early Adult Transition: Ages 17 to 22. During this time, the young man must terminate his adolescent "life structure"—his relationships and activities—by modifying existing relationships he has formed with persons and institutions. He must also begin to explore the possibilities that exist for him in the adult world.

Entering the Adult World: Ages 22 to 28. In this period, a new life structure must be built to link the young man's valued self to the adult world. Internally, he desires stability and feels external pressure to grow up, define his direction, and get married. At the same time, his youthful vitality creates in him a strong sense of adventure. Life offers him many avenues to explore so he tries to keep his options open. Although the balance of emphasis placed on the two tasks varies tremendously among different men, both tasks are evident. For most men, this is a period of considerable crisis.

Age-30 Transition: Ages 28 to 33. The age-30 transition terminates the entering period and initiates the settling down period. A man has several years to reappraise the past and reconsider the future. For most men, this is a very stressful period. They feel a great urgency to change their lives, but they have difficulty changing. They feel stuck in life and experience an imminent threat of chaos, dissolution, and loss of their future. Once a man begins to commit himself to some choices for a new life structure, he moves into the settling down period.

The Settling Down Period: Ages 33 to 40. The underlying task of this period is to create a life structure around a few key choices, invest oneself as fully as possible in this structure, and pursue long-range plans and interests within it. A man tries to establish a niche for himself in society and deepen his roots in his community. He wants competence, a home, advancement, and affirmation by society. He wants to build a better life and strives to fulfill his dreams. Not all men work for advancement in occupational areas, but most plan for advancement in some area of their lives.

The latter part of the settling down period is called "becoming one's own man" (BOOM). Between the ages of 36 and 40, a man's concern with death and decline grows. He has an urgent desire to become independent and to express his own thoughts and feelings. This desire is healthy, but can also be upsetting. The urgency of his desires at this time brings about a resurgence of the little boy in the man. The boy's elemental struggles with dependence, sexuality, and authority come to the forefront. In this period, relationships with mentors are likely to be stormy and are usually terminated.

The Midlife Transition: Ages 40 to 45. As in the previous transition periods, a man in this time of life reappraises his past and reconsiders his future. His reappraisal is induced by an increasing sense of his mortality and a desire to use his remaining time better. The physical declines around the age of 40 are generally moderate, but they are experienced as catastrophic. His somewhat reduced strength and agility and perhaps health impairment are interpreted as his youth dying. He begins to feel that his immortality lies within the larger community and he wants to leave a legacy to be remembered by the generations that follow. This can be done through children, but for many men at midlife, work is the most significant component of the life structure and the major source of the legacy.

Entering Middle Adulthood: Ages 45 to 50. As a man commits to new choices, he enters a new structure-building period. As opposed to earlier years, the self becomes equal to society in importance; a man becomes less dependent on external stimulation. While he enjoys power and the tangible rewards of leadership, he puts less value on possessions and status. He lives more in the present and enjoys the process of living more. By becoming more self-oriented, he grows more objective about society. He has less need to idealize or condemn others. He better appreciates the coexistence of good and evil in humanity and learns to be less tyrannized by his own passions. By becoming more in touch with himself, he can better respond to the developmental needs of his children and other young adults. By working on his developmental tasks, a man can become wise and more loving—more separate and more attached.

Wendy Stewart's Stage Theory

Stewart, a protege of Levinson's, investigated the life cycle of women between the ages of 18 and the mid-30s by intensively interviewing eleven women. Stewart's 1977 study is a useful contribution, particularly since literature on the life cycle of women is so sparse. Her work supports Levinson's contention that there are four age-related developmental periods in this age span and finds many similarities between how men and women change over these years. Stewart's stage theory indicates that men and women develop in very comparable ways in the late teens and early twenties and then begin to diverge.

Transition into Early Adulthood: Ages 18 to 22. Stewart finds that male and female development in this period is practically identical. A notable difference is that a woman's dream of how she would like her life to be tends to emphasize the quality of relationships, while a man's tends to focus more on individual accomplishment.

Getting into the Adult World: Ages 22 to 28. Women in their twenties who are primarily committed to remaining single or forming an occupation are very much like men during this stage. These women establish a new existence away from their home of origin, find ways of living out their dream, form a relationship with a mentor, and tend to balance their commitment with exploration. Similar to men of their age, they try to keep as many doors open as possible, while attempting to appear committed.

For women in their twenties who choose a more traditional path—marriage and a family—this period of life is much less tentative. These women are more firmly committed. The relationship with the mentor, who is usually the mother or another older female relative, is less important than the relationship with the special man who helps her live out her dream.

Age-Thirty Transition: Ages 28 to 33. Occupationally oriented women in this stage feel an increased sense of urgency to stabilize their lives. Traditional women seek a less dependent, more intimate relationship with their husbands and may extend their activities outside the home. As with men, this is a time for deciding and changing some aspects of their lives.

Settling Down: Ages 33 to 40. The desire to "settle down," to invest oneself in a few key aspects of life, seems most applicable to women who did not marry or have children until they were around thirty. In this period, the traditional woman wants to expand beyond family commitments, sometimes at the expense of stability and security.

Using Life Stage Theory to Understand Work Relationships

Life stage theory can help managers to understand their coworkers better and to match jobs and rewards to an individual's development needs. This should result in increased job satisfaction and productivity.

Vaillant (1977) points out that an organization can influence the life course of individuals by providing opportunities and emotional support and by encouraging their development. Knowing what kinds of opportunities and support individuals would appreciate most at a given stage of life would be very useful. Life stage theory helps one gain such an understanding. For example, adults become more interested in education during transition periods because they need to stand back from their lives and reconsider their options. Helping employers become more aware of the characteristics of these transition periods could aid them in designing appropriate training programs and career-planning programs.

A most promising application of life stage theory is to increase understanding of work relationships. Harmony and conflict in a two-person relationship is a function of many factors, some influenced by the intersection of the two individuals' life stages.

Investigation of the dynamics of work relationships indicates that the quality of any work relationship depends strongly upon seven dimensions (Tagiuri and Davis 1982):

1. The degree of agreement between two people on reasons why they are working together and what they and their organization hope to accomplish,
2. The degree of clarity and overlap in the two persons' responsibilities,
3. The type and level of power each has in the relationship,
4. The similarities and differences between the two persons in their objectives, activities, traits, and work styles,

5. The sentiments—basically like, love, and trust—that each person holds for the other,
6. The costs and benefits each person attributes to the relationship measured against their expectations and considerations of alternative work relationships they think they could have,
7. The ability and willingness of both parties to talk and listen to one another.

The position of two individuals in their respective life cycles could, in turn, influence all seven of these determinants of work-relationship quality.

Goals for the company seem highly linked to a person's stage of life. For example, older men are generally more conservative than are younger men. Thus, the extent of agreement on the formal purpose of the work relationship seems sensitive to the respective life stages of the two people.

One's sense of what one should be doing at work changes over the life cycle. For example, the role of apprentice usually feels inappropriate after a certain age. Willingness to accept another's authority also varies with life stage; men in their teens, early twenties, and late thirties are least willing. Therefore, the level and distinctiveness of responsibility and the amount of power a man desires at work can be affected by his life stage, which may lead to harmony or conflict. Bases of power are also likely to change as one ages.

Similarities and differences between two people also appear to be stage-related. One's energy level, skills, interests, needs, and life tasks all vary over the life cycle. Expectations and alternative opportunities change during the course of life, directly affecting the calculation of benefits and costs in a work relationship. Communication, too, could be influenced by stage of life. Certain periods are more turbulent and emotional than others; one's perception and communication may become most distorted during these times.

Life Stage Matrix

To understand how the life stages of two individuals, one older and one younger, influence how they will work together, refer to figure 9–1, the life stage matrix, a tool created for such comparisons (Davis 1982).

In the matrix, the two life spans are divided into age intervals that correspond to Levinson's (1978) conception of the adult male life cycle up to the age of 50 as well as with the stages defined by Buhler (1962), Erikson (1950), and Vaillant (1972, 1977) after that age. In the life stage matrix, the older person's life span is represented horizontally and the younger person's vertically. Each cell in the matrix represents a life stage intersect (LSI) and is defined by two age brackets. A work pair of 63 and 33 years, for example, would be located in cell *N*.

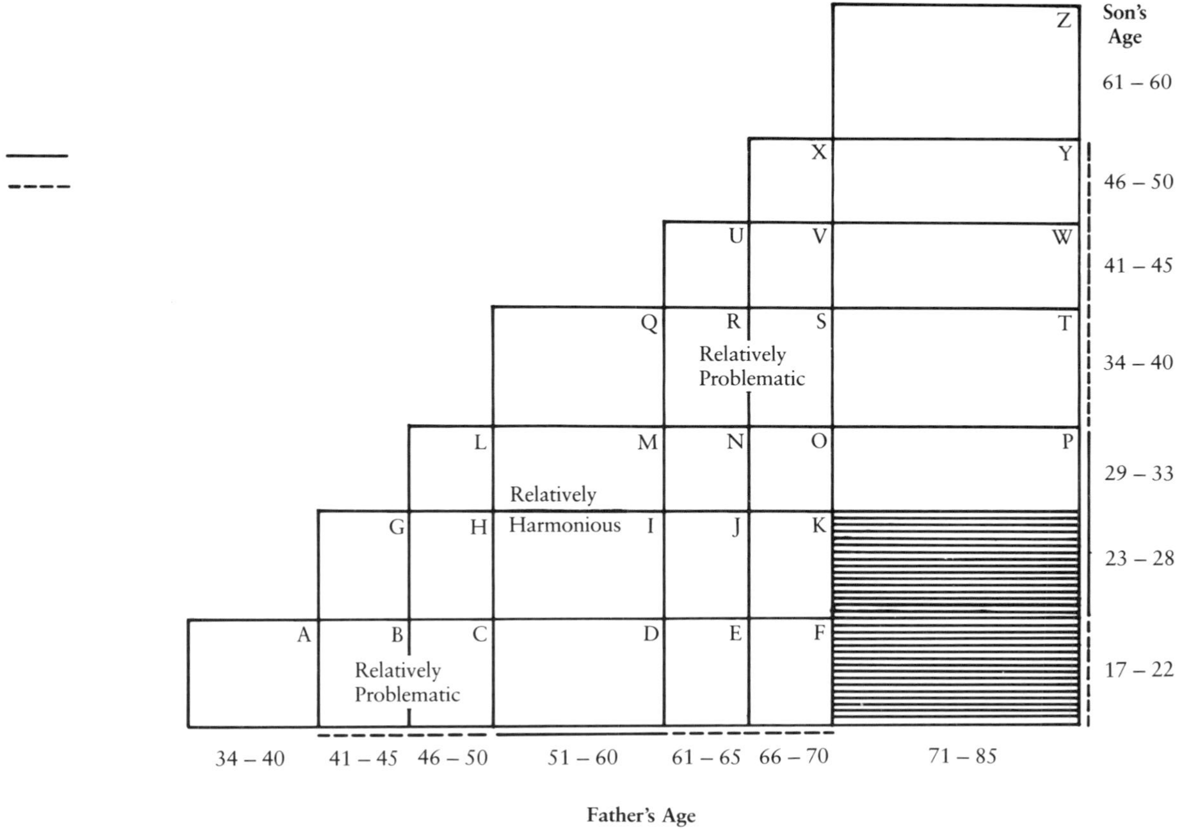

Son's Age

61 – 60
46 – 50
41 – 45
34 – 40
29 – 33
23 – 28
17 – 22

Z
X Y
U V W
Q R S T
Relatively Problematic
L M N O P
Relatively Harmonious
G H I J K
A B C D E F
Relatively Problematic

34 – 40 41 – 45 46 – 50 51 – 60 61 – 65 66 – 70 71 – 85

Father's Age

Source: Davis, J. "The Influence of Life Stage on Father–Son Work Relationships in Family Companies." Ph.D. dissertation, Harvard University. Ann Arbor: University Microfilms, 1982.

Figure 9–1. The Life Stage Matrix

According to life stage theory, the age periods 17–22, 34–40, 41–50, and 61–70 are times when interpersonal relationships, and probably work relationships, can be relatively difficult. These "difficult" times are denoted along the axes by a jagged line. On the other hand, the age intervals 23–33, and 51–60 should be relatively more conducive to harmonious interactions. On the basis of what is known about these male life stages, one would expect that certain cells of the life stage matrix would correspond to relatively poor work relationships, while others to ones of relatively good quality.

Father–Son Work Relationships in Family-Owned Firms

In a study of 89 father-son work pairs in family-owned firms (Davis 1982), there were distinct differences in the quality of the work relationship in father–son pairs of different ages. These changes are predictable on the basis of life stage theory. Consider the life stage influences in the father–son work interactions, as diagrammed in figure 9–2.

In zone I, a typical father and son have much in common—high energy, identity questioning, and their appraising of life. These similarities lead to tensions in the work relationship. Consider first the father's situation. During his forties, a man generally begins to face the fact that there is an end to life and to reconsider what to do with his future. The father-owner-manager can become determined to hold onto his power and fight with those who exacerbate his self-questioning and reduce his feeling of control over his company.

Consider next the son. Young men in their teens and early twenties are still in the process of separating from their family, of trying to establish their identity; they often still have strong conflicts with their parents. To go to work for one's father right after high school or college extends father's control over one's life at a time when a young man can least tolerate the dependence. Entry into the family firm before establishing his independence away from the family may have a regressive or retarding influence on a young man, at least as he sees it.

We both expect and find harmonious father–son work relationships in zone II. In this period, the father is emotionally able to understand and tolerate the son's desire to take on more responsibility. The son wants to learn and grow in competence at the same time the father wants to teach and help the younger generation develop. The two are typically less emotional in this period and communication between them becomes easier.

Fathers in their sixties (zone III) are mindful of the eventually loss of meaningful activities and associations when they retire and leave their companies. Even those who plan to retire in this period of life probably want to stay at the helm and demonstrate their skills and authority until they step down.

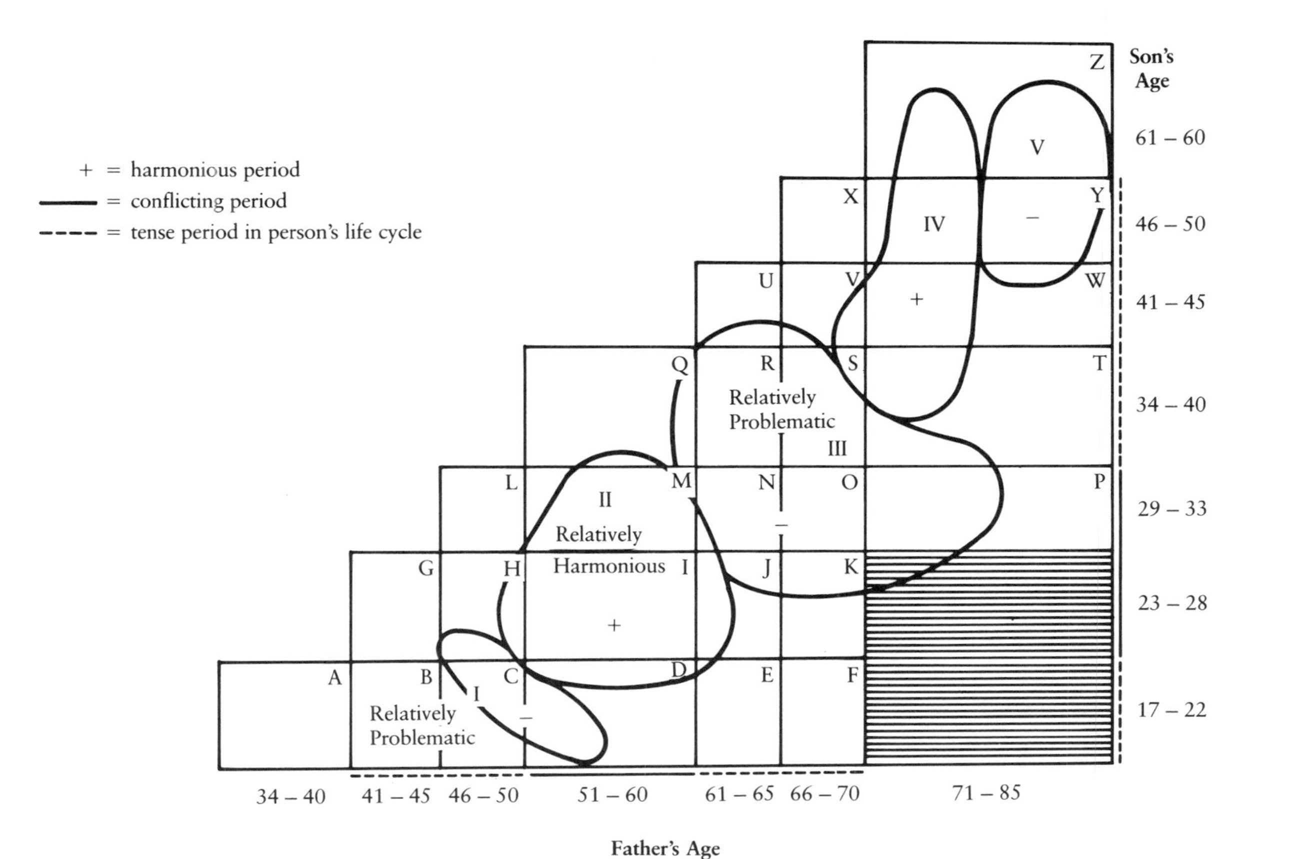

Source: Davis, J. "The Influence of Life Stage on Father–Son Work Relationships in Family Companies." Ph.D. dissertation, Harvard University. Ann Arbor: University Microfilms, 1982.

Figure 9–2. Actual Quality Zones for Father–Son Work Relationships

Sons between ages 34 and 40, meanwhile, are striving to attain competence, recognition, advancement, and security. Approaching 40, these tasks become very pressing. Between the ages of 36 and 40, a man urgently seeks independence and recognition and must become "his own man." The father–son work relationship in this coincidence of life stages will be difficult since the son's renewed struggle with authority would overlap with the father's desire to demonstrate the continuing value of his own authority, skills, ideas and leadership.

If a father in his seventies and eighties continues to work with his son, unless he really relinquishes control (the case in zone IV), the relationship is likely to be difficult (as in zone V).

While relationship history and context are important influences on father–son work interactions, the study of the influence of respective life stages shows that the quality of this relationship varies over its existence in a predictable manner (Davis 1982). Incorporating the life stage factor into a framework for analyzing work relationships improves one's understanding of these interactions.

Managing Work Relationships with Older Workers

As in this study of father–son work relationships, the life stage matrix can be used to help understand the dynamics of any work relationship or social relationship. By locating two individuals in the matrix and examining the concerns and behaviors of their respective life stages, one can infer how the two could be compatible or in conflict.

One should be cautious in using the life stage matrix to predict work relationship quality for several reasons. To begin, age is an indicator, not a determinant, of life stage. Second, an individual's life tasks and concerns may differ from those suggested by the theories. Finally, and most important, life stage is only one influence on a person's behavior. One should not make the mistake of thinking that life stage fully explains a person's behavior or work relationship dynamics. Other influences, (such as the history and the current context of the relationship) also are important factors.

The life stage matrix does help make a point that is vital to thinking about managing a work relationship with an older worker. The difficulty and ease of working with an older person is explained by the intersection of two persons' behaviors—the younger as well as the older. Although difficulty in a work relationship can be attributed more to one person's behavior than the other's, both individuals bring issues and resources to the interaction. It would be useful for younger managers of older workers to consider their own stage of life as well as their coworkers' when diagnosing why problems exist.

What are the developmental tasks each person faces and how does the overlap of tasks influence compatibility or conflict? How do the concerns of both individuals affect the seven determinants of work-relationship quality?

Managers should keep in mind that the seven determinants of work-relationship quality are influenced by historical, contextual, and life stage forces. If some aspect of the two persons' history is contributing to difficulty, the historical cause must be mutually examined, lingering problems rectified, and old tensions made a part of the past. Context problems must also be addressed if they are affecting the quality of a work relationship. There are aspects of context that are difficult or impossible to change—such as an economic recession. Adjustment in the work relationship may involve accepting the current context and deciding to work within it.

If one discovers that life stage is a negative influence on the work relationship, what can one do? First, consider that given enough time, one or both parties will pass into another stage of life and the current life stage tensions may subside. This may be of little comfort if the tensions are anticipated to last for several years. Next, realize that life stage conflict is due to both parties trying to take care of their own developmental tasks rather than to one person purposely attempting to interfere with the life of the other. Unwarranted suspicion that the other person is being malicious encourages defensive behavior—including blaming the other—and distracts from resolving important *relationship* problems. Moreover, once we have a better understanding of our own issues, we should be able to manage our own behavior in a way that might take some pressure off the work relationship. Conflict with an older worker can be used to bring to the surface the developmental tasks of both parties in the relationship and permit coworkers to explore together how those tasks can be accomplished.

Conclusion

As a map of unfamiliar territory, life stage theory allows us to anticipate smooth and bumpy periods of our lives and harmonious and problematic phases in our relationships with others. By appreciating the importance of developmental tasks, by accepting our role in the ups and downs of our relationships, and by understanding how to help others work on their tasks, we can better manage our work relationships.

If we can identify the current life tasks of the older worker, we have a better chance of being useful to that person. By supporting the developmental efforts of others, we help forge an alliance that at any age can make an association more productive and satisfying.

References

Buhler, C. "Genetic Aspects of the Self." *Annals of the New York Academy of Sciences* 96, 1962: 730-764(a).

Buhler, C., and Massarik, F., eds. *The Course of Human Life*. New York: Springer, 1968.

Davis, J. "The Influence of Life Stage on Father–Son Work Relationships in Family Companies." Ph. D. dissertation, Harvard University, 1982. Ann Arbor: University Microfilms, 1982.

Erikson, E.H. *Childhood and Society*. New York: W.W. Norton, 1950.

Gould, R. "The Phases of Adult Life: A Study in Developmental Psychology." *American Journal of Psychiatry*, 129, No. 5 (November 1972): 521–31.

Gould, R. *Transformations: Growth and Change in Adult Life*. New York: Simon and Schuster, 1978.

Levinson, D.J. *The Seasons of a Man's Life*. New York: Knopf, 1978.

Stewart, W.A. "A Psychological Study of the Formation of the Early Adult Life Structure in Women." Ph.D. dissertation, Columbia University, 1977. Ann Arbor: University Microfilms, 1977.

Tagiuri, R., and Davis, J. "A Note on Work Relationships." Unpublished, 1982.

Vaillant, G.E. *Adaptation to Life*. Boston: Little, Brown, 1977.

Vaillant, G.E., and McArthur, C.C. Natural History of Male Psychologic Health. I. The Adult Life Cycle from 18-50. *Seminars in Psychiatry* 4 (4), November 1972: 417–429.

Suggested Readings

Gould, R. *Transformations: Growth and Change in Adult Life*. New York: Simon and Schuster, 1978.

This thought-provoking, easy-to-read discussion concerns how we develop by challenging childhood assumptions about life.

Levinson, H. "On Being a Middle-Aged Manager." *Harvard Business Review* (July-August 1969), 51–60.

This psychological article written for the practicing manager describes the issues of this stage of life and how to cope with them.

Levinson, D.J. *The Seasons of a Man's Life*. New York: Knopf, 1978.

A most detailed description of the tasks and behaviors men exhibit in adult life, this dense but absorbing book is a must for all who want to study life stages. Levinson is currently writing a sequel that discusses both male and female life stages.

Vaillant, G.E. *Adaptation to Life.* Boston: Little, Brown, 1977.

A bit more technical than Levinson's *Seasons of a Man's Life,* this in-depth study of how we evolve psychologically is based on a longitudinal study of Harvard graduates.

White, R.W. *Lives in Progress.* New York: Holt, Rinehart and Winston, 1952.

Three case studies and discussion richly reveal how lives unfold and the many influences on them.

Step 10: Conduct management training on the subject of aging to prevent age discrimination and to encourage effective use of older workers.

Management Training

Helen Dennis

Corporate training is big business. The American Society for Training and Development estimates that companies are spending $30 billion a year on formal courses and programs for their employees. An additional $180 billion is spent annually for informal or unstructured courses (*Wall Street Journal,* August 5, 1986). This growth in corporate education and training has been attributed to a heightened global economy, deregulation, and rapid changes in technology (Lusterman 1985).

In response to these new demands, comprehensive management training programs have been developed. Subjects typically offered include management by objectives (MBO), sexual harassment, conflict resolution, and performance appraisal. A topic conspicuously absent from corporate training programs is aging. The American Management Association publishes yearly catalogues of approximately one thousand different courses in management training, but few, if any, of their offerings are age-related.

When aging is offered as part of a corporate education program, the emphasis is on retirement. The target group usually consists of pre-retirees determining the best time to retire and developing plans to ensure a successful retirement. Sessions on retirement planning have emerged as the accepted forum for discussions about aging in relationship to finances, health, legal issues, housing, and the use of time in retirement.

This chapter focuses on aging and employment and emphasizes a rationale for teaching *managers* about aging. Subjects include reasons to address aging and employment issues, managers' attitudes toward aging, age discrimination, and the role of education and training. Finally, the chapter describes a model management training program on aging and its implications for employers, older workers, and society.

Reasons to Address Aging and Employment

Historically, aging in the workplace has been closely associated with retirement. In the 1980s, the subject of aging has become relevant to the employment and retention of older workers primarily because of legislation, workers' preferences, and employers' needs.

Legislation. Legislation has been the most significant factor influencing management practices regarding older workers. The Age Discrimination in Employment Act (ADEA) prohibits age discrimination in decisions of employment, promotion, retraining, termination, and benefits for most persons 40 years and older. Even though age discrimination is illegal, age discrimination complaints have increased 300 percent since 1978 (American Association of Retired Persons 1986). Since the passage of the ADEA amendments removing the mandatory retirement age in 1986, workers have even more choices and opportunities to continue their employment.

Workers' Preference for Employment. Recent developments in our society have created the need and desire for older persons to remain or reenter the work force. First, inflation has eroded savings and escalated the cost of living, thereby establishing an economic reason for older persons to be employed. Second, increased longevity and good health have enabled older persons to work longer as active contributors in the workplace and society. Third, social contact and job satisfaction have motivated many older persons to seek or retain employment.

Older persons have expressed their desire for continued employment because of economic need or intrinsic rewards of the job. According to a Louis Harris poll, 46 percent of retired persons interviewed expressed their desire to work; and 51 percent of those currently employed who are between 21 and 65 years old preferred to continue working in their later years, rather than retire around the traditional age of 62 to 65 (Harris 1981).

Employers' Needs. An increasing number of employers realize that older workers are an important resource. A number of high technology industries are reporting skilled-labor shortages because numerous older workers with specialized skills are retiring earlier than management anticipated. Consequently, many high technology employers are finding it necessary to offer incentives to retain their older workers.

These changes have presented significant age issues confronting management. Despite these changes, employers have not used their formal education and training programs to meet the challenge of an aging work force. Instead, they have designed generic courses to improve management's ability to motivate employees and enhance their productivity. Although generic training encourages equal treatment for all employees, it does not teach managers about the potential and role of *all older workers,*including minorities and women in their organization (Kieschnick 1981).

Emerging Issues in the Workplace

Several age-related problems are emerging in the workplace that are not usually included in management training.

> Older persons are not recognized by employers as part of the labor market from which employers hire.
>
> Older workers often "level out" with little or no incentive to maintain high levels of performance.
>
> Skilled older workers who are fulfilling a vital role within their company are choosing to take early retirement, thus causing a skilled-labor shortage.
>
> Termination of older workers is resulting in lawsuits because of inadequate evidence of poor performance or, in fact, employers are discriminating against older workers.
>
> Older workers frequently have obsolete skills because technology has advanced while their skills remain static.

In each of these problem areas, managers' attitudes toward aging and older workers' specific skills affect the extent to which these problems are recognized and the manner in which they are reconciled.

Managers' Attitudes toward Aging

Four studies have documented managers' attitudes and skills in managing an older work force.

A survey of corporate managers reported in the *Harvard Business Review* indicated the depth and strength of negative stereotypes about the elderly (Rosen and Jerdee 1977). In this survey of managerial decisionmaking, respondents were asked to make decisions regarding organization and personnel problems. Although the respondents stated that they valued both younger and older workers, their recommended solutions to the problem situations indicated a biased position.

For example, the respondents saw more difficulty in changing the behaviors of older workers; suggested that items be routed around older employees rather than dealing with them; did not attribute positive motives to older workers desiring retraining; favored career development for younger workers, but not for older workers; and saw older workers as less likely to be promoted than younger workers.

A second study, conducted by the Conference Board, surveyed 363 companies regarding their policies and attitudes toward older workers (Rhine 1984). Senior human resource executives were asked to agree or disagree with common perceptions of older workers compared to younger workers. Of the negative perceptions, the one judged valid by at least 50 percent of the responding managers was that older workers tend to be less flexible and more resistant to change. Of the positive perceptions, two-thirds of the responding managers agreed that older workers have lower turnover rates, tend to have greater loyalty to the company, and are more conscientious. One-half of the managers agreed that older workers have better judgment, have fewer accidents, and have better job morale.

Overall, the respondents' age had little relationship to their perception of older workers. The exception was for the 62-and-older age group of respondents. This group agreed with more items that portrayed positive perceptions of older workers (such as "older workers have better job morale and better judgment"). They had fewer agreements with negative perceptions (such as "older workers tend to be less creative and take longer to train") Since the number of respondents in this age category was only nineteen, Rhine suggests that these results may not be statistically significant.

In a third study, Yankelovich, Skelly and White, Inc. (1985) surveyed a random sample of four hundred companies. They concluded that, in general, older workers were viewed positively by human resource decisionmakers and were valued for their experience, knowledge, work habits, and attitudes. Older workers also were ranked particularly highly on characteristics dealing with productivity—attendance/punctuality, commitment to quality, and solid performance records. Older workers were perceived negatively on characteristics that are important to competitiveness—flexibility, adaptability, and aggressiveness. Companies with one thousand or more employees viewed older workers more negatively on these characteristics than smaller companies. The authors concluded that they found "few if any signs of overt or systematic discrimination against older workers" (Yankelovich et al. 1985, p. 5).

A fourth study by Dennis (1983) documented the beliefs of 734 managers regarding older workers. Each of the eight employers participating in the study employed over one thousand persons. Managers were asked to indicate their degree of agreement or disagreement with statements describing older workers. In general, managers had positive attitudes toward older workers. Seventy-five percent agreed that older workers often have good leadership qualities, have valuable experience, and often can help teach younger workers. Seventy-five percent disagreed that older workers often demonstrate less motivation and initiative, are less productive, have higher absenteeism, and have more difficulty coping with stress in comparison to younger workers.

The managers' age was significantly related to the degree of positive attitudes toward older workers. In comparison to younger managers, older managers felt more positive about older workers' contribution to the workplace. These contributions included their efficiency, commitment, competency, leadership qualities, experience, and ability to teach younger workers. Older managers also were less likely to feel that older workers have different needs, experience more difficulties coping with stress, or have conflicts with younger workers. Older managers as a group more often agreed that there are no opportunities for promotion of older workers.

To summarize, research suggests that managers express age sterotypes in making management decisions. In surveys of managers in the workplace, older workers were judged positively in areas of work habits, productivity, and loyalty; they were judged negatively on charcteristics that deal with competitiveness—flexibility, adaptability, and aggressiveness. It is unclear whether managers' age influenced their attitudes toward older workers. Although the surveys generally indicated managers' positive orientation to older workers, age discrimination still remains an issue in the workplace, given the dramatic increase in age discrimination complaints.

Age Discrimination

Age discrimination needs to be counteracted on at least three levels. First, there is a need to address the issue on a *national policy level.* This approach is evident through the enactment of the Age Discrimination in Employment Act and amendments.

Second, there is a need to address age discrimination on the *employee level.* Older adults as job seekers must be competitive in the marketplace. Courses offered by community colleges, job clubs, vocational schools, and adult education programs are designed to improve the job-seeking skills of older adults.

A third approach is to counteract age discrimination on the *management level.* Managers need to be prepared for an aging society and work force. Education and training play a major role in this preparation (Humple and Lyons 1983; Robinson 1983). Legislation can mandate particular organizational behaviors; it cannot mandate attitudes. If managers do not "buy into" the ADEA law and amendments, they are likely to comply only to the extent that they do not incur lawsuits. Without a commitment to the ADEA and an understanding of the law from a human resource perspective, managers may become "creative bookkeepers" who write and state only what is legal without modifying their decisions or behaviors affecting older employees.

Human resource decisions can be made that are highly discriminating yet very subtle so that employees are unable to determine the true reason for the personnel decision affecting them. For example, employers requesting candidates from an employment agency sometimes ask the agency to send them only "younger workers." Younger rather than older workers often are selected for management training programs. Chief executive officers have been quoted in newspapers as wanting "young" creative leadership in their organization. The American corporate culture *is* youth-oriented. Yet, employers are unlikely to be taken to court solely because of a corporate culture. Therefore, it becomes imperative to address the insidious and elusive nature of age discrimination in a way that is concrete, relevant, and acceptable to managers.

Education and Training

Both the private sector and government have requested management training on aging. *Recommendations for Private Sector Initiatives for Older Americans,* a publication from the 1981 White House Conference on Aging, called for the development of management-skills training which specifically deals with older workers and integrates this training into existing programs (1981, p. 7). Congress has recognized the need. The Senate Special Committee on Aging stated that "managers as a group simply are not trained to deal with aging" (Senate Special Committee on Aging 1982, p. 59).

In response to these mandates from the public and private sectors, as well as to these demonstrated needs, the Andrus Gerontology Center developed a model training program on aging specifically geared for managers. The program was designed to discourage age discrimination in the workplace and to encourage managers to use their older workers most effectively.

Age Issues in Management: A National Management Training Program

Development

From 1981 to 1987, the Andrus Gerontology Center was funded by the Levi Strauss Foundation, Atlantic Richfield Foundation, and Administration on Aging (Grant No. 900AM9987/01) to develop, test, and disseminate the first national management training program to address the subject of aging. The program was developed from several sources that provided new information or validated existing data about age issues in the workplace. First, an advisory board consisting of representatives from corporations, government agencies, and universities was selected to assist in the development and testing of the training program. Second, a survey was conducted to determine managers' needs and interests regarding aging and older workers. The survey results provided the foundation for a valid training curriculum and instructional methodology.

In the survey, 750 managers (55 percent response rate) indicated their preferences of topics and issues they would like addressed in a training program. The topics ranked most highly by managers were stress and the older worker, the effects of age on performance, reasons for age biases and ways to change them, motivation, and second-career planning.

The age of the manager was found to be significantly related to topic preferences. Older managers preferred training on second-career planning and were less interested in issues of stress and motivation, while younger managers' interest was high concerning stress and motivation. Older managers' interest in second-career planning may be related to their own needs rather than the needs of their employees. This strong relationship between managers' age and topic preference suggests that the managers' perception of their own age-related needs may be a factor in the perception of needs of their employees.

A third source of information for the management training curriculum was interviews with human resource personnel to determine their definition of issues related to older workers. They expressed two consistent concerns about older workers: age discrimination and the plateau or "leveling out" effect. The latter refers to the worker whose performance has reached a plateau, so consequently the worker is no longer promotable. The following reasons were given for this human resource dilemma: poor communication between supervisors and employees; managers' inaccurate perception of older workers; lack of retraining opportunities; use of ineffective rewards; inability of managers to assess the changing needs of their older employees; reluctance of older workers to continue their education; and a company philosophy that discourages investing in older workers.

Program Description

The management training program "Age Issues in Management" is designed to increase awareness and knowledge about aging and work, enhance problem-solving skills involving an older person, and apply new insights and knowledge to one's own work experience. The program consists of four components. The first is an experiential exercise designed to increase managers' awareness of their own feelings about aging and the feelings of an older person who is the object of age discrimination. The second component is a myths quiz designed to increase managers' knowledge about aging and work. The third component consists of case studies designed to increase managers' problem-solving skills. The cases are based on actual workplace situations that require managers to make human resource decisions involving an older employee. The last component is an application exercise that provides managers with the opportunity to identify and analyze an age-related personnel problem from their own work experience.

Philosophy

The underlying philosophy of the program is that older (as well as younger) employees must be judged as individuals. They must be given equal opportunity to achieve and excel in the work environment, regardless of age. The program does not assume that *all* older workers are competent or that only older workers should be employed. It does assume that given comparable qualifications, older workers have the same potential as other workers, and must be developed and invested in the same way organizations invest in their other employees. Finally, the training program makes the assumption that the productive and effective use of older workers will help employers meet their organizations' objectives while providing significant roles for older persons.

Program Dissemination

The "Age Issues in Management" training program was disseminated nationally through the gerontology departments of five universities: Columbia University, University of Akron, Washington University in St. Louis, Georgia State University, and the University of Southern California. A faculty member from each university trained in-house trainers from employers in their geographic area. These trainers, in turn, presented "Age Issues in Management" to a group of managers within their organization.

Employers participating in this "train the trainer" program represented a diverse group of 60 organizations. Most of the employers were corporations (34), followed by hospitals (9), utility companies (6), universities (5), government agencies (4), a union, and a nonprofit advocacy organization. Of the 60 employers prepared to present the training program, 45 actually conducted the program, reaching 619 managers.

Short-term Effect

The mean age of the 619 managers completing the training program was 54 years. Sixty-four percent of the managers indicated that they supervised an older worker, defined as an employee 50 years or older.

The managers' immediate response to the program was positive:

Ninety percent indicated the program was relevant to their workplace.

Eighty-nine percent indicated the program was meaningful on a personal level.

Ninety-two percent reported they gained at least some new information.

Seventy-seven percent anticipated using their training experience to prevent age-related problems in their work setting.

Of those who anticipated using the training in their work setting, 59 percent expected to use what they had learned in making management decisions, 53 percent in making decisions about their personal lives, and 43 percent in resolving an existing problem in their workplace.

Managers from universities, banks, and hospitals rated the program higher than managers from other employers. Several reasons may explain this difference. First, universities are in the knowledge business, where learning and participating in new educational programs are norms for the environment. Second, hospitals are in the business of human service. They may be more responsive to a program that emphasizes human factors in personnel decisions. Third, financial institutions, in general, conduct ongoing management training programs, and therefore, are likely to be more receptive to training in comparison to those industries that offer few training opportunities. Finally, the collective rating of the remaining employers was somewhat lower than for the previously mentioned groups. The probable reason for this result is the wide variation in responses which is most likely attributable to the diverse industries, organizational structures, and sizes among the employer organizations.

The short-term evaluation results clearly indicate that managers found the program relevant to their work experience. Since many managers indicated that they planned to apply what they had learned to making management decisions, to resolving an existing problem, and to their personal lives, the prospect of managers applying their training experience to management and human resource decisions was promising.

Long-term Effect

Three months after completing the program, 357 managers (58 percent response rate) reported the following results:

Sixty-six percent stated that the training had affected their relationships in the workplace.

Fifty-seven percent indicated that the training affected their feelings about their own aging. Of these, 68 percent had a better understanding of what to expect; 30 percent felt more positive; and 27 percent felt more concerned.

Forty-one percent reported that the training had affected their decisions in human resource planning. Of these thirty-five percent intended to consider using retirees; 23 percent planned to recruit older workers.

Thirty-seven percent of the managers who supervised an older worker and had had the opportunity to make a management decision during the three months after the training indicated that participating in the training program influenced their decision making. The training experience was used predominantly in the areas of *performance review, retraining, and retention.*

For example, managers who applied the training experience to *performance reviews* of older workers made the following statements:

"I listened from their point of view."

"I was sensitive to the need of the older employee."

"Enabled me to set goals for an employee that were realistic and achievable."

"I have increased respect for the knowledge and reliability of the person."

Managers who used their training experience in the area of *retraining* said:

"Broke down some of the myths about aging."

"Would be more inclined to retrain older employees."

"I am taking time to introduce change; more patient with the length of time given [to older workers] to learn."

"I realized that the informal training I was providing wasn't clear and I was assuming more than I should have. I sent the employee to a formal training [program] and she clearly has a better understanding [of her work].

The following statements were made by managers who used the training experience for *retention* of older workers:

"Tried to retain an employee over 50 who was leaving."

"I will use [the employee] on a part-time basis."

"I will consider reassignment of responsibility."

"The company may have been remiss in not providing retraining of the employee."

"An older employee's skills and knowledge can be of value beyond retirement."

Discussion of Long-term Effect. The training effect evident three months after the program is an indication of the relevance and timeliness of the "Age Issues in Management" program. It usually is difficult to document the impact of a training program because of the number of intervening variables that occur between the time of training and the follow-up evaluations. The strength of a training effect must be great to be measurable several months later. The "Age Issues in Management" program met this criterion.

As previously indicated, two-thirds of the managers stated that the training affected their *relationships* in the workplace three months after the training. According to the evaluations, the training helped individuals increase their awareness of others' needs and feelings, enhanced an existing relationship, and helped identify a problem previously unnoticed. It is not clear whether the changes in relationships were only with older persons. Regardless, improved relationships in the workplace is a desirable outcome from the perspective of both the employer and employee.

The impact of the program on managers' *feelings about their own aging* is of equal interest. Over half reported the training affected feelings about aging. Some felt more positive about their own aging, some felt more concerned. One possible explanation for the increased concern is that managers may have felt more vulnerable as older or future older workers because of their new awareness and knowledge about aging. For this particular subgroup, it would be useful to have a follow-up program addressing the age-related concerns.

As a result of the training program, over one-half of the managers intend to *involve older persons* in their human resource planning. Most managers are considering the employment of retirees and the recruitment of older workers. This intention is a first step in acknowledging an older human resource pool that can be used to meet corporate objectives.

Finally, *management decisions* directly affecting older workers were influenced by manager participation in the program. In most cases, management decisions in areas of performance reviews, retraining, and retention favored increasing opportunities for older employees. This outcome is the bottom line of the training program.

The Relationship between Outcomes and Manager Characteristics. Responses to evaluations completed three months after the training were examined according to two manager characteristics—whether or not a manager supervised an older worker and the manager's age. Fifty-seven percent of the managers who completed the evaluations supervised an older worker; the mean age of these managers was 44 years. There was no statistically significant relationship between evaluation responses and whether or not a manager supervised an older worker. Managers' age only affected one variable—planning to use the training experience for future human resource planning. Younger managers plan to use their training experience for future human resource planning more than older managers. Perhaps this is not surprising. It is likely that younger managers with less experience had not recognized older workers as a valuable resource. Older managers, who also are older workers, most likely realized and had identified the experiences and capabilities of their older employees.

Implications. These results have far-reaching implications. Education and training of managers does make a difference in management decisions regarding older workers. The evaluation results do not imply that managers should or will hire and retain all older persons. However, they do suggest that training on aging does affect a management decision-making process, attitudes and, in many cases, the management decision. It also suggests that workers—old and young—must be judged as individuals without preconceived notions about their potential or worth. As a result of the training, managers reported becoming more sensitive to work-related needs of their older employees, the role and responsibility of the organization, and the diverse methods that can maximize older employees' potential and contribution to the organization.

Current management practices that work against older workers may be a function of a youthful corporate culture that had no empirical basis, managers' lack of awareness and knowledge about the potential of older employees, and management practices that favor younger employees for promotion and retention. Training is a simple and relatively inexpensive way of assisting managers and, therefore, organizations to increase their utilization of a significant human resource while increasing employment and retention opportunities for older persons. Given a global economy and increased competition, older workers can help organizations continue to meet their corporate objectives in a complex and changing society.

Conclusion

Age discrimination continues to be pervasive in the American workplace (Mackaronis 1986). Strict adherence to the Age Discrimination in Employment Act is necessary to avoid costly lawsuits. However, a commitment to the law is not sufficient. Management must also be committed to the principle behind the law—that each person is judged on individual merits and is provided with equal opportunity to make the best contribution to the workplace.

Management training can play an important role in assisting managers to examine their management behavior in relationship to older workers. For example, the "Age Issues in Management" program increased managers' awareness about age discrimination, dispelled myths about aging and work, and increased problem-solving skills in situations involving older workers. Since aging is inevitable for all workers, every employer should include the subject of aging, from both legal and human resource perspectives, in general management and supervisory training or affirmative action programs.

With continued education and training about aging and work, managers are likely to avoid age discrimination complaints and lawsuits as well as to increase the effective use of their mature work force. The use of older workers can both help corporations meet their growing and changing company objectives in a global economy, and provide meaningful work roles for middle-aged and older Americans.

References

American Association of Retired Persons. *Working Age* 1, no. 6 (May/June 1986).

Dennis, H. *Managing an Aging Work Force - A Six Month Report.* Los Angeles: Andrus Gerontology Center, University of Southern California, 1983.

Harris, L., and Associates, Inc. *Aging in the Eighties: America in Transition.* Washington, D.C.: The National Council on the Aging, Inc. 1981.

Humple, C.S., and Lyons, M. *Management and the Older Workforce: Policies and Programs.* New York: American Management Association, 1983.

Kieschnick, W.F. *Recommendations for Private Sector Initiatives for Older Americans.* Washington, D.C.: White House Conference on Aging, 1981.

Lusterman, S. *Trends in Corporate Education and Training.* New York: The Conference Board, 1985.

Mackaronis, C. "The U.S. Age Discrimination in Employment Act." *Ageing International* (Autumn/Winter 1986): 15–16.

Rhine, S.H. *Managing Older Workers: Company Policies and Attitudes.* New York: The Conference Board, 1984.

Robinson, P.K. *Organizational Strategies for Older Workers.* Work in America Institute Studies in Productivity. New York: Pergamon Press, 1983.

Rosen, B. and Jerdee, T.H. "Too Old or Not Too Old." *Harvard Business Review* 55 (6), 1977, 97–106.

U.S. Senate, Special Committee on Aging. *Aging and the Work Force: Human Resource Strategies,* Sen. Rep. No. 96-294. 97th Cong., 2nd sess. 1982.

Wall Street Journal. "Corporate Training," August 5, 1986.

Yankelovich, Skelley and White, Inc., *Workers Over 50: Old Myths, New Realities.* Washington, D.C.: American Association of Retired Persons, 1985.

Suggested Readings

Butler, R.N., and Gleason, H.P., eds. *Productive Aging: Enhancing Vitality in Later Life*. New York: Springer, 1985.

This book is a summary of papers presented at the Salzburg Seminar that focused on health and productivity in later life. The book emphasizes the triumph of survivorship as it relates to health, productivity, the environmental influences on aging, creativity, wisdom, work past retirement, and health care. The information is particularly relevant to aging, employment, and retirement issues.

Doering, M., Rhodes, S.R., and Schuster, M. *The Aging Worker: Research and Recommendations*. Beverly Hills: Sage, 1983.

The authors present a summary of research about the aging worker based on a comprehensive literature review.

Jacobson, B. *Young Programs for Older Workers*. New York: Van Nostrand Reinhold, 1980.

This book describes innovative model corporate programs that affect older workers in areas of employment, retraining, work arrangements, reentry, outplacement, and retirement planning.

Step 11: Use community resources for future employment and career-development opportunities for older employees.

Resources for Managers of an Aging Work Force

Carol A. Cronin

In working with older employees, managers are in a position to prevent and resolve work-related problems by utilizing a variety of services within both their own organization and the broader community. These services can be used to remotivate the "plateaued employee," help an employee keep skills current, prepare an employee for retirement, conduct an exit interview, fill job vacancies with experienced workers, and assist an employee in establishing a second career.

The Employer as a Resource

The employer can attain information about services from at least two sources. The first source consists of those services provided by the company. These frequently include employee assistance, retraining, wellness, and preretirement planning programs. The second source consists of community services, particularly educational and counseling programs.

Information on these programs is usually found in public affairs and human resource departments, as well as in company foundations. If department personnel are unaware of community resources, one cannot assume that they do not exist. Many service-providing agencies are nonprofit and have a small public relations budget that frequently minimizes their visibility in the community.

Older-worker Resources

Community resources that are useful to managers of older workers are categorized into the following sections:

Older-worker coordinating councils

Job-referral programs

Retraining programs

Career-counseling services

Retirement-planning programs

Rehabilitation agencies

Self-employment services

Age-discrimination information

Other national resources

Addresses and telephone numbers of specific resources are given in the resource section at the end of this chapter.

Older-worker Coordinating Councils

When looking for available employment and training services for the older adult, one can begin the search by approaching coordinating councils that serve as centralized sources of information about local older-worker programs. Operation Able in Chicago is a model coordinating council linking older workers, employers, and senior-employment agencies into a network throughout its metropolitan area. Similar programs are available in Boston (Careers for Later Years, Inc.), Detroit (Project Able), Little Rock (Arkansas Able), Los Angeles (Los Angeles Council on Careers for Older Americans), New York City (Senior Employment Services), and San Francisco (California Able).

Job-referral Programs

Job-referral programs help older workers secure employment. The programs are helpful to both the employer and the older job seeker. Employers can utilize job-referral agencies to locate experienced applicants while older employees may use them when they want to continue to work after leaving their place of employment.

Job-referral programs for older job seekers include the following agencies and services:

Forty Plus. This organization for upper-level managers and executives provides intensive job counseling and job referral. Forty Plus requires a membership fee and is available in numerous large cities in the United States.

Senior Community Service Employment Program (Title V). This federally funded program for older adults provides work experience in nonprofit agencies prior to job placement in the private sector. Participating contractors nationwide include the American Association of Retired Persons, the National Council on the Aging, the National Urban League, and the U.S. Forest Service. In some cases, these organizations subcontract with local agencies in urban and rural areas nationwide. For more information, contact a local Area Agency on Aging, a public agency that funds local programs for older adults, or the national Title V contracting agencies listed under *Resources* in this chapter.

Senior-center Job Desks. In many communities, senior center "job desk" staff match the skills of older workers registered with the service to job orders from employers. For more information, request a list of senior centers from the Area Agency on Aging.

State Employment Services. An older-worker specialist is frequently designated by the state employment service to provide services to older clientele. To inquire if this special service is available, call the local branch of the state employment service.

Other job-referral programs for older workers are available through some YWCAs, YMCAs, city manpower departments, United Ways, and religious-sponsored groups such as the Jewish Vocational Service, Catholic Charities, and Ecumenical Councils. Additional job-referral programs are offered by educational institutions including community colleges, universities, and community centers.

The National Association of Older Worker Employment Services (NAOWES). This organization is a consortium of nonprofit and public older-worker employment services. NAOWES publishes a quarterly newsletter and acts as a national information referral source. In addition, the National Association of State Units on Aging sponsors the National Clearinghouse on State and Local Older Worker Programs that provides consultation to private employers on the recruitment, training, and retention of older workers.

A growing number of cities are hosting job fairs for older workers to provide a forum for employers to meet older applicants and become familiar with community resources. Older-worker job fairs have been conducted in New York, Philadelphia, Chicago, Hartford, and Los Angeles. Call the Area Agency on Aging to check if there is a job fair in your area.

Retraining Programs

Given the rapid nature of technological change, many employers and employees are recognizing the importance of updating skills or learning new skills to prevent obsolescence. Although many large employers offer training programs to their employees, employers are not the only source for training. Education and training programs are offered by community colleges, unified school districts, and extension programs affiliated with universities. These programs can substitute or supplement training programs offered by employers.

Training programs designed specifically for older workers are available through the Job Training Partnership Act (JTPA). Effective in October 1983, JTPA has two provisions that emphasize older workers:

1. States are mandated to use 3 percent of their federal allocation to establish programs and services for older workers.
2. A primary target group for JTPA consists of workers dislocated from employment because of factory closings or technological changes. Many of these dislocated workers are older with long-term experience.

Qualified employers who volunteer their work site for the training receive partial reimbursement for their training costs. Local program development under JTPA is the responsibility of *private industry councils* primarily composed of local business representatives. For more information, contact the private industry council in your area.

Career-counseling Services

The relationship between aging and work is difficult to define, given the varying degrees of importance that work assumes in an individual's life. The incidence of midlife crises, career plateauing, second careers, and early retirement seem to indicate that attitudes toward work change over the life span. Though not always associated with older employees, the terms *deadwood, burned out,* or *put on the shelf* too often refer to long-service employees who seem to have lost interest in their work. The waste in productivity resulting from a mismatch between employer expectations and employee motivation can be tremendous. Fortunately, career-planning resources exist in the community to help employees assess their skills and interests to define better their role in the labor market.

An excellent resource available to employees of all ages is the career center affiliated with most educational institutions. In some cases, particularly at the community or junior college level, career services are available to the general public for free or for a moderate charge. These services include career testing, individual counseling, a career library, and workshops.

Public and private universities and colleges also offer career-counseling services through their extension programs. Some colleges and universities are improving career services to their alumni, adding another resource for older college graduates. State employment services are good resources for career-counseling referral. In many states, vocational counselors are available by appointment through the state job service. They often conduct workshops on assessing career strengths and on the job-search process. Though primarily geared toward women, programs affiliated with college and university women's centers and YWCAs usually are open to both midlife and older men and women reassessing their career interests. Peer counseling and vocational testing are some of the services available through many of these centers.

Many professionals in the field of career counseling, vocational guidance, and outplacement are developing special expertise in helping midlife and older adults reenter the job market or change career directions. National organizations and resources that are helpful in locating professionally qualified personnel include the American Personnel & Guidance Association, American Society for Training and Development, and American Society for Personnel Administrators.

Retirement-planning Programs

Retirement-planning programs are increasing in number as a popular new employee benefit for middle-aged and older workers. The programs provide information relevant to retirement decisions and life-style including financial planning, health issues, housing, leisure activities, and legal concerns.

Generally available through commercial consulting firms, nonprofit organizations, and individual consultants, retirement-planning programs are tailored to meet the needs of middle-aged and older workers who are preparing for the latter part of their lives. In some communities, retirement planning is directly available to older individuals through educational institutions such as community college older-adult programs or university extension courses. Banks and other service industries are beginning to offer retirement-planning programs to older consumers as part of their overall financial service plan. For more information about retirement programs, contact the International Society of Preretirement Planners.

Rehabilitation Agencies

Older workers who become physically, mentally, or emotionally disabled may benefit from programs offered by the state department of rehabilitation. These services include vocational and personal counseling, job training, job placement, and transportation aid. In addition, the department offers employers information on access laws and standards, specialized services for people injured on the job, referral to other community organizations, and consultation on adapting equipment and working conditions to meet the needs of the disabled. For more information, look up the department of rehabilitation in the state government section of the telephone book.

Another program designed to meet the needs of older people with disabilities is the Projects with Industry program of Aging in America, Inc. The program consists of a two-week session on job seeking and skills training designed specifically to enable older disabled persons to obtain employment. Currently, there are several program sites: New York, Wichita, Philadelphia, New Haven, Cleveland, Topeka, Minneapolis, Tampa, Las Vegas, San Antonio, and four cities in upstate New York. For more information, contact Projects with Industry.

Finally, the Institute for Rehabilitation and Disability Management of the Washington Business Group on Health can provide technical assistance to employers on managing older-worker disability. As an additional service, the institute catalogues innovative corporate job-accommodation and return-to-work programs that are available to the public.

Self-employment Services

Many older employees are interested in putting their skills to work in their own business upon retirement. In some cases, the business relates to their previous employment and may involve establishing a consulting firm. In others, hobbies might be turned into money-making ventures.

There are several community resources that help train people to become self-employed. Frequently, community colleges offer courses that cover start-up procedures. Many local Chambers of Commerce have a division that offers advice and materials for small businesses. Two national programs offer services to those who want to start their own business. The Service Corps of Retired Executives (SCORE), staffed by volunteers, offers free business counseling. For more information, contact SCORE through your area Chamber of Commerce or Small Business Administration. The second resource is the National Association for the Cottage Industry, a nonprofit national membership organization that sponsors a home-business information clearinghouse, a periodic newsletter, workshops, and conferences on all aspects of working in the home.

Age-discrimination Information

Under the Federal Age Discrimination in Employment Act, private employers of twenty or more persons are prohibited from discriminating against almost all individuals 40 years and older. The law applies to all aspects of the employment process, including hiring, retraining, promotion, and termination. For more information, contact the Equal Employment Opportunity Commission in your area.

State or municipal laws are often more strict in their prohibition of age discrimination. To check the law in your area, contact the state or city fair employment, human rights, human relations, or civil rights commission.

Other National Resources

Several national organizations have developed an expertise on older-worker issues and resources.

The Worker Equity Department of the American Association of Retired Persons (AARP) provides a variety of resources to employers, including a free bimonthly newsletter titled *Working Age* and management information on such issues as age discrimination and retirement planning. AARP also sponsors The National Older Worker Information Service (NOWIS), which offers computerized information on community resources and innovative employment practices relevant to the aging work force.

The Institute on Aging, Work and Health of the Washington Business Group on Health provides information on health-benefit issues relevant to an older work force, health-promotion programs for older workers and retirees, and community resources that maximize the productivity of an aging work force.

Other national organizations that provide information about older workers include the federally funded Administration on Aging, the House and Senate Committees on Aging, the National Alliance of Business, the National Commission for Employment Policy, the National Institute for Work and Learning, and the National Association of Area Agencies on Aging.

Conclusion

A final resource offered by many agencies is their expertise on aging. Staff from community agencies often are available to provide management information about the demographics and implications of an aging society. With the growth of industrial gerontology as a specialty, future managers will be more sensitive to age-related issues and resources relevant to an older work force.

The aging of America ensures that companies will be evaluating their current programs and practices affecting older workers and retirees. Community resources will play an increasingly important role in providing information to managers and direct services to older workers and job seekers in areas of employment, retraining, promotion, and retirement planning. Given the number and diversity of resources available, managers are in a position to prevent and resolve age-related problems in the workplace by directly obtaining information from these resources or recommending them to their mature employees.

Resources

Older-worker Coordinating Councils

Arkansas Able
P.O. Box 34032
Little Rock, Arkansas
(501) 374-1318

California Able
870 Market Street
San Francisco, California 94102
(415) 391-5030

Careers for Later Years, Inc.
Suite 306
World Trade Center Boston
Commonwealth Pier
Boston, Massachusetts 02210
(617) 439-5580

Los Angeles Council on Careers for Older Americans
Suite 204
5225 Wilshire Boulevard
Los Angeles, California 90036
(213) 939-0391

Operation Able
36 South Wabash Avenue
Chicago, Illinois 60603
(312) 782-3335

Project Able
51 West Warren
Detroit, Michigan 48201
(313) 833-0622

Senior Employment Services
62 West 14th Street
New York, New York 10011
(212) 206-8921

Job-referral Programs

Forty Plus is available in the following cities: New York, Chicago, Denver, Honolulu, Houston, Los Angeles, Oakland, Philadelphia, Washington, D.C., San Diego, Raleigh, London, and Toronto.

National Association of Older
Worker Employment Services (NAOWES)
c/o National Council on the Aging
600 Maryland Avenue, S.W.
Washington, D.C. 20024
(202) 479-1200

National Clearinghouse on State
and Local Older Worker Programs
National Association of State Units on Aging
600 Maryland Avenue, S.W., #208
Washington, D.C. 20024
(202) 484-7182

Senior Community Service Employment
Program National Contractors

American Association of Retired Persons
1909 K Street, N.W.
Washington, D.C. 20049
(202) 662-4800

Green Thumb, Inc.
5111 Leesburg Pike
Falls Church, Virginia 22041
(703) 820-4990

National Association for the Spanish Speaking Elderly
2727 West 6th Street
Los Angeles, California 90057
(213) 487-1922

National Center on the Black Aged
1424 K Street, N.W.
Washington, D.C. 20005
(202) 637-8415

National Council of Senior Citizens
925 15th Street, N.W.
Washington, D.C. 20005
(202) 347-8800

National Council on the Aging
600 Maryland Avenue, S.W.
Washington, D.C. 20024
(202) 479-1200

National Urban League
500 East 62nd Street
New York, New York 10021
(212) 310-9202

U.S. Forest Service
P. O. Box 2417
Auditors Building
Washington, D.C. 20013
(202) 382-1703

Career Counseling

American Personnel & Guidance Association
5999 Stevenson Avenue
Alexandria, Virginia 22304
(703) 823-9800

American Society for Personnel Administrators
606 North Washington Street
Alexandria, Virginia 22314
(703) 548-3440

American Society for Training and Development
600 Maryland Avenue, S.W., Suite 305
Washington, D.C. 20024
1-800-424-9106

Retirement-Planning Programs

International Society of Preretirement Planners (ISPP)
11312 Old Club Road
Rockville, Maryland 20852
1-800-327-ISPP

Rehabilitation Agencies

Institute for Rehabilitation
and Disability Management
Washington Business Group on Health
c/o The National Rehabilitation Hospital
102 Irving Street, N.W.
Washington, D.C. 20010
(202) 877-1196

Projects with Industry
Aging in America, Inc.
1500 Pelham Parkway
Bronx, New York 10461
(212) 824-4004

Self-employment Services

National Association for the Cottage Industry
P.O. Box 14460
Chicago, Illinois 60614
(312) 472-8116

Service Corps of Retired Executives (SCORE)
Small Business Adminstration
1111 18th Street, N.W.
Washington, D.C. 20417
(202) 653-6279

Other National Resources

Administration on Aging (AoA)
300 Independence Avenue, S. W., #4760
Washington, D.C. 20201
(202) 245-0724

American Association of Retired Persons
1909 K Street, N.W.
Washington, D.C. 20024
(202) 872-4700

National Older Workers
Information System (NOWIS)
1909 K Street, N.W.
Washington, D.C. 20024
(202) 872-4700

National Alliance of Business
1015 15th Street, N.W.
Washington, D.C. 20005
(202) 289-2910

National Association of Area Agencies on Aging
Suite 208
600 Maryland Avenue, S.W.
Washington, D.C. 20024
(202) 484-7520

National Commission for Employment Policy (NCEP)
Suite 300
1522 K Street, N.W.
Washington, D.C. 20005
(202) 724-1545

National Institute for Work and Learning
1200 18th Street, N.W.
Washington, D.C. 20036
(202) 887-6800

U.S. House of Representatives
Select Committee on Aging
712 House Annex #1
Washington, D.C. 20515
(202) 226-3375

U.S. Senate
Special Committee on Aging
SDG-33
Washington, D.C. 20510
(202) 224-5364

Washington Business Group on Health
Institute on Aging, Work and Health
229 1/2 Pennsylvania Avenue, S.E.
Washington, D.C. 20003
(202) 547-6644

Suggested Readings

Doering, Mildred, Rhodes, S.R., and Schuster, M. *The Aging Worker: Research and Recommendations.* Beverly Hills: Sage, 1983.

The text provides a comprehensive, well-documented overview of research on the aging worker. Beginning with an analysis of the demographics of an aging work force, the authors present such topics as the work behavior of older adults and the performance evaluation, training, retirement planning, and pension/benefit provisions of older employees.

Jacobsen, Beverly. *Young Programs for Older Workers: Case Studies in Progressive Personnel Studies.* Work in America Institute Series. New York: Van Nostrand Reinhold, 1980.

In this landmark study, the author presents over sixty case examples of innovative programs for older workers. Included are alternative work options (such as part-time work and phased retirement), retraining, second careers, and retirement counseling. Many of the programs cited in this 1980 text are still in operation.

National Alliance of Business. *Invest in Experience: New Directions for an Aging Workforce.* Washington, D.C.: National Alliance of Business, 1985.

Chapters of this booklet, which is designed for corporate managers, include management objectives for utilizing older workers, work force demographic changes, barriers to older-worker labor-force participation, and corporate strategies and current initiatives to promote older-worker employment. A resource section and bibliography are included.

Ragatz, Jill. *Needs of Older Employees and Retirees: Task Force Results of the Corporate Volunteerism Council of Minneapolis and St. Paul,* 1985.

This report is the result of a survey and focus group analysis of the policies and programs of Corporate Volunteerism Council members in the twin cities. Topics include older-worker needs, corporate assistance for older workers, the promotion of volunteer opportunities, and retirement planning.

Yankelovich, Skelly and White, Inc. *Workers Over 50: Old Myths, New Realities.* Washington, D.C.: American Association of Retired Persons, 1985.

This study documents management perceptions of older workers. Included in the study findings are that older workers are perceived positively by managers, that little age discrimination exists in the workplace, and that management attitudes differ according to the size of the employer.

Step 12: Examine Labor's History, Policies, Needs, and Services Regarding Older Union Workers.

Age Issues in the Workplace: A Labor Perspective

Judith Wineman

Whether one sits on the labor or management side of the bargaining table, the variable of age in today's workplace needs to be considered as one factor in planning for the future of American workers. Age should be of concern to union leaders and staff as much as it should be to bank managers or corporate vice presidents because the work force is aging and retiring without comparable replacement of older workers.

The following specific concerns are addressed in this chapter:

What is the history of age issues in the workplace as defined by organized labor?

Why should organized labor be concerned about age in today's workplace and what are the issues of age confronting labor?

What are labor and management doing together to address the variable of age in the workplace?

How can a management training program emphasizing age issues in the corporate workplace be applied to a union setting?

The History of Age as a Labor Issue

Although the mandate of unions is "to improve the lives of those they represent by improving their conditions of work and insuring respect for their dignity as workers" (AFL-CIO 1985, p. 5), this mandate has not addressed specific concerns for older workers. Instead, labor's involvement has been with historically significant but general contract issues of seniority and pensions.

Seniority

Seniority initially surfaced as an issue for railroad workers whose tenure was disturbed by frequent layoffs or transfers from one site to another. After the right to collective bargaining was established in 1935, the union became the instrument that controlled job favoritism and discrimination. Seniority provisions in skilled trades, such as printing, helped to control the number of itinerant crafts people.

From its inception, the trade union concept of seniority was not related to chronological age, but rather to years spent on the job. Contract language dating back to 1938 that reviews various types of seniority (including temporary layoffs, work sharing, and promotions) gives no indication that labor felt obligated to protect workers on the basis of chronological age.

Layoffs. "When laying off employees, the *oldest in point of service* shall be retained." The phrase *oldest in point of service* indicates that a worker will be retained based on length of time worked, *not* chronological age (International Brotherhood of Paper Makers) (U.S. Department of Labor 1938, p.1)

Rehiring.

> Whenever the Firm stops working because of the slack period it is agreed by said Firm that upon resumption of work, it shall give work to those employees who were laid off at the end of the preceding season before engaging new help. (International Fur Workers Union) (U.S. Department of Labor 1938, p.2)

From 1941 to 1975, the definition of seniority expanded or contracted in response to variables of unemployment, inflation, and federal government policy. However, a worker's age still did not appear as a relevant priority.

> Seniority is the principle of granting employees preference in certain phases of employment in accordance with *length of service*. The principal aim of a seniority program is to afford the maximum security and reward to those who have rendered longest service. (U.S. Department of Labor 1941, p. 1)

> The seniority system is a cornerstone of the American labor movement. It is the worker's answer to arbitrary decisions by management in determining employee rights and promotion priorities. Because seniority translates *length of service* into a vested right, it is a tangible asset for any worker. Next to the union card itself, seniority is a worker's most valued possession. Seniority is a contractual right, and, as such, is indivisible. (AFL-CIO Executive Council 1975)

Interestingly, an early reference to chronological age is found in that part of the labor movement where seniority provisions in contracts were almost completely absent because of the irregular availability of work. This sector includes coal mining, clothing manufacture, and building construction. These are highly seasonal and mass-production industries that were widely organized by the late 1930s.

> In these industries, seasonal fluctuations [i.e. built-in unemployment] in production mean frequent layoffs. Since the great majority of jobs are semi-skilled or unskilled, most of the workers can be easily replaced, thus increasing the feeling of insecurity. The *emphasis on youth and speed* in these industries also has tended to cause a feeling of uncertainty of tenure on the part of older workers. (U.S. Department of Labor 1941, p. 1)

Work Sharing

These predictable and profound variations in the availability of work led to the preference and subsequent contract language for "work sharing," rather than layoffs based on seniority. Theoretically, work sharing or rotation made age irrelevant because whatever work was available was to be "divided among regular employees to prevent layoffs" (*Monthly Labor Review* 1941, p. 9). Work sharing provided greater flexibility, higher morale, and better stabilization of a worker's wages than a rigid seniority system.

Today, the 1941 concepts of work sharing and job sharing are reemerging in the literature (McConnell 1980; National Commission for Employment Policy 1985) as recommended work alternatives for older employees. Ideas once applied indiscriminately to all workers are being redefined for chronologically older workers. Despite these recommendations, 50–year-old file clerks or waitresses may still be concerned about the "emphasis on youth and speed" (*Monthly Labor Review* 1941, p. 1) and its effect on their job security.

Age Issues Confronting Labor

Labor must be prepared to respond to the growing numbers of older workers and the concern expressed by employers for their productive, cost-effective integration into the work force. Four factors will influence labor's response: the demography of the U.S. work force; competition among age groups; skill and industry obsolescence; and unemployment.

Demography

Older workers, defined by the Bureau of Labor Statistics as age 45 or older, numbered 32 million in 1980 (National Commission for Employment Policy 1985). This figure is expected to rise to 38 million by 1995. The largest increase in the older work force is expected to be in the 45–54 age range.

Of the approximately 22.5 million workers (23 percent of the work force) represented by organized labor in 1980, over 7 million employed workers (31 percent of those represented) were age 45 to 65. Approximately one-quarter million employed workers (8.8 percent of those represented) were age 65 and over (U.S. Department of Labor, Bureau of Labor Statistics 1981).

The 1981 report by the Bureau of Labor Statistics provides further insight into the median age and labor representation of employed older workers. The median age of employed represented workers was 37.7 years—nearly four years older than the median age of the nonrepresented work force. "Employed workers represented by labor organizations were . . . older than their nonrepresented counterparts in each of the major occupational groups" (p. 3). These figures remained stable when linked to race and sex.

The median age of all men represented by labor organizations in 1980 was 37.9 years. The median age of all represented women was 37.3 years (Bureau of Labor Statistics 1981). Overall, labor represents nearly 50 percent fewer women than men, although certain widely unionized industries (such as clothing in the blue collar trades and clerical in the public service sector) have been traditionally female-dominated. The *oldest* workers represented by labor in 1980 were women. Represented workers in personal household services had the highest median age (52.2 years), followed by women in the apparel industry (45.6 years). In both service and apparel groups, the largest concentration of employed workers represented by labor was in the 45–65 age range (Bureau of Labor Statistics 1981). These demographics impel labor to begin to develop programs and policies that attend to the needs of its aging work force.

The concerns of a specific group of older workers, women in the apparel industry, further demonstrate that those represented by labor face many of the age-related problems experienced by their nonrepresented counterparts. Average earnings in apparel are subject to tremendous seasonal variations and the generally poor state of the industry. Yearly earnings fall in the $8–9,000 range for those who can manage to work full-time (forty weeks a year) (ILGWU Research Department 1986).

In 1983, the median income of all American women age 65 and older was $5,599 (American Association of Retired Persons 1984, p. 9). What, then, does the average woman of average age in the apparel industry have to look forward to? Is she destined to fit the "too old to work, too young to retire" stereotype? Does she have skills that can be retooled *if and when* jobs are available? Are her parents elderly or her children teenagers? Do the caretaker stresses of home affect her productivity, the speed that is so essential in a mass production industry? Are her hands numb from working a machine for thirty years or is she going deaf from the noisy demands of shop life?

As current literature and study have begun to focus more intensively on the business response to the older white collar and service work force, the need for opportunities for "phased retirement" or the innovation of "retiree labor pools" is being emphasized. Yet, the women previously described represent a cross section of older American workers, male and female, who do not have the luxury of choice in making retirement decisions. The lives of thousands of older workers, regardless of union representation, are subject to the stresses of occupation and the aging process in industries that themselves are failing.

These older workers without options must be labor's current and future challenge. Labor's ability to meet this challenge lies in its history as well as its long experience representing the blue collar work force. Industries such as autos, steel, textiles, apparel, construction, and mining have traditionally been labor strongholds. In 1980, for example, approximately 41 percent of all blue collar workers were represented by labor organizations, compared to only 18 percent representation each for white collar and service industries (Bureau of Labor Statistics 1981).

Finally, labor's ability to further assist these older workers will be particularly influenced by the degree to which it recognizes the variable of age as central to the needs and problems of the American workplace.

Competition among Age Groups

The largest increase in the older work force in the coming decades is expected to be in the 45–54 age range. Morrison calls this group "the largest cohort of middle-age workers in U.S. history" (1983, p. 19). Consequently, he also suggests that the predicted demand for workers age 65 and over during the next twenty years may prove to be unfounded. "The growth of the middle age to older workforce (particularly women) will be the most important characteristic of the future labor market" (p. 19).

Particularly in the aging industrial sectors of the economy such as steel, mining, textiles, apparel, and typography, organized labor is facing competition for jobs among groups of older workers separated from one another by no more than ten or twenty years. Additionally, these labor-intensive industries face competition for business from new corners of the world employing more modern, sophisticated, and less expensive technologies. When jobs are scarce in industries such as steel and mining, who will be retrained by a union-sponsored skills-development initiative? Will it be an older worker with an established work history and a battery of skills to build upon or a younger, less skilled worker who can offer the employer a longer period of productivity for the training investment? Is a younger worker more valuable to the company and more able to learn? Is an older worker less flexible and less able to learn?

Inability to distinguish between myth and reality surrounding its older constituents can exacerbate competition issues for labor. Consider the situation at the negotiating table when benefit contributions are in question.

An employer wants to limit certain contributions to a disability fund for workers over 55 in exchange for increased pension fund contributions for those workers. The employer's rationale to the union is that once older workers get sick, they never recover. They are absent for prolonged periods of time and therefore should probably just retire, "enjoy what time is left," and collect a bigger pension instead of a smaller disability payment.

To effectively and equally represent constituents age 55 and over in the described scenario, the union negotiators would need to recognize the following myths and realities:

> Data indicate that older workers have attendance rates that are at least as good as those of their younger coworkers (U.S. Department of Health and Human Services 1984).
>
> Those who stay in the work force may exemplify a self-selection process whereby only the healthy continue to work (U.S. Department of Health and Human Services 1984).
>
> Work and leisure time are *both* important in the lives of older workers. Many variables, including the adequacy of retirement income and job availability, influence the older worker's decision to work (U.S. Department of Health and Human Services 1984).

To ignore or examine superficially the economic, social, and health circumstances affecting the status of older workers is to promote less than full representation of labor's constituency.

Skill Obsolescence and Unemployment

Issues of skill obsolescence and unemployment become increasingly acute as workers age. A 1984 Bureau of Labor Statistics survey indicated that unemployment for those age 55 to 64 was 30 percent, the highest figure for any age group. Further, 27 percent of this age group had completely withdrawn from the labor force (American Association of Retired Persons 1986).

> Once unemployed, the older worker runs the greatest risk of being without work for long periods of time. . . . Millions of older men and women have withdrawn from the labor force unwillingly because they could not find jobs and eventually gave up looking for them. (Kirkland 1982, p. 12)

Skill obsolescence may be a cause of unemployment as well as a contributing factor to the protracted periods of joblessness experienced by such high percentages of older workers. "An issue of concern to employers and union . . . is maintaining work productivity and preventing skills obsolescence" (National Commission for Employment Policy 1985, p. 45). The following are typical of the problems of skill obsolescence faced by increasing numbers of older workers in industrial areas throughout the nation.

> A dress factory in a small southeastern town has employed 100 female sewing-machine operators for over 20 years. The average age of the workers in this group is 48 years. The shop and the manufacturer shut down, drowned by foreign imports. The town has few other jobs to offer and the nearest big city has no apparel industry. Some jobs may exist for clerks and typists.
>
> A family-owned manufacturing concern in a midsize city in the Northwest has employed 25 men, average age 55 years, as draftsmen for the past 30 years. The company was recently sold and the new owners, seeking to modernize, will soon install a sophisticated computer graphics system. Its operation requires only half the staff now employed. All similar companies in the area, especially those that are nonunion firms with no enforceable seniority requirements, are hiring very young workers, training on-site, and paying substantially lower wages.

These examples offer several options for labor response and intervention. Of course, labor should be immediately involved in securing the worker's negotiated benefits such as severance pay or pensions. An age-based labor response to these situations also would attend to such issues as retraining needs and job redesign, centralized job listings for possible relocation to other plants, and both union and community social services for the worker and the family, particularly for the duration of the unemployment period.

Increased participation of members in their unions is a recently reiterated goal of the AFL-CIO (AFL-CIO 1985). One way to increase labor's traditional proximity to membership and to strengthen the quality of its representation is for it to take a more active role in confronting potential age crises in the workplace. The crises include skill deterioration and obsolescence, the psychological trauma of job dislocation, and competition among older workers for new jobs and training opportunities.

Labor should be prepared to prevent job insecurity caused by economic or age factors. Between 1980 and 1986, the declining U.S. steel industry laid off 25,000 people. More than one-third of those laid off were over 40. Fewer than one-half of those workers were able to find new, full-time jobs (*New York Times,* August 5, 1986). Even among growing or stable sectors of the economy, employers may find disincentives for retaining older workers. Labor's preventive role in these instances might be to dispel myths regarding worker age and productivity relative to benefit costs. Labor's protective role is always to defend against arbitrary employer practices, one of which might be age discrimination. These attitudes and actions are especially critical for labor representatives when seniority agreements are not enforceable or do not exist.

Labor–Management Initiatives in the Workplace

> Today . . . labor unions are [also] interested in assisting older workers as the workforce represented by unions age, and as industry restructuring threatens displacement of workers of all ages. (National Commission for Employment Policy 1985, p. 37)

> In general, older workers are perceived quite positively by American business. They are widely valued for their knowledge and experience, work habits and attitudes and emotional maturity. (Yankelovich et al. 1985, p. 6)

Labor–management initiatives directed at older workers may be the result of contractual or extracontractual (informal) agreements. Union policies, employer attitudes, and industry constraints will influence the availability of older-worker programs. The scope of labor's cooperation with these efforts will be shaped by several conditions in the workplace: (1) job-sharing/work-sharing options that may be in conflict with union seniority agreements, (2) part-time options that may deny the older worker other benefits such as health insurance and pensions, (3) the economic health of some industries, such as steel or textiles, that may prevent bargaining efforts targeted to skills-development programs because there are too few jobs anywhere in those industries in which to relocate. Labor has been historically reluctant to simply train for training's sake.

The following examples focus on older-worker and labor–management initiatives in areas of training, benefits, and alternate work options.

United Auto Workers (UAW)

As imports continued to batter the big U.S. automobile companies in the early eighties, job security for auto workers became a key demand in negotiations.

In 1982, the UAW and the Ford Motor Company negotiated the Guaranteed Income Stream (GIS) Benefit Program as part of their overall collective bargaining agreement. The goal of the program was to provide additional benefits to employees with high seniority who might be laid off, in the event that the industry decline did not improve or stabilize. The GIS provides income and insurance benefits to eligible older workers until retirement or age 62. These workers eligible for assistance must agree to accept new job assignments for which they are qualified when the employer makes them available. The jobs may be within Ford or in another company. GIS recipients must also be available for training opportunities. Failure to accept these provisions results in termination of GIS benefits.

The UAW/Ford GIS program was designed to satisfy the union by "preserving the income security of older workers . . . in all phases of the program" (National Commission for Employment Policy 1985, p. 39) and to offer the company economic incentives to rehire, relocate, and train older workers as quickly as possible or continue to pay GIS benefits. The company has assured them of jobs; those who return to Ford are given increased health and life insurance benefits and the opportunity to amass greater pension credits compared to those they might have received had they not been laid off.

United Steelworkers of America

Provisions in the union's contract with a wire company in Rhode Island allow for reallocation of older workers through the use of the seniority system (McConnell 1980). An older worker may shift from a job that might be physically too demanding to one which is less so, replacing a younger worker with less seniority in the process, if that job is more suited to the older worker's abilities. However, a job-reallocation program can be difficult to implement. "It often means demotion and lower pay and frequently denies the value of the accumulated skills of older employees" (McConnell 1980, p. 83).

American Federation of Government Employees

The federation's contract contains trial retirement provisions for workers at the Equal Employment Opportunity Commission (EEOC). The program allows up to five employees a month to try retirement for a full year in order to decide if they wish to do so permanently. Age and seniority determine eligibility for the program.

A job at the EEOC is guaranteed for employees who wish to return to work. If the original job is available, the worker may return there. Otherwise, a comparable job at the same site is arranged. The worker returns at the same pay level regardless of job description.

Communication Workers of America (CWA)

In 1983, CWA negotiated an agreement with American Telephone and Telegraph (AT&T) providing skills retraining and development programs for workers affected by the rapid technological changes in the communications industry. Employer contributions are the basis for program funding.

The focus of the program is to enable workers to adapt their skills to new jobs, as old jobs and skills are phased out. A career-development approach is encouraged in an attempt to lessen the older worker's feelings of task or skill dislocation. The CWA/AT&T program does not restrict eligibility on the basis of age. Younger workers facing displacement also may participate.

Examples of other unions involved in labor–management older-worker initiatives include the Service Employees International Union (SEIU), which has a work-sharing program; the American Federation of Teachers (AFT), which uses job sharing; and the International Brotherhood of Teamsters (IBT), which retrains unemployed older workers.

A Training Program for Union Leaders

Purpose and Structure

In July 1985, the International Ladies' Garment Workers' Union (ILGWU) offered a seminar to its General Executive Board entitled "Age Issues in the Workplace." Several months earlier, the staff of the nation's Retiree Service Department participated in a training program entitled "Age Issues in Management" developed by the Andrus Gerontology Center at the University of Southern California. The program was designed to train midlevel corporate managers to recognize age as a significant issue in the workplace, to understand its behavioral implications for their employees and to prevent age discrimination. (See Chapter 10.)

The leadership of the ILGWU had agreed to participate in this training program for two reasons. The 85–year-old union had a long history of involvement with its older and retired workers. Second, recognizing that the average age of its constituency was over 45, the union viewed this program as a natural opportunity to expand the understanding of its membership.

The Retiree Service Department staff presented the program to the union's General Executive Board for its approval. The board, consisting of union vice presidents, was trained by Retiree Service Department staff and subsequently evaluated the program's appropriateness for use with midlevel staff such as local managers, organizers, and business agents. The latter group was most critical for the Retiree Service Department to reach because business agents are the frontline troops, the most direct union link to the membership. The business agents' job is to be in the workplace—on the shop floor. Their primary function is to interpret and enforce the union contract.

The goal of the Retiree Service Department was twofold: to persuade the union's executive leadership that the training program was critical to effective staff performance; and to offer it as an additional resource that could be used to represent members, either to address contract violations or to identify and mediate age-related disputes between workers themselves. Ideally, the department envisioned local managers or business agents as able to understand age issues in the same way as they understand price setting for a garment or utilization of health and welfare benefits to more effectively represent their membership.

From the outset, the Retiree Service Department realized that selected training materials would have to be adapted in order to present this management-based program to a group of union vice presidents. These changes were minimal. The program title was changed from "Age Issues in Management" to "Age Issues in the Workplace." Job titles such as "managers" were changed to "officers" (elected union leaders) and "staff" (nonelected leaders).

It became increasingly clear that new nomenclature and several subtle semantic variations in the training materials eased the program's transition from a management to labor auspice. These variations reflected the obvious philosophical differences in approach to workers—emphasizing the union rather than employer role in workplace issues. The conceptual framework for teaching about age in the workplace was retained. New case studies were developed to reflect union, industry, and contract issues of layoffs, pay reductions, job transfers, and rehiring. Existing case studies were also used to highlight the differences, if any, between labor and management response.

The Retiree Service Department staff trained board participants, ranging in age from 39 to 68, to "feel" the aging process and to evaluate well-known garment-industry contract issues in light of that training experience. For example, a case study was developed in which an older female worker with over twenty years in a particular factory was transferred, with no prior notice, from one machine to another on which she was not as fast. The shift occurred, according to her supervisor, because the worker was slowing down and had been absent from work so often in past weeks that overall production in the shop was affected.

Board participants initially evaluated this situation solely on the basis of the union contract that protected the worker from arbitrary employer practices. Her pay rate as well as the history of her position at the original machine were critical contract issues. Board members were also able to identify age stereotypes such as lowered productivity and increased absences as especially relevant to the successful resolution of the worker's grievance.

The ILGWU has thirteen geographic regions nationwide and in Canada, although the bulk of its 200,000 members are in the northeastern United States. Following the pilot training with the ILGWU General Executive Board, the Retiree Service Department conducted similar training programs for midlevel staff in five other regions. Two of these programs were run in cooperation with the regional directors who were also union vice presidents who participated in the General Executive Board training session.

Nearly seventy-five evaluations were completed from three training sessions. The board and staff indicated that the training program was theoretically and practically relevant and applicable to the effective representation of the membership. In particular, participants felt that the materials would be useful in preventing and resolving age-related problems in the garment shops.

Implications

One would not insist that the positive ILGWU experience with "Age Issues in the Workplace" should be replicated in every union. However, it might serve as a blueprint from which others in labor could build. The ILGWU experience points to the continuing need for increased labor receptivity to gerontology and the variable of age in the workplace.

The "business" of labor is to offer equal representation to all constituents. The legal vehicle for this representation is the union contract. *Any* form of discrimination runs contrary to this mandate and must be addressed in contract language that defines the prohibition and the means for a remedy, such as the grievance procedure.

Conclusion

> No serious observer [of organized labor] denies that unions have played and continue to play a civilizing, humanizing, democratizing role in American life.
>
> —AFL-CIO 1985, p. 5

As American labor once developed English and citizenship programs for newcomers to the U.S., set standards for minimum wage requirements for all workers, and pioneered health and safety programs in the workplace, labor now must address the needs of its rapidly aging work force.

The subtlety of age discrimination requires direct response and concrete action. An age-based labor agenda must include criteria for the education and training of staff and membership. Action begins with leadership commitment to programs such as "Age Issues in the Workplace" that will help staff to integrate understanding of the aging process with its effect on the older worker and the workplace. In addition, age factors also should be examined in light of their applicability to contract negotiation and enforcement. Positive, valid expectations of the capabilities of older union workers can develop only if they are rooted in negotiated contracts and labor–management policies derived from those contracts.

An effective age-based labor agenda also requires that all constituents be given opportunities to learn about the aging process. Both younger and older workers can benefit from a more realistic understanding of age and its effect on, for example, physical abilities, job security, and alternative work options.

It is difficult to predict whether or not organized labor will be able to respond consistently to age factors in the workplace in the years ahead. As their resources are strained by shrinking memberships and failing industries or government abrogation of its responsibilities to workers and the work site, unions may place a low priority on older worker education and training. These variables also will shape labor–management cooperation and older-worker–program initiatives. However, labor will continue to represent a rapidly aging work force, with or without such collaboration. Maximum effective representation of this constituency demands the recognition of age as a permanent influence on today's workers and the workplace.

References

AFL-CIO Committee on the Evolution of Work. *The Changing Situation of Workers and their Unions*. Washington, D.C.: AFL-CIO, 1985.

AFL-CIO. *Seniority and Lay-Offs*. Executive Council Resolutions. October 1975.

American Association of Retired Persons. *A Profile of Older Americans: 1984*. Brochure prepared by AARP Program Resources Department. Washington, D.C.: 1984.

American Association of Retired Persons *Working Age* 2 no 1 (July/August) 1986.

Clague, E., Palli, B., and Kramer, L. *The Aging Worker and the Union*. New York: Praeger, 1971.

Fowles, D. "The Numbers Game: Older Workers." *Aging*, No. 348. Washington, D.C.: U.S. Department of Health and Human Services, ILGWU Research Department 1986.

Kaplan, B.H. "Alternative Work Options for Older Workers: Part III—The Union and Professional Association View." *Aging and Work* (Summer 1981).

Kirkland, L. "Employing the Older Worker: A Labor Perspective." *Generations* 6 (1982).

Lueck, T. "After Manville: Middle-Aged and Jobless." *New York Times*, August 5, 1986.

McConnell, S.R. "Alternative Work Patterns for an Aging Work Force." In *Work and Retirement: Policy Issues,* Ragan, P.K., ed. Lexington, Mass.: Lexington Books, 1980.

McConnell, S.R. "Assessing the Health and Job Performance of Older Workers." *Business and Health* (June 1984), Washington Business Group on Health.

Morrison, M.H., "The Aging of the U.S. Population: Human Resource Implications." U.S. Department of Labor, Bureau of Labor Statistics, *Monthly Labor Review.* Washington, D.C.: U.S. Government Printing Office, May 1983.

National Commission for Employment Policy. *Older Worker Employment Comes of Age: Practice and Potential.* Menlo Park, Calif.: Public Policy Center, SRI International, 1985.

Paul, C. "Company Productivity and Worker Age: A Technical Report." A report prepared for the Administration on Aging and the Department of Health and Human Services. Washington, D.C., 1984.

RAI (Retirement Advisors). "Selected Older Worker Policies and Issues." RAI Workshop Training Materials. New York, 1985.

U.S. Congress, Congressional Budget Office. *Work and Retirement: Options for Continued Employment of Older Workers.* Washington, D.C.: U.S. Government Printing Office, 1982.

U.S. Department of Health and Human Services, Office of Human Development Services, Administration on Aging. *Older Workers: Myths and Reality.* Publication No. (AoA) 84-20515. Washington, D.C.: U.S. Government Printing Office, 1984.

U.S. Department of Labor, Bureau of Labor of Statistics. *Earnings and other Characteristics of Organized Workers, May, 1980.* Bulletin 2105. Washington, D.C.: U.S. Government Printing Office, 1981.

U.S. Department of Labor, Bureau of Labor Statistics. *Seniority Provisions in Union Agreements.* Serial No. 1308. Washington, D.C.: U.S. Government Printing Office, 1941.

U.S. Department of Labor, Bureau of Labor Statistics. *Some Seniority Provisions in Union Agreements.* Serial No. 5849. Washington, D.C.: U.S. Government Printing Office, 1938.

Wineman, J. "Services to Older and Retired Workers." In *Handbook of Gerontological Services,* Monk, A., ed. New York: Van Nostrand Reinhold, 1985.

Work in America Institute, Inc. *The Future of older Workers in America.* Report of a symposium. Arden House, Harriman, New York, 1981.

Yankelovich, Skelly and White, Inc. *Workers Over 50: Old Myths, New Realities.* Washington, D.C.: American Association of Retired Persons, 1985.

Suggested Readings

AFL-CIO Committee on the Evolution of Work. *The Changing Situation of Workers and their Unions.* Washington, D.C.: AFL-CIO, 1985.

This report offers both the current AFL-CIO policy on the state of unions today and the needs of workers of tomorrow as well as concrete recommendations for organized labor's arrival into the next century. Recommendations include increasing member participation, improving communications, and improving organizing activity. It is a forcused self-examination of both the positive and negative characteristics of the American labor movement today.

Clague, E., Palli, B., and Kramer, L. *The Aging Worker and the Union.* New York: Praeger, 1971.

This book offers a broad-based view of twelve AFL-CIO unions and their programs for older and retired workers. Seniority and pension issues are discussed in each of the twelve unions and are also considered in greater depth in the final section of the book. Although dated, it should still serve as an essential reference and historical guide to the provision of services to older and retired union members.

McConnell, S.R. "Alternative Work Patterns for an Aging Work Force." In *Work and Retirement: Policy Issues,* Ragan, P.K., ed. Lexington, Mass.: Lexington Books, 1980.

This chapter provides one of the few discussions of work patterns for older workers that includes both labor and business perspectives and responses. Traditional concepts of work and leisure are described, followed by a comprehensive examination of alternative work patterns ranging from common forms such as part-time work to periodic sabbaticals and phased retirement. It offers a challenging conceptual framework from which both business and labor could creatively proceed to further address age in the workplace.

Wineman, J. "Services to Older and Retired Workers." In *Handbook of Gerontological Services,* Monk, A., ed. New York: Van Nostrand Reinhold, 1985.

An overview of the provision of services to older and retired union workers from the perspective of industrial gerontology and social work. Types of services examined include social services, educational and leisure programs, and retraining and employment options both within unions and in the community. The target population for this discussion is primarily female, single, immigrant, low-wage, and semiskilled—a rapidly growing yet underserved portion of older America and its work force.

Step 13: Capitalize on older workers' desires and abilities to extend their working career

Continued Work Contributions in Late Career

Jeffrey Sonnenfeld

Retirement

Many of the attributes that describe fulfillment in life are also associated with a successful work relationship. The feeling of belonging, a sense of worth, the satisfaction of involvement, and the achievement of continuity, status, and identity are all expressions of a positive work experience. Retirement disrupts these attributes of work. Therefore, it is understandable that for many people, retirement is a difficult event that comes at a sensitive stage in life, at which time losses of identity, health, and vitality are major concerns.

Large-scale surveys of top executives indicate that almost three-quarters of the respondents would continue in their jobs even if they were financially independent (Korn and Ferry 1985). Polls by Louis Harris and Associates indicate that over half their respondents would continue to work beyond age 65. Among retired workers, 46 percent still wish they were working. Several studies indicate a reversal in trends toward early retirement (Boss et al. 1985). In a cornerstone study of fifty stressful life events, retirement ranks tenth (Holmes and Rahe 1967).

More recent reviews of research on retirement suggest that the study of retirement had really been a surrogate for the study of the distress over aging (Behr 1986). In a modern achievement-oriented society, many people measure their lives using their career accomplishments as an indicator that their existence had value. Career extensions through continued normal employment or part-time and phased reductions in workload are relied upon to ease the trauma of aging.

The reports of early-retirement trends require careful examination with regard to occupational patterns. Top leaders, performers, self-employed professionals, independent artisans, and others with high personal discretion are not eager to quit. In a recent survey of one hundred retired corporate leaders, virtually all denied that they had "really retired." They wanted to be recognized as busy and important people with continued professional worth. In particular, institutional leaders, facing retirement may suffer emotional stress due to loss of power, misgivings about timing and goal achievement, and concerns about the successful perpetuation of their organizations.

Acting Your Age

Over the past two decades, scientific investigations by physiologists and psychologists have revealed that chronological age (the time that has passed since birth) is an inadequate measure of functional age (what an individual can do) or social age (what an individual is obliged to do). This finding supports the lack of correlation between abilities that change with age and the biased social pressures to require people to act their age.

Paul Mazursky's film *Harry and Tonto* provides an example of society's expectations from a retiree. Through the eyes of Harry (a fairly healthy, retired school teacher), the viewer experiences the frustrations of a community of aged and lonely people facing a hostile and disintegrating environment. Harry, attached to the familiar surroundings of the past, has become accustomed to the ruins and dreariness of his life. At first, Harry resists change and is evicted from his apartment before the building is razed. His embarrassed middle-aged son coming to the rescue admonishes his father angrily to "act your age, Pop." To which Harry responds, "I am acting my age."

Once having been aroused to exert his own wishes, he continues to rebel and rejects his son's plans for his life. Harry, liberated from the mournful shackles of the past, embarks on a trip to visit his children around the country and renews family associations. He meets new friends, learns new survival techniques, refines personal skills, and adapts gracefully to a changing world. Although bitter in the beginning, his relocation, opportunity to tutor young people, and chance to understand the problems of adolescents facilitates his own rejuvenation. Harry is criticized by his children and patronized by middle-aged people. However, his decision to opt for a full life until the end is inspired by the welcome and warmth of his young friends and grandchildren.

The contest between the middle-aged and the combined forces of old and young is observed vividly in the conspiratorial union of grandparents and grandchildren. Author Ronald Blythe commented in his book *The View in Winter,* "The old challenge authority because they have exercised its pretensions, the young because they cannot believe they will ever have to" (p. 72). The middle-aged, meanwhile, see both groups as a personal but unconscious threat.

> The middle-aged frequently find themselves timidly—yet compulsively—measuring their assets against those of old age to see what has yet to go. . . . The old are ever conscious of the lengths to which self-preservation in the not-so-young will go, and frequently fear them. (Blythe 1979, p. 73)

Exposure to the elderly reminds the middle-aged of future loss. At midlife, one may thus undergo a reorientation to time. Instead of measuring the years behind, one contemplates how little time remains. This can lead to a resentment of older people as their presence reminds younger people of their own aging at the same time that older workers appear to block the opportunity of the younger.

Such intergenerational hostilities are intensified within managerial hierarchies. Each cohort targets the other generation as the cause of their own diminished opportunity. This was demonstrated in a pioneering study of age bias drawn from a broad-based sample of managers who read the *Harvard Business Review* (Rosen and Jerdee 1977). The managers were asked to recommend action regarding three employees. For half the study participants, the employee was described as being "older," and for the other half of the participants, the employee was described as being "younger." The participating managers who thought the employee was younger were far more willing to supply opportunity for training, promotion, and helpful feedback. Those described as "older employees," but with descriptions identical to the younger ones, were judged to be more rigid, resistant to change, and deserving of less management attention or organizational opportunity (see figure 13–1).

Most participants stated that they favored improved treatment for older workers even though their management recommendations were biased. The "in-basket" (an exercise with simulated decision pressure) format of the study, however, revealed hidden age stereotypes that support self-fulfilling prophesies. The pronouncements of equal opportunity for older workers is not reflected in their decisions. Not surprisingly, those study participants over age 50 were far more conscientious about fair treatment of older workers. I have replicated this study with almost one thousand of my students each year and find repeated bias toward helping the younger worker, consistent with the original study.

Age and Retirement

Older workers were not always forced into retirement at prescribed ages. A decade ago, Congress passed legislation extending retirement from age 65 to age 70. Many employers and journalists were opposed to this measure. Columnist William Safire cautioned in a *New York Times* article entitled "The Codgerdoggle," "Old people get older and usually less productive, and they ought to retire so that business can be better more economically served[sic]. We should treat the elderly with respect which does not require treating them as if they were not old" (Safire 1977, p. 29).

Five years later, after losing a $2 million lawsuit brought by three fired employees in their late fifties and sixties, Norman Wexler (the 68–year-old chairman of the I. Magnin department stores) defended the firm claiming,

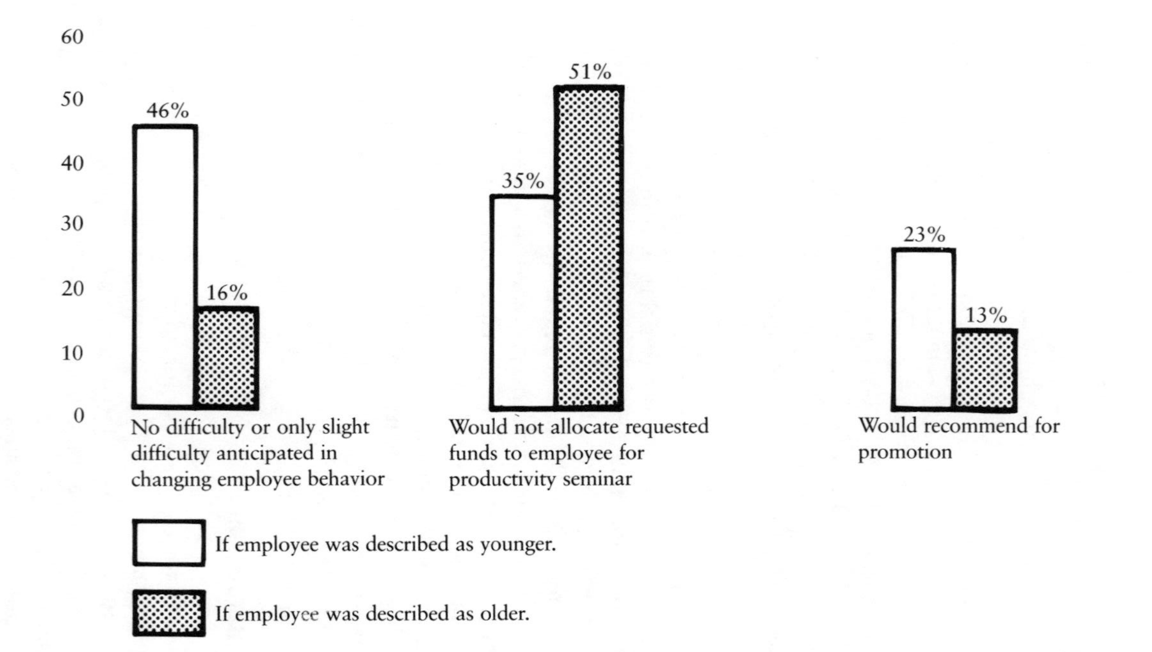

Source: Rosen, B. and Jerdee, T.R. "Too Old or Not Too Old." *Harvard Business Review* 55 (November-December 1977): 96–106.

Figure 13–1. Age-Bias Survey of Managers

"I'm different. . . . Old people don't want to work as hard. The young people are better. . . . It's an evolutionary fact" ("60 Minutes" 1984). Such misconceptions are inconsistent with scientific research and company experience. For example, Macy's department stores never have felt the need to introduce a mandatory retirement age.

The tradition of age-related retirement is a twentieth century practice. Although the *American Dictionary* in 1828 listed the word *retirement,* it was not applied to the elderly. Old workers were valued for their wisdom and moral stability, and company policies did not require people to stop working (Graebner 1980; Acherbaum 1978; Fisher 1977). At age 81, Benjamin Franklin negotiated the great compromise that preceded the adoption of the U.S. Constitution.

But, a new era opened—the beginning of the twentieth century. William Osler, the chief physician of Johns Hopkins University Hospital introduced an especially gloomy perspective in his influential farewell address. Osler praised "the effective, moving, vitalizing work of the world . . . accomplished by people . . . between the ages of 25 and 40" (Graebner 1980, pp. 4–5). Meanwhile, he deplored the uselessness of men above 67 years of age and warned of calamities that may befall men during their seventh and eighth decades (Graebner 1980).

These declarations set off a storm of public frenzy as more workers moved from farm and craft shops to jobs in fast-paced factories. In 1904, President Theodore Roosevelt amended the Civil War veterans' pension to define old age as a disability, thereby rendering 60– and 70–year-old veterans eligible for benefits if they quit work. The purpose, in part, was to encourage their exit from the work force (Treas 1986). Later on, the influence of the Progressive Movement's humanitarian concern for the condition of workers drove older workers from dangerous manufacturing jobs. Preferential personnel policies favored young workers in the 1920s, and massive unemployment in the 1930s led to collective bargaining agreements. New Deal legislation established formal retirement provisions. The Social Security Act of 1935 selected age 65 as a basis for normal retirement. Consequently, participation in the U.S. labor force by men over age 65 fell from 68.3 percent in 1890 to 55.6 percent in 1920, 41.8 percent in 1940, and then to a low of 19.1 percent in 1980 (see figure 13–2).

Age Discrimination

Concern about rampant age discrimination descended to the midcareer level by the 1960s. This prompted President Lyndon Johnson to urge congressional action to oppose the waste of human potential and unemployment payments through arbitrary age discrimination. Such challenges to age bias led to the

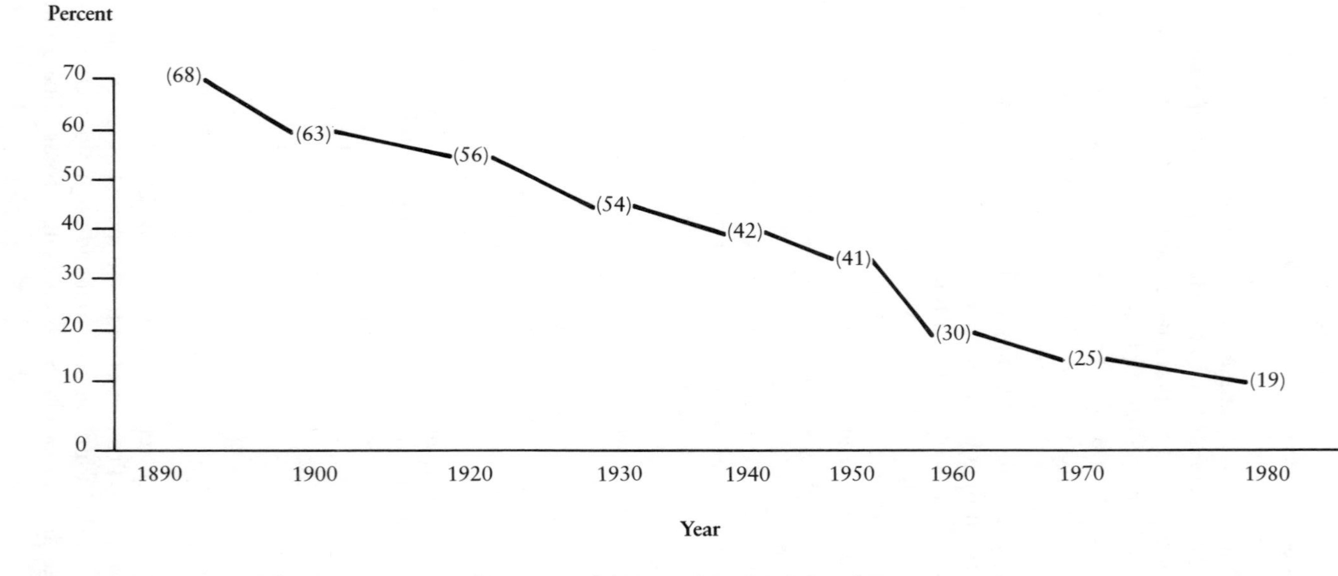

Source: U.S. Bureau of the Census, *Historical Statistics of the United States: Colonial Times to 1970,* Bicentennial ed., Part 1. Washington, D.C.: U.S. Government Printing Office, 1975, p. 132.
U.S. Bureau of the Census, "Population Profile of the United States, 1980," *Current Population Reports,* Series P-20, No. 363. Washington, D.C.: U.S. Government Printing Office, 1981.
For more detail, see Treas, J., "The Historic Decline in Late-Life Labor Force Participation in the U.S." In *Age, Health, and Employment,* Birren J., et al., eds. Englewood Cliffs, N.J.: Prentice–Hall, 1986.

Figure 13–2. Labor Force Participation for Those 65 and Over, 1890–1980

1967 Age Discrimination in Employment Act, which, after the 1978 amendments, protected most workers 40 to 70 years of age from personnel discrimination and abolished mandatory retirement for federal workers.

A study of the growing number of age-discrimination suits over the past decade found that employers were successful in 73 percent of cases (Hergenrather 1985). Many of the suits lost were brought by employees of the largest companies in major industries, such as Eastern Airlines, Chevron, and Trans World Airlines. By the mid-1980s, 40 percent of the Fortune 500 companies had withdrawn personnel policies calling for mandatory retirement at any age. By early 1986, 16 states had passed laws banning mandatory retirement. In October 1986, Congress finally passed similar legislation banning all mandatory retirement, thus restoring a vital civil right to workers of all ages. The measure will exclude state and local police officers, firefighters, and prison guards.

The American Council on Education succeeded in getting an amendment to delay inclusion of college professors for seven years, during which time federal studies would be conducted on the impact of abolishing mandatory retirement in colleges and the feasibility of developing age-related fitness tests for police officers and prison guards. Florida Democratic Congressman Claude Pepper's 1986 bill was backed by senior citizens and was opposed by the U.S. Chamber of Commerce, which stated that the bill could cause stagnation in the work force. A Department of Labor spokesman said the legislation would add 195,000 employees to the nation's work force by 1990.

Demographic Pressures

These legislative changes are inspired by the shifting power of older workers. Important changes in the demographic pattern have emerged, including the anticipated 16–20 percent midlife bulge of the baby boomers as well as the radical acceleration of the aged population segment. While the 18-to-24–year-old category will decline by 10 percent by 1990, the number surviving beyond age 65 will grow by 10 percent (U.S. Bureau of the Census, July 1977). Clearly, the over-65 age sector is growing twice as fast as other groups—it is now in excess of 24 million. By the year 2040, this segment will double again to reach a peak of 55 million. From movements that have already commenced, it is apparent that the maturing of the baby-boom population will have a great impact on all our institutions.

The rise in generational special interest groups, career tension clashes, and the emergence of a vibrant consumer force have their genesis in this expansion of older community members during the past three decades. The over-60 citizens have doubled in number since 1950 and grew by a fourth again in the 1970s. The over-75 age group has grown tenfold since 1900, while the over-85 members have grown 17 times since the turn of the century. As we make progress in understanding the full potential of this new distribution of human resources in our midst, we will be in a better position to resolve problems such as retirement, work tenure, alternative career opportunities, and issues of adaptation of the retired worker.

Older people have startled consumer marketers by their purchasing behavior. Householders headed by an over-50 age-group member now hold more than one-half of all the discretionary income in the United States, roughly $150 billion (Rosener and Prout 1986).

It has been suggested that Florida, with 17 percent of the population over age 65 as well as 33 percent over age 50, provides a glimpse into the year 2000 for the rest of the nation. Therefore, Florida has become a principal laboratory for consumer research. By the year 2020, one-third of the U.S. population is expected to be over age 55. The major packaged goods firms now market new foods, cosmetics, and health items for this population (Gilman 1986). Advertisements now prominently feature active older people as models. Major Hollywood studios have found box office success placing old people on center stage in films such as *Cocoon* starring septuagenarians Don Ameche and Hume Cronyn, *On Golden Pond* with Henry Fonda and Katherine Hepburn as a retired couple, and *Going in Style* with George Burns as a restless retiree.

Similarly, television—which formerly broadcasted primarily youth-oriented adventure series and midlife family comedies—now presents several shows, such as "Golden Girls," directed toward an older audience. Brandon Tartikoff, president of NBC Entertainment and sponsor of "Golden Girls," explains his change: "Take some women around sixty. Society has written them off and has said they're over the hill; we want them to be feisty . . . and having a good time" (Harmetz 1985, p. H–25). The show deals with themes such as career trials, faltering health, and death; it has consistently high market ratings.

Individual Variation in Abilities and Aging

Such changes toward the elderly in general, and toward mandatory retirement in particular have been part of a larger transformation. Leading gerontologists suggest that a quiet revolution has taken place that has liberated people from having to "act their age." The rigid timetable for guiding major life events has been reset.

Attitudes toward older workers are changing. Rigidly enforced age grading is disappearing. Gerontologist Bernice Neugarten commented,

> The whole internal clock I used to write about that kept us on time, the clock that tells us whether we're too young or too old to be marrying, or

going to school, or getting a job or retiring, is no longer as powerful or compelling as it used to be. (Neugarten 1980, p. 35)

Mountaineering to Management

Popular journals regularly confuse us with paradoxical anecdotes about age and competency on the job. For example, a nationwide newspaper ran a story in 1986 on a likely future entrant into the baseball Hall of Fame. The player, Steve Carlton, refused to recognize that he might have passed his peak at age 41. While a pitcher for the Philadelphia Phillies, he struck out 4,000 batters, won 319 games, and received the Cy Young Award (for pitching) four times. However, he refused to retire when his performance fell even though the team president urged it. The team president regretfully fired Carlton, calling this "the most agonizing time I spent in baseball" (Bodley 1986, p. 5c). Rehired by another team, he had to quit in embarrassment when his performance did not improve.

However, the same issue of the paper featured an article on Hilda Crooks, a 90–year-old mountain climber who had just completed her twenty-third annual ascent up Alaska's Mount McKinley. She climbed 100 high peaks since the age of 66 (Archibald 1986, p. 2A). Moreover, the street-smart Guardian Angels have even opened patrols to crime fighters approaching their eighties (*Newsweek* July 1, 1985). Albert H. Gordon, the vibrant 84–year-old chairman of the investment bank of Kidder Peabody, has continued to run 10 miles a day and ran the London Marathon in his eighties. Gordon commented in an interview with me, in July 1984, "People don't realize the potential of the human mind or body. Physical health greatly affects your occupational flexibility. You must prepare to fight physical decline by planning challenging exercise."

Nonetheless, we often carry a deeply planted bias against older workers, because we associate aging with decline in performance and with a swiftly approaching withdrawal from work. Depressing realizations of personal and professional loss are emphasized. Career-stage theorists label late career a time for "decline and disengagement." For example, MIT management professor Edgar N. Schein has pointed out that organizations expect older workers to adjust to their circumstances by learning to accept reduced levels of power, learning to accept and develop new roles based on declining competence and motivation, and learning to manage a life that is less dominated by work (Schein 1978).

Similarly, the prominent adult-life–development theorists such as psychologists Erik Erikson, George Vaillant, Roger Gould, and Daniel Levinson discuss the later years as a time for coping with reduced physical capacity, reacquaintance with family and friends, and reviewing one's life work and contribution (Erikson 1963). Erikson described late life as a time for resolving the balance between a sense of integrity and completeness in life versus a sense of despair over lost opportunity and mistakes.

Such preparation for societal expectations and critical personal tasks are important in understanding the emotional needs of older workers. However, exclusive reliance upon this approach may lead to a dysfunctional preoccupation with the longer-run future. At every life stage, we must wrestle with appropriate anxieties, but our lives are not limited to these concerns. By premature overemphasis upon the need to prepare for the end of work or the end of life, we may rob individuals of a full life in the present.

Controlling Physical Declines

The emphasis upon full use of existing capabilities does not deny that certain physiological changes become more pronounced with age. Bodily functions that decline most commonly with age are the senses of vision and hearing plus the immune system, which can exacerbate cardiovascular and kidney problems and degenerative diseases. However, while 85 percent of workers over 65 suffer from chronic diseases, the onset is gradual; diseases do not suddenly appear at the age of 65 (Robinson 1986). In fact, there is a 75 percent prevalence rate of these conditions between ages 60 and 64. Many can be treated and controlled.

The McArthur Foundation funded a multidisciplinary project to study the great variations in the rate of aging. Robert Butler, a geriatric specialist at Mt. Sinai Hospital, has prescribed a regimen that will be of assistance in limiting or compensating for age-related disabilities (Hallowell 1985). According to research by the Andrus Gerontology Center at the University of Southern California, people who maintain regular exercises can set the clock back 25 to 45 years. This can produce a 35 percent increase in work capacity (de Vries 1986).

Psychological Changes

Physiological changes in older people also can be accompanied by psychological changes. This involves some cognitive skills and attitudes that may affect judgment and learning. For example, neurological decay has been linked to random brain activity or "neural noise." A higher percentage of mental errors occur when the brain fails to respond promptly to neural signals. This slowing occurs throughout adult life, but can be slight until late life. Generally, older people employ far more rigid decision-making criteria and require a 75 percent chance of certainty before committing themselves to any final action. In general, they are more deliberate in making mental links and take fewer risks than younger people.

Judgment and Learning

If time pressure is not a relevant factor, the cognitive performance of older people tends to be at least as strong as that of younger people. For example, self-paced learning and self-paced tests, where individuals do not have to make speed-versus-accuracy trade-offs, are free of age-related performance problems. These self-paced tests show no decline with age in problem solving, number facility, or verbal comprehension (Welford 1976). A major study on human perception concluded that wisdom through experience can help correct for slowed response time: "While some perceptual processes exhibit age-related declines in adulthood, other processes, such as higher order selectivity may come to play a more significant role in accounting for perceptual experience" (Hoyer and Flode 1980). Perception, of course, is a psychological as well as a physiological process. Expectations and needs have an impact on what is perceived. In this sense, experienced older workers bring some advantage.

Most of the learning difficulties of older people relate to acquisition and recall failures rather than to actual retention of new information. The human memory system is thought to be a two-step process involving initial information entry and later storage. Older people may have more trouble holding newly entered information in short-term memory. Thus, it is not coded properly for retention. In retrieval as well, short-term memory blockages cause problems. Many memory blockages can be overcome by training in appropriate mental techniques (Birren and Schaie 1977). New research from MIT, Harvard, Tufts, and the National Institute of Mental Health suggests that memory loss may further be limited by changes in diet. While brain damage may not be reparable, the addition of choline found in the food additive lecithin may increase the vital neurotransmitter acetycholine, which carries signals across synapses (Mog et al. 1980).

Researchers at University of California at Irvine and Harvard Medical Schools have found that the brain continues to grow in late life if a person is presented with a stimulating situation in an enriched environment. Pioneering research suggests that learning a new language, for example, may lead to a significant growth of nerve dendrites (*New York Times* 1985, pp. C1, C7). Research by psychologist Ellen Langer has found that many supposedly natural consequences of aging are due to a debilitating "mindless" state, when people surrender independence and are placed in a helpless state. She found that nursing home patients with increased control over their situation showed significant improvement in measures of alertness, active participation, and mental and physical well-being (Langer and Rodin 1976).

This emphasis upon shaping one's environment to conquer age-related challenges to physical and intellectual performance also applies to the work attitude of older workers. Theories of aging that emphasize continuous activity, rather than disengagement from work, draw upon the evidence of strikingly high morale among older workers. A recent government study suggested that economic advantages of employing older workers are largely due to lower turnover and lower absenteeism which follow from such high morale (U.S. Senate 1984). Research on all sectors of the American work force positively relate age with job satisfaction (Hunt and Saul 1975).

As these strengths are recognized, one also must recognize the forms of resistance to change in older workers. For example, sudden changes in job structure and social networks can be threatening to older workers. The job represents friendships, routines, a sense of self-worth, and a niche in society. A colleague and I recently completed a three-year study of middle-management retraining in the financial services industry (Hill and Sonnenfeld 1986). In this industry, the threat of obsolescence to the older worker was very real due to changing strategic markets, business operations, and technologies.

Older managers were generally as receptive as younger managers to retraining. Although older workers found retraining relevant to their jobs and the changes in the company, they did not find it relevant to their own career progress. They felt that learning would not enhance their career progress as in the case of younger people. Therefore, older employees need opportunities to develop through new assignments as well as provision of updating and retraining.

Age in Various Occupations

In reviewing studies of performance by occupation for different age groups, it is important to be aware of biases built into the performance appraisals themselves. In particular, even the word *potential* in performance appraisals often is used to measure time remaining more than anticipated productivity or likely advancement. In addition, many of these studies are cross-sectional and do not compare the same individuals over a lifetime.

Fifty scholarly studies of age and work performance over the past two decades report no substantial overall relationship. Exceptions include slight variations corresponding with occupation and by methods of performance assessment (Waldman and Avolio 1986; McEvoy and Cascio 1986).

Many well-publicized reports from companies that never have introduced mandatory retirement and have workers in their seventies and eighties substantiate these findings. The president of Globe Dye Works commented that “as long as a man can produce, he can keep his job” (Moore 1977, p. 1). The 87–year-old president of a small General Foods subsidiary where the average age is 70 commented, “Older people are steadier, accustomed to the working discipline” (Atlas and Rees 1977, p. 64). Sales workers at Hart

Marx have never faced mandatory retirement and show no decline in performance attributable to age. Banker's Life and Casualty Company proudly promotes its tradition of open-ended employment, retaining top executives, clerks, and secretaries through their eighties. The company reports that these workers show wisdom and are helpful to others. Polaroid and United States Steel have both had good experiences with older workers and rated their performance and attendance as exemplary, even among workers whose jobs entail heavy demand. At Travelers Insurance Company, older workers have been found valuable enough to be urged to return from retirement and to fill the office's need for temporary help where possible.

Age has surprisingly little effect on manual workers. In several studies, performance remained steady through age 50, with subsequent decline of less than 10 percent of peak performance. Attendance was not significantly affected and the separation rate (quits, layoffs, and discharges) was high for those under 25 and very low for those over 45. The high variations between manual labor studies and those of clerical workers show considerable differences within age groups, compared to the variation between age groups. Generally, older workers show a steadier rate of work and accuracy than younger workers (U.S. Department of Labor, 1957, 1960, 1965). As in previous work settings, attendance records were as good for older workers as for younger ones, and rates of turnover were lower.

Older workers seem to have superior performance in sales positions. Insurance companies, auto dealers, and large department stores regularly report that age, if a factor at all in performance, is an asset (Cron and Slocum 1986; Keller and Quirk 1973). The accumulated technical knowledge and interpersonal skills are best utilized at this career stage. A notable exception to this trend is the salesperson's experience at several high-technology companies. Here, morale frequently declines with length of service. Studies of performance of scientists and engineers show peaks at age 40 and again at age 50 (Pelz 1966; Dennis 1966).

Finally, looking at managers, we can see that the cognitive predisposition toward caution has been identified in work settings. Management researchers found a relationship between age and risk taking as well as between age and the value placed on risk. A study of 1,484 managers across 200 corporations found older managers less willing to take risks and holding lower estimates of the value of risk in general. A study of 80 lower-level decisionmakers also found that older managers tended to take longer in reaching decisions and were less confident of them. However, older managers were better able to appraise the value of new information (Vroom and Pahl 1971).

Additional research suggests that younger managers tend to be the most autocratic in making quick decisions without consulting coworkers, while middle-aged managers are more consultative. Research suggests that older managers are most efficient because they could act as decisively as the young, but took better advantage of information-gathering activities than did younger managers (Pinder and Pinder 1974). Thus, while older managers may be more cautious and slow, they can make firm decisions based on superior information.

The psychologist B.F. Skinner told me that his eighties were his most prolific decade. He stated, "You have to work to shape your physical world so that you can create." He encouraged artists whose work is "getting a little tight . . . to try a new touch . . . and paint with a longer brush."

Career Longevity of Public Figures

The potential to make great contributions in the late-career stage indicated by the research reviewed in the previous section has been especially well demonstrated in the outstanding accomplishments of older public figures ranging from artists and performers to political leaders.

Celebrities

Artists. For example, artist Grandma Moses continued painting past age 100, and Pablo Picasso continued to draw and engrave into his nineties. When Marc Chagall died at age 97 in 1980, he was hailed as one of the giants of modern art with over three-quarters of a century of unbroken productivity (Russell 1985; Taylor 1985). Michelangelo was 88 years old when he drew up the architectural plans for the Church of Santa Maria Degli Angeli.

Musicians. Similarly, we can find many examples of late-career musicians. Pianist Arthur Rubinstein performed one of his greatest recitals in Carnegie Hall at age 89. Pianist Rudolph Serkin maintained a full performance schedule at age 81, while running a summer music school in Vermont. Vladimir Horowitz and Claudio Arrau both have maintained active performance schedules around the world. Ragtime pianist Eubie Blake performed publicly up to his hundredth birthday. Choreographer Martha Graham wrote an inspiring description of her fulfillment through her work at age 91 (Graham 1985).

Authors. Turning from art to writing, George Bernard Shaw wrote the play *Farfetched Fables* at age 93. Winston Churchill authored *A History of the English Speaking People* at age 82. In Isaac Bashevis Singer's eighty-first year, the Nobel Prize winner launched two new plays Off Broadway, while publishing four books plus articles in five journals (Matchan 1985). He continued to receive acclaim for his uncluttered prose. In 1985, Dr. Benjamin Spock revised his 1945 blockbuster book on child care with 38 new sections. It continues to be a best seller (Hager 1985).

Filmmakers. Turning to films, internationally renowned filmmaker Luis Bunuel made some of his most esteemed movies, such as a *Dairy of a Chambermaid* and *Belle du Jour,* in his sixties and seventies. Actress Ruth Gordon's astounding number of magnificent performances on film and on stage from 1911 until her death at age 88 showed a continued development and refinement of her craft. Ninety-one–year-old George Burns continues to be active in television and film.

Public Policy Leaders

There are many late-career leaders in public policy making. The long list of older executive and legislative leaders includes President Ronald Reagan, who will complete his second term at age 77, and near-90–year-old Senator John Stennis and Congressman Claude Pepper, who has championed the needs of older Americans for decades. In October 1986, Pepper won another landmark battle with the passage of legislation he sponsored that bans mandatory retirement based on age, giving older Americans "new hope, new courage and a new feeling of meaningfulness." He stated in a recent interview I had with him that "I am not old enough to retire. Furthermore, I don't believe anyone is entitled to my job just because he or she is younger."

A number of septuagenarians and octogenarians are among the public servants that have contributed to maintaining continuity in U.S. foreign policy. Prominent in this category are Henry Cabot Lodge, Ellsworth Bunker (who brilliantly led the negotiations of this century's most historic international agreements), and Secretary of State George Marshall, who drafted and implemented the famous Marshall Plan to resurrect war-torn Western Europe. Averell Harriman spent half a century in service to presidents from the 1930s until his death in 1986. In 1968, at age 76, he began the Paris negotiations to end the war in Vietnam (Oser 1986).

Qualities of Late-Career Leaders

In all these cases, there was a new triumph around every corner. With no concern for reaching the ultimate peak and then retiring, these people continued to make valuable contributions in postpeak performances long after they passed traditional retirement age. Common qualities of these late-career leaders and others I am researching is that they are motivated, achievement-oriented people with a great deal of discretion over the conditions of their employment (Sonnenfeld 1987). They continue to share the benefits of their accumulated wisdom. Mark Twain is supposed to have once commented,

"Wouldn't life be glorious if it began at age 80 and progressed to age 18!" These people enjoy their work and they enjoy their lives. Work is not drudgery that they hope to escape. At the same time they are not workaholics. They do not have a compulsive need to keep up with peers. Rather, they are "work intensives," people who are renewed through their contributions. We can rejuvenate instead of waste the talent of older workers by providing opportunities to tap their potential.

Conclusion

This chapter has looked at the continued potential contribution of workers as they age. The discussion of the psychological meaning of retirement as a terminal career event is really a discussion of the psychological meaning of work. For people of all ages, work provides far more than financial compensation. It provides many of the same functions as family and community—namely, personal identification, group belonging, and a purpose for our efforts. While many retire early, it is often an escape from unpleasant or uninteresting work situations. For some people, such as leaders, artists, and performers, work is so important in providing benefits that a life without work appears to be impossible.

Retirement as a desirable or desired institution for *all* of society is being reconsidered. It is largely a twentieth century creation that addressed several concerns. First, there was increased concern over the ability of people to perform, especially given the stepped-up production technologies of this century. Second, the emphasis upon retirement grew as a way to bypass older workers who had become fearful of unnecessary risk. Third, there was a concern that older workers could clog vital channels of promotion and growth for younger people. Related to this third point is the tendency during retrenchments to favor the young, who presumably have longer potential employment in the firm. Therefore, encouraging retirement allows the firm to retain valuable future resources at the expense of current talent.

These concerns may only be partially accurate and can be overcome. Physical deterioration cannot be halted, but its occupational impact can be minimized. A challenging physiological and psychological environment for older workers prevents the common self-fulfilling prophecy of obsolescence. This continued challenge in the work environment does not require older workers to monopolize power or opportunity. New job placements through promotion, lateral moves, or demotions can sometimes help the older worker find needed new opportunity for renewal while creating job vacancies for younger successors. Converging streams of current gerontological research on the mind, the body, and the behaviors of older workers suggest that age can be an asset. Demographic shifts and legislative change are not the key threat. If our companies atrophy, it is through poor utilization and revitalization of resources.

In general, this chapter suggests that we all look more closely at the frontier of possible contributions that can be made by the thoughtful assignment of older workers to the appropriate jobs. Crude stereotypes, misplaced paternalism, and the eagerness of ambitious younger people to displace older workers in search of opportunity for themselves all threaten our chances of using more imaginative methods for fully utilizing and challenging older workers in American society.

References

Acherbaum, A.N. *Old Age in the New Land Since 1790.* Baltimore: Johns Hopkins University Press, 1978, pp. 20–22.

Archibald, O.M. "Grandma High on Climbing: Mountain Kneels to 90-Year Old." *USA Today,* April 8, 1986, p. 2A.

Atlas, S.T., and Rees, M. "Old Folks at Work." *Newsweek,* September 26, 1977, p. 64.

Behr, T.A. "The Process of Retirement: A Review and Recommendations for Future Investigation." *Personnel Psychology* 39 (1986): 31–55.

Birren, J.E., and Schaie, K.W., eds. *Handbook of the Psychology of Aging.* New York: Van Nostrand Reinhold, 1977.

Blythe, R. *The View in Winter: Reflections on Old Age.* New York: Harcourt Brace Jovanovich, 1979.

Bodley, H. "Charlton Bows Out with His Mind at Ease." *USA Today,* August 8, 1986, p. 5C.

Boss, D.J., Bosse, R., and Glynn, R.J. "Period Effects on Planned Age for Retirement, 1975–1984." *Research on Azin* 3 (1985): 395–407.

Cron, W.L., and Slocum, J.W. "The Influence of Career Stages on Salespeople's Job Attitudes, Work Perceptions, and Performance." *Journal of Marketing Research* 23, (1986): 119, 129.

de Vries, H. *Fitness After 50.* New York: Charles Scribner's Sons, 1986.

Dennis, W. "Creative Productivity Between the Ages of 20 and 80 Years." *Journal of Psychology* 21 (1966): 1.

Erikson, E. *Childhood and Society.* 2nd edition. New York: W.W. Norton, 1963.

Fisher, D.H. *Growing Old in America.* New York: Oxford University Press, 1977.

Gilman, H. "Marketers Court Old Consumers as Balance of Buying Power Shifts." *Wall Street Journal,* April 23, 1986, p. 33.

Graebner, W. *A History of Retirement: The Meaning and Function of an American Institution, 1885–1978.* New Haven: Yale University Press, 1980.

Graham, M. "Martha Graham Reflects on Her Art and a Life in Dance." *New York Times,* March 31, 1985, pp. H–1, H–8.

Hager, M. "Practicing with Doctor Spock." *Newsweek,* March 4, 1985, p. 10.

Hallowell, C. "New Focus on the Old," *New York Times Magazine,* March 1985, pp. 48–50, 109–11.

Harmetz, A. "NBC's Golden Girls' Gamble on Grown-Ups." *New York Times,* September 22, 1985, pp. H–2, H–25.

Hergenrather, E.R. "The Old Worker: A Golden Asset." *Personnel* (August 1985): 59.

Hill, L.A., and Sonnenfeld, J.A. "Renewal within Financial Service Firms: Managers' Reflections on Retraining." Paper presented at Harvard Business School Colloquium on Contemporary Developments and Changes in the U. S. Financial Service Sector, chaired by S.L. Hayes, III, Boston, June 24, 1986.

Holmes, T.H., and Rahe, R.H. "The Social Readjustment Rating Scale." *Journal of Psychosomatic Research* 11 (1967): 213–18.

Hoyer, W.J., and Flode, D.J. "Attention and Perceptual Processes in the Study of Cognitive Aging." In *Aging in the 1980s: Psychological Issues,* Poon, L.W., ed. Washington D.C.: American Psychological Association, 1980.

Hunt, J.W., and Saul, P.N. "The Relationship of Age, Tenure and Job Satisfaction in Males and Females." *Academy of Management Journal* 20, (1975): 690.

Keller, C.H., and Quirk, D.A. "Age, Functional Capacity, and Work: An Annotated Bibliography." *Industrial Gerontology* 19 (1973): 80.

Korn, L.B., and Ferry, R.M. *Korn/Ferry International's Executive Profile.* Los Angeles: Korn Ferry, 1985.

Langer, E.J. and Rodin, J. "The Effects of Choice and Enhanced Personal Responsibility for the Aged," *Journal of Personality and Social Psychology* 34, 1976: 191–198.

Matchan, L. "A Singer of Stories." *The Boston Globe Magazine,* August 25, 1985, pp. 15, 65–73.

McEvoy, G.M., and Cascio, W.F. A Meta-Analysis of Age Differences in Job Performance: Replication and Extension. University of Colorado, unpublished manuscript, 1986.

Mog, R.C., Davis, K.L., and Parley, C. "Cholinergic Drug Effects on Memory and Cognition in Humans." In *Aging in the 1980s: Psychological Issues,* Poon, L.W., ed. Washington, D.C.: American Psychological Association, 1980.

Moore, J.L. "Unretiring Workers, to These Employees, the Boss is a Kid." *Wall Street Journal,* December 7, 1977, p. 1.

Neugarten, B. "Acting One's Age." *Psychology Today* (April 1980): 66.

New York Times. "Data Point to Growth of Brain Late in Life," July 30, 1985, pp. C1, C7.

Newsweek. "Texas's Aging Angels (July 1, 1985): 45.

Oser, A.S. "Ex-Governor Averell Harriman, Advisor to Four Presidents, Dies." *New York Times,* July 27, 1986, pp. 1, 23.

Pelz, R.C. "The Creative Years in Research Environment, Industrial and Electrical Engineering: Transaction of the Professional Technical Group." *Engineer Management* 11, 1964. As referenced in L. W. Porter's "Summary of the Literature on Personnel Obsolescence," Conference on Personnel Obsolescence, Dallas, Stanford Research Institute and Texas Instruments, June 21-23, 1966.

Pinder, C.C., and Pinder, P.R. "Demographic Correlates of Managerial Style." *Personnel Psychology* 27 (1974): 257–70.

Robinson, P.K. "Age, Health, and Job Performance." In *Age, Health, and Employment,* Birren, J.E., Robinson, P.K., and Livingston, J.E., eds. Englewood Cliffs, N.J.: Prentice-Hall, 1986.

Rosen, B., and Jerdee, T.H. "Too Old or Not Too Old." *Harvard Business Review* 55 (1977): 97–106.

Rosener, M., and Prout, L.R. "Targeting the old Folks: Florida Leads the Way in Marketing to the Elderly." *Newsweek* (January 6, 1986): 54.

Russell, J. "Marc Chagall is Dead at 97, One of Modern Art's Giants." *New York Times,* March 29, 1985, p. A-1.

Safire, W. "The Codgerdoggle." *New York Times,* October 3, 1977, p. 29.

Schein, E.H. *Career Dynamics.* Reading, Mass.: Addison-Wesley, 1978.

Sonnenfeld, J. *The Hero's Escape: The Retirement and Renewal of Chief Executives.* New York: Oxford University Press, 1987 (expected).

Taylor, R. "Marc Chagall—An Appreciation." *The Boston Globe,* March 3, 1985, p. 2.

Treas. J. "The Historical Decline in Late Life Labor Force Participation in the United States." In *Age, Health, and Employment,* Birren, J.E., Robinson, P.K., and Livingston, J.E., eds. Englewood Cliffs, N.J.: Prentice-Hall, 1986.

U.S. Bureau of the Census. "Projection of the Population of the United States: 1971–2000." Series P-25, no. 704. Washington, D.C.: U.S. Government Printing Office, 1977, pp. 10–11.

U.S. Department of Labor. *The Older American Worker, Report to the Secretary of Labor.* Washington, D.C.: U.S. Government Printing Office, 1965.

U.S. Department of Labor, Bureau of Labor Statistics. *Comparative Job Performance by Age: Office Workers.* Bulletin No. 1273. Washington, D.C.: U.S. Government Printing Office, 1960.

U.S. Department of Labor, Bureau of Labor Statistics. *Comparative Performance by Age: Large Plants in Men's Footwear and Household Furniture Industries.* Bulletin No. 1223. Washington, D.C.: U.S. Government Printing Office, 1957.

U.S. Senate, Special Committee on Aging. *Costs of Employing Older Workers,* Sen. Rep. No. 37.1160. Prepared by 98th Cong. Washington, D.C.: U.S. Government Printing Office, 1984.

Vroom, V.H., and Pahl, B. "Age and Risk-Taking Among Managers." *Journal of Applied Psychology* 12, (1971): 22.

Waldman, D.A., and Avolio, B.J. "A Meta-Analysis of Age Differences in Job Performance." *Journal of Applied Psychology* 71 (1986): 33–38.

Welford, A.T. "Thirty Years of Psychological Research on Age and Work." *Journal of Occupational Psychology* 49 (1976): 129.

Wexler, N. Interview comments on M. Wallace, *The I. Magnin File.* On CBS's "60 Minutes," April 1984.

Suggested Readings

Rosen, B., and Jerdee, T.H. *Older Employees: New Roles for Valued Resources.* Homewood, Ill.: Dow Jones-Irwin, 1985.

The general situation of older workers (regardless of industry, job function, location, or prior career history) is addressed here. This book interprets for managers the current research findings, legislative changes, and shifts in societal expectations that affect an aging U.S. work force. The authors provide many brief cases to illustrate practical constructive responses from the individual supervisor and executives charged with changing an entire work system of a company. Tips on job design, assessment, human resource planning, and organizational development are provided.

Schein, E.H. *Career Dynamics: Matching Individual and Organizational Needs.* Reading, Mass.: Addison-Wesley, 1978.

To best appreciate the priorities at late career, we must look at older workers from the perspective of their individual career histories. This book takes a serious and applied approach drawing upon the scholarly research addressing the role of a career within people's total ecological context through their lives. The dynamics of family, work, and more personal development are integrated so that the spillover across life sectors can be appreciated. Careers are defined as both organizational creations and personal creations. The practical implications address age-related priorities regarding the recruitment, selection, development, planning, and exit.

Schoenstein, R. *Every Day is Sunday.* Boston: Little, Brown, 1985.

The world without work for those with ample money and good health is explored in this book. The author provides a humorous, but cutting review of life within some of the nation's most prominent retirement communities: Arizona's Sun City, California's Leisure Villages and Leisure Worlds, and New Jersey's Clearbrook and Concordia. The author lived in each community for a period of time, joining in the many planned activities and talking with residents about their segregation from younger people and the world of productive labor. The convenience and playfulness of these retreats is juxtaposed with a resentment over the isolation from general society and the commercial packaging of late-life uselessness.

Sonnenfeld, J. *The Hero's Retreat: The Retirement and Renewal of Chief Executives.* New York: Oxford University Press, 1987.

Late-career leaders feel a sense of frustration similar to that felt by other older workers who must leave the work force before they have contributed all that they believe they can. Unlike most other workers, top leaders continue to face pressure to retire at or before age 70. Late-career leaders must conquer two sets of personal barriers to exit from high office for constructive, personal, and organizational transitions: (1) those due to one's heroic stature and (2) those due to one's heroic mission. Top leaders overcome their late-career challenges in very different ways. Four common departure styles are presented. They are supported by original interviews with fifty prominent chief executives plus surveys of another three hundred top leaders, along with historical references and anthropological research on some folk heroes' retirement. Implications are drawn for both personal and organizational handling of the retirement and renewal of top leaders.

Step 14: Offer comprehensive retirement-planning programs.

Retirement Planning

Helen Dennis

The field of retirement planning has evolved in response to the growing needs of middle-aged and older adults who frequently spend approximately 10 to 30 years in retirement. Both the amount of time and proportion of the life span spent in retirement have increased during the past 80 years. In 1900, the average male spent 3 percent of his lifetime in retirement; in 1980, he spent 20 percent of his life in retirement (U.S. Senate 1985). With the recent increase in early retirements, the amount of time spent in retirement is likely to increase.

Retirement planning is an emerging specialty that incorporates information from diverse disciplines such as business, education, gerontology, economics, social work, and psychology. To reflect the broad perspective of this field, this chapter will present definitions of retirement, an overview of retirement planning, reasons to offer retirement-planning programs, barriers to providing such services, and what needs to be done to meet current and future retirement-planning needs of middle-aged and older persons.

Definitions of Retirement

The term *retirement* has assumed a number of different meanings over the years. In fact, the concept of retirement is a recent one. Noah Webster did not include the term in its modern usage among his definitions in his 1828 dictionary. In 1967, the term retirement was defined in the *Random House Dictionary of the English Language* as the "removal or withdrawal from service, office, or business; a withdrawal into privacy or seclusion" (1967 p. 1224). Essentially, this definition means giving up one's work or going into seclusion, definitions that have little relevance to retirement in the 1980s and 1990s.

In contrast to the passive approach to retirement, more recent definitions stress an active orientation. For example, retirement may be considered a process, event, role, or phase of life. Retirement as a *process* begins with informal planning that can start during middle age or earlier and continues until one leaves the work force. It is an *event* when an individual separates from the job. The event is often accompanied by a ceremony and gift; it may be considered a right of passage. Retirement as a *social role* has rights and duties. Retired persons are expected to manage their own affairs without assistance, live within their income, and avoid becoming dependent on their families or communities (Atchley 1976). Finally, retirement as a *phase of life* begins with the retirement event and ends when the individual becomes dependent and/or institutionalized and is unable to carry out retirement roles (Atchley 1976).

The noted sociologist Robert Atchley believes that a necessary feature of retirement is the receipt of a pension. He views retirement as a condition in which an individual is forced or allowed to retire, is employed less than full-time, and has some income from a retirement pension earned through previous years of service as a job holder. Using this definition, a part-time worker who receives a pension is considered retired. Kaplan (1979) defined a retiree as an individual who withdraws, temporarily or permanently, from an activity, interest, or commitment. Kaplan's definition recognizes that retirement can be temporary, but does not include the notion of partial retirement (Parker 1982).

The definition of retirement continues to undergo revision to reflect the realities of American society. For example, Maurice Lazarus in a dialogue with Betty Friedan states that "the concept of retiring at a particular age is an anathema to the concept of productive aging" (Butler and Gleason 1985, p. 78). He notes that when people complete college, they are commencing, not retiring from college. When they complete graduate school, they are graduating, not retiring from graduate school. Therefore, he suggests that we find a substitute for the word *retirement* that means continuing participation rather than withdrawal.

In *The Complete Retirement Planning Book* (Dickinson 1976) advises the reader not to use the term *retirement.* Dickinson states that retirement calls to mind "retreat, withdrawal, seclusion . . . and elastic stockings" (1976, p. ix). He suggests calling retirement "refinement" or the "elective years." A *Wall Street Journal* article (November 3, 1986) gives advice to those providing job references for retirees seeking employment. Rather than stating that Mr. X has retired from the company, references were advised to state that "Mr. X has decided to explore opportunities outside the company because of changes due to our recent merger."

Clearly, the negative connotations about retirement reinforce common myths and stereotypes. These misconceptions frequently are perpetuated by institutions, families, and individuals. Fortunately, the meaning and image of retirement are changing because of greater awareness of the opportunities in retirement, increased press coverage of positive retirement stories, greater knowledge and understanding of the retirement process, and the positive experience of millions of Americans.

Retirement

Individuals have diverse responses to retirement. For most individuals, retirement conveys both gains and losses in various proportions. Many look forward to this period of life because it means more choices, less stress, no commuting, freedom, and greater control over one's life. For others, retirement may signify a period of loss—losses of income, social contacts, role, challenges, and structure. The extent and impact of these gains and losses and subsequent adjustment to retirement are affected by several variables.

Thompson (1958) investigated these variables in a research study to determine the elements of a good adjustment to retirement. He found that good adjustment was affected by three variables. First, it is important for the pre-retiree to have a *positive attitude* toward retirement; second, a pre-retiree should have a *realistic view* of retirement; and third, the pre-retiree should make *realistic plans* for the future. These attitude and planning variables that influence adjustment to retirement frequently are the basis for retirement-planning programs.

Research studies indicate that retirees who participate in retirement-planning programs report achieving high levels of personal competence (Charles 1971), self-actualization (Meyer 1977), and adjustment (Palmore 1982). Therefore, the development and implementation of plans are an important aspect of preparing for retirement (Kasschau 1974).

Retirement Planning

Retirement planning essentially is planning for one's future. The process frequently is referred to as life planning because effective planning depends on decisions made over a lifetime. Individuals who plan for retirement can prepare for this process independently or by attending retirement-planning educational programs.

Those who prepare for their future without attending formal retirement-planning educational programs frequently plan for all aspects of their lives over a period of time. Information they need on financial and estate planning and other areas is obtained through libraries, newspaper articles, and conversations with professionals and those already retired. These individuals may be thought of as independent learners—those who learn what they need to know without participating in formal instructional programs.

Many adults plan for their retirement by participating in retirement-planning educational programs. These programs typically are presented to a group of pre-retirees.

History

Retirement-planning services can be traced back to conversations between employer and employee about pension benefits and insurance coverage. Early surveys indicated that many companies had well-established individual retirement-planning programs before 1950.

The group type of retirement-planning program is traced to the pioneering work of several universities including the University of Michigan, University of Chicago, Duke University, University of Southern California, and Drake University. One of the first educational programs for older adults was conducted in 1948 at the University of Michigan by Clarke Tibbitts. The course was not called preretirement, but rather "Problems and Adjustment in Later Maturity and Old Age." It was designed to help pre-retirees adapt to the social and psychological changes frequently accompanying aging and retirement. In the 1960s, Woodrow Hunter, a pioneer and outstanding contributor to the field who also was at the University of Michigan, developed a comprehensive retirement-planning program and conducted research on the impact of retirement planning on adjustment in later life.

Other organizations followed the university efforts and developed programs and services for pre-retirees. These organizations included adult education services, government departments, libraries, YMCAs, churches, industries, community colleges, and labor unions.

Retirement-Planning Programs

A typical comprehensive retirement-planning program sponsored by a corporation covers approximately six to eight topics in a period of twelve to sixteen hours. Topics usually addressed include financial and estate planning, health promotion, living arrangements, use of time, interpersonal relationships, and, sometimes, employment and career development.

Retirement-planning programs frequently are provided by employers and are developed by individuals within the organization. Professionals who are in-house specialists may have retirement-planning programs as their sole responsibility. More often, specialists combine their retirement-planning function with other responsibilities such as retiree relations, corporate benefits, and pension planning.

Retirement programs also can be provided by an outside consultant. In some cases, these consultants are hired to design a program, select speakers, and coordinate all related activities. In other cases, consultants are used only for program development and design or only to address a specific content area.

Employers or consultants may purchase a retirement-preparation program that has been developed by a profit or nonprofit group. These programs consist of instructional and audiovisual materials and are referred to as packaged programs. Some address the broad needs of middle-aged adults preparing for their future, while others emphasize more specialized needs for groups such as single adults and women.

Packaged Programs. Today, employers have a wide choice of packaged programs in terms of purpose, materials, and cost. The following programs have been selected as examples.

The American Association of Retired Persons (AARP) developed a comprehensive program entitled "Think of Your Future." It is designed to motivate middle-aged and older adults to plan for their future. Topics for this program are challenges of the future, dynamic fitness, attitude and role adjustments, meaningful use of time, housing, lifestyle, work options, financial security, legal affairs, and estate planning. The program was updated in 1986 to reflect the changing times and needs of pre-retirees.

The National Council on the Aging (NCOA) designed a comprehensive program for middle-aged adults entitled "Retirement Planning Program." It consists of six sessions including life-style planning, financial planning, interpersonal relations, living arrangements, and leisure. Videotapes, participant's workbooks, and leaders' guides are part of the instructional materials. A series of slide tapes address significant topics in retirement planning, thereby eliminating the need for outside speakers.

Another program developed by NCOA, "Facing Our Future," focuses on the retirement-planning needs of women in midlife. It consists of six two-hour sessions and is designed to be facilitated by a peer leader. A leader and participant manual, audio tape cassettes of interviews with women, and a slide/tape presentation that can be used for recruitment are part of the educational materials.

A video-based seminar developed by Life Planning Management is entitled "Taking Charge of Your Retirement." The modules include retirement transitions, financial independence, health and wellness, housing, legal issues and life-style designs. Instructional materials include a participant's manual, facilitator's manual, and a computer-assisted financial software program (FIND PRO).

A packaged program that has a variety of materials on retirement planning has been developed by Retirement Advisors, Inc. (RAI). Services include retirement publications, retirement-planning seminars, and programs designed for specialized groups such as women, senior-level executives, and those taking early retirement in response to company incentives. Additionally, RAI provides data-base services, in-house training, and program evaluation.

Internally Developed Programs. Some programs are developed within the organization and are used exclusively for the organization's employees. Two examples are described—one that has been developed by a corporation and another developed by a labor union.

The Levi Strauss Corporation developed a program entitled "Discovery Unlimited." Seven topics are presented: "it gets better after fifty," "to your health," "make it legal," "home sweet home," "have the time of your life," "the financial plan," and "the benefits of your retirement." Outside speakers are used to present information on financial, legal, and health components. Narrated slide presentations focus on factory scenes at Levi companies to personalize the program for Levi employees.

The United Auto Workers (UAW) developed a program, "Planning for Successful Living," with support from the Fund for the Improvement of Postsecondary Education. The six-part program addresses subjects of planning, social security, budgeting, health, consumer rights, and housing. Information is presented through slide-tape presentations, participant's notebooks, coordinator's manuals, and other resource material. Participants' workbooks contain quotations from UAW leaders, specific exercises, checklists, and case histories.

Reasons to Offer Retirement-Planning Programs

Employers offer retirement-planning services for a number of reasons—to meet employee expectations, to respond to employees' need for financial independence in later life, to encourage early retirement, to improve morale and the corporate public image, and to respond to legislative imperatives.

Employee Expectation. Many employees expect retirement-planning services from their employer as a company benefit. In fact, retirement planning is considered one of the more recent benefits provided by employers (Perham 1980). As employees become aware that decisions made during their working years will affect the quality of their retirement years, they will continue to look toward employers for information and guidance.

Need for Financial Independence in Retirement. Financial vulnerability of retirees is a driving force behind retirement-planning services. The *Wall Street Journal* (September 9, 1986) reported the results of a survey of chief executive officers who were asked to respond to the statement "employees should take more responsibility for provision of their own retirement income." Of those responding to the survey, 84 percent agreed, 11 percent disagreed and 5 percent had no opinion. According to an article in the *Harvard Business Review*, employers should assume the responsibility of helping workers increase their understanding of the individual's responsibility to finance postwork income (Underwood 1984).

Increasing health care costs, instability of pensions, uncertainty about social security income, and the 1986 tax reform act eliminating the deductability of many people's IRAs are strong signals to Americans that they must have other financial resources for their retirement. Some employers are aware of this need for greater financial independence in retirement and are responding by providing financial-planning assistance to employees of all ages.

Early Retirement. A standard method used by employers in the 1980s to reduce their work force is to offer their employees financial incentives for early retirement. This downsizing or reduction in force is designed to reduce personnel costs, at least on a short-term basis.

Although retirement-planning programs were not developed primarily to encourage the early exit of employees from the labor force, in recent years, programs have been used to encourage retirement of qualified employees, those who have a specified number of years of service. These individuals may be as young as 50 years. Employees who attend a retirement-planning seminar frequently make their retirement decision based on information learned at financial and estate-planning sessions sponsored by the employer. In fact, retirement-planning seminars have been recommended as a retirement incentive and overall strategy for employers (Robinson et al. 1984).

A 1981 survey (Mercer) documents the use of retirement-planning programs as a method to encourage early retirement. The survey indicated that 36 percent of responding companies believed that their retirement-planning programs were effective in encouraging early retirement. Incentives consisted of offering financial packages that increased pensions, benefits, and insurance coverage.

Improved Morale. Although difficult to support with research evidence, retirement-planning programs have been viewed as an effort to improve morale and alleviate some anxiety about retirement decisions and subsequent retirement experiences. This is particularly true in organizations that offer early-retirement opportunities. It also is believed that the improved morale affects the quality of performance in the years remaining before retirement.

Public Image. Employers are aware of their public image. Companies want a positive reputation to attract the best and brightest employees. The book *The 100 Best Companies to Work For* (Levering et al. 1984) lists a wide range of company benefits. Retirement-planning programs are noted among the benefits that made working for an employer more desirable.

Legislation. Legislation has encouraged companies to provide retirement-planning services. The Employee Retirement Income Stabilization Act (ERISA) of 1974 was designed to correct the shortcomings of the private pension system. Part of the law requires employers to communicate upon request pension benefits to employees on a yearly basis. This communication is part of retirement planning.

The 1986 amendments to the Age Discrimination in Employment Act (ADEA) removed the mandatory retirement age for most employees. Companies often explain to employees the meaning of the law and its implications for their tenure with the company and its relevance to seeking employment after retirement. These explanations often are part of a retirement-planning program.

Barriers to Providing Retirement-Planning Services

A corporate philosophy, economic conditions, and personnel shortages may hinder employers from providing retirement-planning services to their employees.

Corporate Philosophy. A corporate philosophy, in part, reflects the organization's attitude and sense of responsibility toward its employees. For purposes of this discussion, the focus will be on long-term employees. A positive corporate philosophy toward long-term employees is reflected in the organization's awareness of their needs and a sense of responsibility to provide information and other supportive services to ensure their successful retirement. A neutral philosophy toward long-term employees is reflected by the organization's attitude that retirement is a private matter and employees should assume complete and independent responsibility for preparing for later life. The positive corporate philosophy would support the offering of retirement-preparation services; the neutral corporate philosophy would not. Most corporations seem to embrace a neutral philosophy which hinders the offering of such a program.

Economic Climate. The economic environment strongly influences the amount of funds an employer allocates for benefits and services. The cost of presenting retirement-planning programs can range from very modest to very high. In some cases, the amount of money budgeted for retirement services determines whether or not a company offers retirement-planning programs.

In a period of belt-tightening non–revenue-producing services frequently are eliminated. Unfortunately, retirement planning often falls into this category.

Personnel Available. Staff must be available to present and manage the retirement-planning function. If downsizing and cost-cutting measures are underway in the organization, staff time may either be eliminated or decreased for this function. When down-sizing is not occurring, the lack of personnel who are interested or skilled in retirement planning will prevent the offering of retirement-planning services.

Trends in Retirement Planning

Several trends in retirement planning are evident in the 1980s and have implications for the next decade.

Formal retirement-planning programs are increasing. In a survey of Fortune 500 corporations, 51 percent of 142 responding companies had programs; 75 percent of all Fortune 500 companies are projected to have programs by 1989 (Siegel 1986). These figures have increased in comparison to previous survey findings that indicate approximately one-third of large companies offer programs (Research and Forecasts, Inc. 1979; Underwood 1984).

Planning for retirement is beginning at earlier ages. Adults are planning for their retirement earlier in their lives than they did in the 1970s. Two reasons are suggested for this phenomenon. First, employees are becoming eligible to retire at younger ages because of the financial incentives offered to them by large corporations. Second, middle-aged adults are becoming increasingly aware of the need for economic self-sufficiency in later life.

Retirement-planning programs are used to encourage retirement. Although it is illegal to force individuals to retire because of age, some programs are used to reinforce the attributes of retirement with the hope that participants will make a decision to retire within a short period of time. This is particularly true in organizations that offer financial incentives for early retirement. Typically, these organizations offer brief financial discussions of retirement, including information about amount of pension and social security funds available to those qualified to receive these benefits. In some cases, consultants have been asked to stress the positive aspects of retirement so that attendees will be more eager to make a retirement decision. According to a survey of 529 companies by Hewitt Associates (1986), nearly three-fourths of voluntary separations from the work force take the form of early retirement that has been encouraged by the offering of financial incentives.

New content is being introduced in programs. Several new content areas are being addressed in retirement planning. The first is the subject of employment during retirement. As employees continue to take early retirement and find they need additional income, the part-time employment option becomes very attractive.

A second content area that is beginning to be introduced is the subject of caring for aging parents. This subject is becoming relevant to an increasing number of middle-aged adults. According to a survey conducted by Retirement Advisors, Inc. (1986), 30 percent of the respondents had responsibility to care for their aging parents. A Travelers Co. (Travelers Companies 1985) survey indicated that 20 percent of their employees over the age of 30 had care-giving responsibilities for aging parents.

A third content area being developed for retirement-planning programs is alcohol abuse (Hansen and Dennis 1987). It is believed that the incidence of late onset of alcohol abuse is growing among retirees. Educational models are being developed to introduce information about risk factors, changes in tolerance, and social pressures that will discourage the misuse of alcohol in later life.

The field of retirement planning is growing. One indication of the growth of retirement planning as a profession is the increase in the membership of its professional society, the International Society of Preretirement Planners (ISPP). This organization is composed of health educators, gerontologists, social workers, adult educators, financial planners, corporate-benefits specialists, psychologists, estate planner, and others. Between 1983 and 1986, the organization grew in membership from 150 to 700 and from one chapter to nearly ten across the country. As the need for retirement-planning services continues to increase, more professionals will be offering planning, education, and counselling services to middle-aged adults taking early retirement as well to those taking a later retirement.

Meeting Retirement-Planning Needs

Although these trends indicate broadened services to employees, much remains to be done. The following seven recommendations are directed to employers, managers, retirement specialists, and employees.

1. *All employers should offer some type of retirement-preparation service to their employees.* Despite the increase in retirement-planning programs, 90 percent to 95 percent of eligible workers receive no formal training or assistance in retirement planning (Monk and Donovan 1978–79; Migliaccio

1986). Data from the national longitudinal surveys conducted in 1981 found that less than 2 percent of men 60 to 74 years old reported that they participated in a retirement-planning program at work (Beck 1984). In a survey conducted for the American Association of Retired Persons (1986), only 23 percent of employees 40 years and older stated that their employers offered education on retirement planning. Approximately half of those surveyed worked for companies with fewer than 500 employees.

Retirement-planning programs are most frequently offered by large corporations employing only a minority of U.S. employees. Most employees in the United States work for medium-sized to small companies who are less likely to offer retirement-planning services. The survey results provide a strong rationale for small to medium-sized employers to provide some type of retirement-education services. The services may range from the distribution of printed material to the offering of a comprehensive retirement-planning program.

2. *Employers should offer retirement-planning services early in the careers of their employees.* This applies to individuals taking either the standard of "planned-for" retirement or the early retirement induced by financial incentives. A comment often made by retirees is that they wished they had started the planning process earlier in their work lives. Adequate financial preparation and the development of new goals for the latter part of life require time and appropriate action.

3. *Employers should encourage financial responsibility and planning for all employees, regardless of age.* Effective financial planning cannot start at the age of 59. Employees must be educated to take responsibility for their retirement income. Employers can provide tools to help their employees become more self-reliant and can motivate them to use these tools (Underwood 1984).

4. *Employers should address specific needs of the "early retiree" who is being encouraged to retire.* Nusberg refers to this group as "premature retirees" (1986, p. 30). She notes that few retirement-training programs have addressed the needs of this group. Typically, finances are stressed in their seminars without addressing issues of role change, use of time, relationship with spouse, and the psychological and social impacts of not working at 50 or 55 years. Clearly, the financial *and* nonfinancial issues are significant.

Employees need adequate time to make a retirement decision. It has been reported that employees complain about not having enough time to decide whether or not to take the financial-incentive package for a voluntary early-retirement exit. For example, Polaroid employees were given three months to make a decision; AT&T employees were given three weeks (Kessler 1985).

5. *Evaluation of program effectiveness needs to be included in retirement-planning programs.* One reason that employers are reluctant to provide retirement-preparation services is that they are not convinced that these services make a difference in the lives of their employees (Coleman 1986). Evaluations will document program effectiveness and show that reasonable outcomes can be attained. In an environment of mergers, reductions in force, and conservative spending on services, program accountability is of increasing importance.

6. *Specialized needs of pre-retirees should be addressed.* For example, individuals retiring in poor health require services. This group is considered one of the most vulnerable and neglected (Palmore et al. 1985). Programs are needed to reduce the negative effects of retirement for those who must confront ailing health and disability.

Individuals in the lower socioeconomic level need services. They tend to have the least freedom and need assistance to retain an adequate income in retirement (Palmore et al. 1985). Beck suggested that those who would benefit most from retirement planning have less education, lower occupational status, no pension coverage, and, therefore, lower income. These individuals have the least access to retirement-planning services (Beck 1984).

Women need programs designed for their needs. A stereotype about women is that work is not meaningful to them (Block 1984). An extension of this belief is that women face less of a dilemma in retirement than men because women are giving up a secondary role, while men are giving up a primary role. Empirical studies on meaningfulness of work do not support this belief (Block 1984). Women are likely to spend many of their retirement years without their husbands because the average life span for women is longer than for men. Therefore, women have special issues of economic self-sufficiency and role changes that should be addressed in retirement planning. Some programs are addressing these issues, such as "Facing our Future" developed by the National Council on the Aging. Another program for women is being developed by Long Island University.

The special needs of minorities must be acknowledged and addressed. Blacks, Hispanics, Asians, and Native Americans who plan to retire must deal with specific social, cultural, and economic issues that typically are not included in comprehensive retirement-planning programs. Common barriers to minorities planning for retirement include a greater probability that they will be employed in jobs without adequate pension coverage; health problems forcing early retirement; the need to work into old age for income; low level of education; and a feeling that retirement planning is not relevant to them (Torres-Gil 1984).

7. *Retirement specialists should participate in continuing education.* Retirement specialists need to have up-to-date information on subjects including

finances, health, housing options, and career opportunities. This will enable them to develop, present, and administer effective retirement-planning programs. In addition to being knowledgeable in these areas, specialists need skills in group process, adult education, administration, and evaluation. Participation in workshops, conferences, seminars, and credit courses should be encouraged by employers.

Conclusion

Betty Friedan suggested that "people over 65 should have the widest possible choice of options for productive participation in society" (Butler and Gleason 1985, p. 77). Employers can play a major role in preparing their employees today to be in a position to exercise these options in the future. The adequacy and self-sufficiency of tomorrow's retirees will have an impact on society that affects business, government, and families. Employers have the opportunity to create an environment that will allow their employees to continue as vital retirees in the future. That opportunity is relatively simple—providing educational services in retirement planning. The investment is relatively small, and the payoff is large and long-lasting for retirees, their employers, and society.

References

American Association of Retired Persons. *Work and Retirement: Employees Over 40 and Their Views.* Washington, D.C.: American Association of Retired Persons, 1986.

Atchley, R.C. *The Sociology of Retirement.* New York: Wiley, 1976.

Beck, S.H. "Retirement Preparation Programs: Differentials in Opportunity and Use." *Journal of Gerontology* 39 (1984): 596–602.

Block, M. "Retirement Preparation Needs of Women." In *Retirement Preparation,* Dennis, H., Ed. Lexington, Mass.: Lexington Books, 1984.

Butler, R.N., and Gleason, H.P. eds. *Productive Aging: Enhancing Vitality in Later Life.* New York: Springer, 1985.

Charles, D.C. "Effect of Participation in a Preretirement Program." *Gerontologist* 11 (1971): 22–28.

Coleman, A. "The Management of Change: A Focus on Retirement." *Training Officer* (October 1986) 298–301.

Dickinson, P. *The Complete Retirement Planning Book.* New York: E.P. Dutton, 1976.

Hansen, W.B., and Dennis, H. "Alcohol Problem Prevention Among Retiring Adults." Submitted to the National Institute of Alcohol, Abuse, and Alcoholism as part of a proposal for the study of age and alcohol, February 1987.

Hewitt Associates. *Plan Design and Experience in Early Retirement Windows and in Other Voluntary Separations,* 1986.

Kaplan, M. *Leisure: Lifestyle and Lifespan*. Philadelphia, Penn.: Saunders, 1979.

Kasschau, P.L. "Reevaluating the Need for Retirement Preparation Programs." *Industrial Gerontology* (Winter 1974): 40–55.

Kessler, F. "Managers Without a Company." *Fortune* (October 28, 1985): 51–56.

Levering, R., Moskowitz, M., and Katz, M. *The 100 Best Companies to Work For.* Reading, Mass: Addison-Wesley, 1984.

Mercer, W.M. *Employer Attitudes: Implications of an Aging Work Force*, 1981.

Meyer, S.L. "Androgogy and the Adult Learner." *Educational Gerontology* 2 (1977): 115–22.

Migliaccio, J.N. "Falling Short of Pre-retirement Training." *Training and Development Journal* (May 1986): 6–8.

Monk, A., and Donovan, R. "Pre-Retirement Preparation Programs." *Aged Care and Service Review* (1978–79): 5–6.

Nusberg, C. "Early Retirement Ubiquitous in Western Nations." *Aging International* (Autumn/Winter 1986): 26–32.

Palmore, E.B. "Preparation for Retirement: The Impact of Pre-retirement Programs on Retirement and Leisure." Paper presented at annual meeting of the Association for Gerontology in Higher Education, Washington, D.C., February 1982.

Palmore, E.B., Burchett, B.M., Fillenbaum, G.C., George, L.K., and Wallman, L.M. *Retirement: Causes and Consequences*. New York: Springer, 1985.

Parker, S. *Work and Retirement.* Boston: George Allen and Unwin, 1982.

Perham, J.C. "The Newest Employee Benefit." *Dun's Review* (May 1980): 72–80.

Random House Dictionary of the English Language. New York: Random House, 1967.

Research and Forecasts, Inc. *Retirement Preparation: Growing Corporate Involvement*. New York: Corporate Committee for Retirement Planning, 1979.

Retirement Advisors, Inc. *RAI Employee Eldercare Survey.* RAI: May 1986.

Robinson, P., Paul, C., and Coberly, S. *Timing the Retirement Exit.* Los Angeles: Andrus Gerontology Center, University of Southern California, 1984.

Siegel, R. "Preretirement Programs in the 80's." *Personnel Administrator* (February 1986): 77–83.

The Travelers Employee Care Giver Survey: A Survey on Caregiving Responsibilities of Travelers Employees for Older Americans. Hartford, Conn.: Travelers Companies, June 1985.

Thompson, W.E. "Pre-Retirement Anticipation and Adjustment in Retirement." *The Journal of Social Issues* 14, no. 2 (1958): 35–41.

Torres-Gil, F. "Retirement Issues that Affect Minorities." In *Retirement Preparation*, Dennis, H. ed. Lexington, Mass.: Lexington Books, 1984.

Underwood, D. "Toward Self-reliance in Retirement Planning." *Harvard Business Review* (May-June 1984).

U.S. Senate Special Committee on Aging, American Association of Retired Persons, Federal Council on the Aging, and Administration on Aging. *Aging America: Trends and Projections*. Washington, D.C.: U.S. Department of Health and Human Services, 1985.

Wall Street Journal. "Early Retirement May Lead to Lucky Break," November 3, 1986.

Wall Street Journal. "Employees should take more responsibility for provision of their own retirement income," September 9, 1986.

Suggested Readings

Dennis, H., ed. *Retirement Preparation.* Lexington, Mass.: Lexington Books, 1984.

This book for the retirement planner, educator, and counselor is designed to help these specialists develop, implement, and evaluate their programs and services. Chapters include the aging process, selected characteristics of the aging, health promotion, financial planning, instruction for adults, program evaluation, preretirement counselling, issues affecting minorities, retirement-planning needs of women, and retirement and the family. An annotated list of audiovisuals and books relevant to retirement planning is included.

McCluskey, N.G., and Borgatta, E.F, eds. *Aging and Retirement: Prospects, Planning, and Policy.* Beverly Hills, Calif.: Sage, 1981.

Multiple aspects of aging and retirement are presented, focusing on demography and economics of aging, aging and retirement planning, and personnel and federal policies.

Montana, P.J. *Retirement Programs: How to Develop and Implement Them.* Englewood Cliffs, N.J. Prentice-Hall, 1985.

This book is a guide to developing and implementing preretirement programs. It focuses on elements needed for developing a program for specific organizations and concerns of human resource managers regarding retirement planning. An annotated bibliography, forms, checklists, and directory of vendors of products and services are included.

Szinovacz, M. *Women's Retirement: Policy Implications of Recent Research.* Beverly Hills, Calif.: Sage, 1982.

This book consists of research specifically devoted to women's retirement. Subjects include the employment status and work history of women, attitudes and plans in preparation for retirement, and the female experience in adjusting to retirement.

Epilogue

Helen Dennis

The final pages of a book typically are used to summarize chapters, to select the most important thoughts, and to leave a message with the reader. Instead of presenting a traditional epilogue, I would like to use this space to challenge the reader.

If you are a *manager,* the challenge is to examine your employer policies and practices for age biases. What are the assumptions your organization is making regarding older employees? Is your organization conveying subtle messages to older employees about their opportunities for advancement, retraining, or new assignments? As a manager, what can you introduce in your work setting that will increase objective assessment of older (and younger) workers? How can you encourage the effective use of older persons that will help meet company objectives?

If you are a *faculty member* of a business school, examine how your students are learning about aging. Is it only a legal issue? How do courses on human resource management address the older worker? Is aging acknowledged as an issue in the workplace? Do courses present positive models of aging such as new roles for older workers and successful models of older leaders or senior managers? Your MBA students of today will be the middle and senior management of the future.

If you are involved in the field of *industrial gerontology* or *industrial social work,* how can you encourage the continued growth and productivity of older employees and fair management practices?

If you are a *retirement planner,* how can you assist older workers to increase their employment options and encourage management to use their skills?

If you are involved with organized *labor,* what are the needs of your older union workers? How can management participate in joint efforts that will maximize the skills and talents of older union employees?

Finally, consider *your own work life.* What are the choices you want in mid- and later life? What are your career visions? How long would you like to work? What must you do to ensure that you have the skills to continue contributing in the workplace? What do you need to bring to management's attention about their attitudes, policies, and practices that affect older persons?

The ultimate challenge is to make a difference—one that begins to create age-neutral work environments. Such environments truly provide equal opportunity for all workers and value contributions from the individual, regardless of age.

Index

About the Contributors

Ralph A. Alexander, Ph.D., is a professor of psychology at the University of Akron, Akron, Ohio. His research and professional interests focus on individual differences and personnel psychology with particular emphasis on valid, nondiscriminatory employment practices.

Carol A. Cronin, M.S.G., M.S.W., is vice president of policy and director of the Institute on Aging, Work, and Health at the Washington Business Group on Health in Washington, D.C. She is responsible for both the overall coordination of health-policy activities and for program initiatives in the areas of postretirement medical benefits, health promotion for older workers, and productivity issues relating to an aging work force.

John A. Davis, D.B.A., is an adjunct assistant professor in the Department of Management and Organization, University of Southern California. His research has examined the influence of adult life stages on work relationships. He consults with managers in developing companies and family-owned businesses.

Dennis Doverspike, Ph.D., is with the Psychology Department at the University of Akron. He is active in both the industrial/organizational and industrial/gerontological graduate programs. His research and teaching interests include personnel psychology and training and organization development.

Martin Lyon Levine, J.D., LL.D., is the UPS Foundation professor of law, gerontology, psychiatry, and the behavioral sciences at the schools of law, gerontology, and medicine of the University of Southern California. He is also director of the Oxford-USC Institute of Legal Theory. He is honorary president of the National Senior Citizens Law Center, founding president of the International Society of Aging, Law, and Ethics, and past chairman of the Aging and Law section of the Association of American Law Schools. He is author of *Age Discrimination and the Abolition of Mandatory Retirement* and editor of *Elderlaw: Legal, Ethical and Policy Issues of Aging Individuals and an Aging Society.*

Phoebe S. Liebig, Ph.D., is senior analyst on the economic team of the Public Policy Institute, American Association of Retired Persons and an adjunct assistant professor at the Leonard Davis School of Gerontology, Andrus Gerontology Center of the University of Southern California. Previously, she was planning director of the Andrus Center and served on the faculties of the USC Schools of Medicine and Gerontology. Her research interests focus on pensions, retirement policy, older-worker employment, and education and training in aging.

Roger B. McDonald, Ph.D., is a National Institutes of Health postdoctoral fellow in the Department of Nutrition, University of California at Davis. His research focuses on the effects of exercise on biological aging and includes studies describing these effects on bone metabolism and thermoregulation.

Carolyn E. Paul, Ph.D., is Assistant Professor of Gerontology and Director of the Business Institute on Aging at the Andrus Gerontology Center, University of Southern California. Her doctorate is in Sociology with a specialty in Social Gerontology. Her research has focused on Industrial Gerontology issues related to older workers, retirees, and older consumers.

Jeffrey Sonnenfeld, D.B.A., is an associate professor at Harvard Graduate School of Business Administration. He is a past president of the Careers Division of the Academy of Management and an editor of three professional journals. He is currently completing a book on chief executives in late career, *The Hero's Escape: The Retirement and Renewal of Chief Executives* (Oxford University Press, 1987).

Harvey L. Sterns, Ph.D., is a professor of psychology and director of the Institute for Life-Span Development and Gerontology at the University of Akron. He also is research professor of gerontology at the Northeastern Ohio University College of Medicine, codirector of the Western Reserve Geriatric Education Center, and chairperson of the Ph.D. program in industrial gerontological psychology at the University of Akron. His research and teaching interests include training and retraining, career development, cognitive and motor skills, and aging.

Robert M. Tager, M.D., is a neurologist with a practice involving workers' compensation disability evaluations in Santa Cruz, California. He is an adjunct associate professor of gerontology at the Leonard Davis School of Gerontology, Andrus Gerontology Center, University of Southern California. He has lectured and written on the subjects of stress and stress management since 1975.

Renato Tagiuri, Ph.D., is professor emeritus of social sciences in business administration at Harvard Graduate School of Business Administration. He has been faculty chairman of the "Seminar on Management in Industrial Research" of the Industrial Research Institute since 1973. He is a member of the Assemblea of the Associates of the Centro di Ricerca sull'Organizzazione at Bocconi University, Milan, Italy; consulting editor of *Harvard-Espansione* (The Italian edition of *Harvard Business Review*); president of Auerbach/Christenson/Tagiuri, Inc.; and a member of the board of directors of a high technology company.

Judith Wineman, M.S.W., is associate director of the Retiree Service Department of the International Ladies' Garment Workers' Union. She administers all social service, education, cultural, preretirement/postretirement, and legislative programs for 127,000 retired union members in the United States, Canada, and Puerto Rico. Currently, she is developing a series of programs designed to assist older workers displaced by plant closings.

About the Editor

Helen Dennis, M.A. is project director and lecturer at the Leonard Davis School of Gerontology, Andrus Gerontology Center, University of Southern California. She developed and directed the first national management training program to address the subject of aging in the workplace and is working with major corporations in California to introduce aging in their management training curriculum. She teaches a course on retirement planning at the Leonard Davis School and is editor of the book *Retirement Preparation: What Retirement Specialists Need to Know.* Ms. Dennis currently is national president of the International Society of Preretirement Planners.

Fourteen Steps in Managing an Aging Work Force

Helen Dennis

Frequently, the topic of aging and the workplace is addressed too late in the career of most employees or in relation to avoiding costly age discrimination lawsuits. Clearly, policy issues regarding age must be established early in the career cycle so that employers may reap the best performance from employees and aging workers may attain the highest level of job satisfaction and compensation.

People are living longer, healthier, and more productive lives. Many individuals are continuing to work in their later years because they enjoy their work opportunities or because they have financial needs. The workplace, however, is not set up to deal with this unprecedented aging workforce, resulting in an increase in age discrimination complaints.

This useful handbook is designed to provide you with information you will need to manage the ever increasing aging workforce and to respond to this complex personnel opportunity. Contributors from gerontology, business, law, medicine, psychology, sociology, public administration, and social work provide the background, guidelines, and information necessary to implement clear and enlightened corporate policy.

The book contains fourteen chapters addressing specific changes, problems, and issues: psychological and physical aspects of aging, stress-related disorders, training and retraining older workers, performance appraisal, alternative work schedules, retirement planning, and more. The ADEA (Age Discrimination in Employment Act) is clearly and concisely explained, helping managers make better employment, retention, termination, retraining, and promotion decisions. Additional resources, such as information on management